How Odd of God

Also by William H. Willimon
from Westminster John Knox Press

Acts (Interpretation series)
The Collected Sermons of William H. Willimon
Concise Encyclopedia of Preaching (with Richard Lischer)
The Early Preaching of Karl Barth: Fourteen Sermons with Commentary
    by William H. Willimon (with Karl Barth)
A Guide to Preaching and Leading Worship
Preaching about Conflict in the Local Church
Preaching and Leading Worship
Preaching to Strangers: Evangelism in Today's World (with Stanley Hauerwas)
United Methodist Beliefs: A Brief Introduction

How Odd of God

Chosen for the Curious Vocation of Preaching

The 2014 Macleod Lectures on Preaching,
Princeton Theological Seminary

William H. Willimon

WESTMINSTER
JOHN KNOX PRESS
LOUISVILLE · KENTUCKY

© 2015 William H. Willimon

First edition
Published by Westminster John Knox Press
Louisville, Kentucky

15 16 17 18 19 20 21 22 23 24—10 9 8 7 6 5 4 3 2 1

Scripture quotations from the New Revised Standard Version of the Bible are copyright © 1989 by the Division of Christian Education of the National Council of the Churches of Christ in the U.S.A. and are used by permission. Scripture quotations marked KJV are taken from the King James Version of the Bible. Scripture quotations marked NKJV are taken from the New King James Version. Copyright © 1982 by Thomas Nelson. Used by permission. All rights reserved.

Excerpts from Karl Barth, *Church Dogmatics: The Doctrine of God*, II/2 (Edinburgh: T. & T. Clark) are © Karl Barth 1957 and are used by permission of Bloomsbury Publishing PLc. Excerpts from Marcus Borg, "What's Christianity All About," in *Day One*, February 6, 2011, http://day1.org/2544-whats_christianity_all_about. Used by permission. Excerpts from Stanley Hauerwas, *Without Apology: Sermons for Christ's Church* (New York: Seabury Books, 2013) are used by permission of Church Publishing Inc. Excerpts from John Piper, "Pastoral Thoughts on the Doctrine of Election," sermon © 2015 Desiring God Foundation. Website: desiringGod.org are used by permission.

"The Call of St. Matthew" painting by Michelangelo Merisi da Caravaggio is used by permission of Alinari / Art Resource, NY. "The Crucifixion" painting by Mathias Gruenewald is used by permission of Erich Lessing / Art Resource, NY. Photo of the tympanum from the abbey at Vézelay is © Holly Hayes and is used by permission.

Book design by Sharon Adams
Cover design by Eric Walljasper

Library of Congress Cataloging-in-Publication Data

Willimon, William H.
  How odd of God : chosen for the curious vocation of preaching / William H. Willimon.
— First edition.
    pages cm
  Includes index.
  ISBN 978-0-664-25974-7 (alk. paper)
  1. Clergy—Appointment, call, and election. 2. Vocation, Ecclesiastical. 3. Barth, Karl, 1886-1968.
  4. Election (Theology) 5. Willimon, William H. I. Title.
  BV4011.4.W55 2015
  251.0092—dc23

                                                                                    2015009073

♾ The paper used in this publication meets the minimum requirements of the American National Standard for Information Sciences—Permanence of Paper for Printed Library Materials, ANSI Z39.48-1992.

Most Westminster John Knox Press books are available at special quantity discounts when purchased in bulk by corporations, organizations, and special-interest groups. For more information, please e-mail SpecialSales@wjkbooks.com.

Oddities do not strike odd people. This is why ordinary people have a much more exciting time; while odd people are always complaining of the dullness of life.

—G. K. Chesterton, *Orthodoxy*, 16

How odd of God
 to choose the Jews

—William Norman Ewer, journalist and sometime poet

But not so odd
 As those who choose
A Jewish God
 Yet spurn the Jews

—Leo Rosten, American humorist, teacher, and scriptwriter

The Jew, so miraculously preserved, . . . through the many calamities of this history, who as such is the natural historical monument to the love and faithfulness of God, who in concrete form is the epitome of the [one] chosen and blessed by God, . . . is the only convincing proof of God outside the Bible.

—Karl Barth, *Church Dogmatics* IV/3–2, 877

Bishop Willimon is the worst thing that has happened to the Methodist Church in Alabama. His know-it-all attitude, "my way or the highway" style of dictatorial leadership. He has been an embarrassment in his criticism of our Governor. Liberal and un-American. Insensitive. Why he ever thought God wanted him to be a preacher is beyond me. Willimon has the wrong disposition for the job of bishop. I know that most of the pastors in this Conference agree with me, but they don't say anything because they are afraid of him.

—Email from a United Methodist received in June 2012

Where is the one who is wise? Where is the scribe? Where is the debater of this age? Has not God made foolish the wisdom of the world? . . . Consider your call, brothers and sisters: not many of you were wise by human standards, not many were powerful, not many were of noble birth. But God chose what is foolish in the world to shame the wise; God chose what is weak in the world to shame the strong; God chose what is low and despised in the world, things that are not, to reduce to nothing things that are.

—1 Corinthians 1:20, 26–28

Contents

Introduction   ix

1. The Oddness of God   1
2. Karl Barth and Election   25
3. The Vocation of the Elect   50
4. Called for Mission   57
5. The Witness of Preaching   105
6. Preaching as Public Truth   128
7. Homiletical Implications of Election   137

Notes   164
Index of Names   187
Index of Subjects   191

Introduction

This book ensued from my rereading of Karl Barth's doctrine of election.[1] Without intending to do so, Barth reminded me of the wonder of the preaching vocation and the oddity of a God who would call the likes of me to preach. Election is God's act whereby our lives are wrenched out of our control and we are commandeered to witness, thereby enabling the joy of talking about something more important than ourselves, our families, or our churches.

Beginnings are tricky. In sermons, theological trouble often occurs early. Barth was notoriously opposed to sermon introductions.[2] Experienced preachers are chary of introductions; we loathe to give away too much too early. Every sermon is a journey in time, and the sermon that gives away the destination too soon is a dull trip.

Barth was opposed to introductions not simply because they give away too much too soon but because introductions are often indicative of preachers attempting to limit God's speech to what we, on our own, are able to say and what our congregations, on their own, are able to hear.

Election is a biblical event for which there is no human, experientially based introduction, an idea much like resurrection. The hunch that God not only exists but also chooses, elects, and summons a few to carry out diverse intentions for all is unsubstantiated by anything within us. Election is an idea that is available only through revelation.

The preacher, in spite of personal limitations and faults, has been elected by God and the church to risk God talk. Preaching is public speech that is rigorously disciplined in its studied attentiveness to the subject and the instigator of proclamation—the one God who is the relentlessly revealing Father, the too-close-for-comfort Son, and the wildly unconstrained Holy Spirit. As Barth said, our peculiar joy is to base our speech on "God's work and activity, the actuality of the Word of God, freely preceding and underlying all views and dogmas."[3]

Preaching is responsive to God's initiative; we speak because God does. Even now, toward the end of my preaching life, my best sermons are due to my being given some fresh awareness of God, launched again as if for the first time on an adventure that the Trinity began in me four decades ago when God inscrutably elected me, of all people, to preach.

This book is my extended reflection on the homiletical implications of Barth's *Church Dogmatics*, II/2, specifically chapter 7, §§ 32–35, "The Election of God."[4] Election is the odd but grand public secret to which the church bears witness. Preaching is demonstration, enactment, and performance of the drama of election. God not only elects, without our help or consent, to be our God but also elects the most unlikely people to be partners in God's revelation, witnesses of God's gracious decision to be God for us (as Jesus Christ) rather than God against us (as are many of our self-concocted "godlets").

To be a witness under the control of an uncontrollable God means to have one's words subsumed by "pointing in a specific direction beyond the self and on to another." What makes a person a witness "is solely and exclusively that other, the thing attested."[5] Witness is God's elected means of announcing to sinful humanity, by God's selection of sinful preachers, God's gracious determination to be a God who loves, saves, and employs sinners. What is required of the witness is simple acknowledgment of the wonder who is the Trinity, curiosity and humility before the otherness of a Savior who relentlessly loves people who don't know how to love him.[6]

Here I offer a description of the theological point of view for my work as a preacher in the hope that fellow preachers will be given optimism that the vocation to which God has called us is worth our lives. Barth gave us a wonderful reconstitution of the doctrine of election; I hope to apply Barth's insights to induce in my fellow preachers fresh conviction that our odd vocation is a major way God intends to get back what belongs to God.

Research and writing of this book occurred while I served as pastor of Duke Memorial United Methodist Church and during my Barth and Preaching Seminar at Duke Divinity School. Living in these two worlds (that ought to be one) gave rise to this book in ways I do not fully understand.

I write this book as I near retirement, toward my end, which isn't so bad. Like you, I've been in training for my end since my life's beginning. That is, God has been trying to teach me that I live on borrowed breath; the life I live isn't my own. A redemptive God seems to enjoy making virtue out of necessity, and here, moving relentlessly each day toward my necessary end, I think God is doing just that. For over four decades I've been living the adventurous life of introducing God into the conversation in such a way that does not contradict God. Whether or not this is my last book is up to God; whether or not this is my last anything has always been God's call.

Barth said that it's as difficult to end as to begin a sermon. Every preacher discovers that most of the uncontrollable, adventurous stuff happens once we think we've ended the sermon and we have had our last word. It is then, at the end, that sometimes the Holy Spirit rips the sermon out of our hands and runs wildly throughout the congregation, saying odd things we never intended. Due to divine summons, I've been forced by God to live more audaciously than I would have if I had been left to my own devices, in sermons tossing God into the discourse of people who are uncomfortable with talk of God. They come to church wanting to be comforted rather than called. Then I preach. I speak of a God who has elected to be God for us; then I step aside and watch the fireworks. What a wonderful way to end, and begin.

Will Willimon
Pentecost, 2015

Chapter One

The Oddness of God

Throughout my ministry, I have kept a single painting ever before me. A print hangs over my desk even now, authorizing my work, guarding my faith, rationalizing why I am here rather than elsewhere. It is Michelangelo Caravaggio's "The Calling of Saint Matthew." Caravaggio completed this painting in 1600 for the Contarelli Chapel in the church of San Luigi dei Francesi in Rome. Today it hangs alongside two other Matthew paintings by Caravaggio, "The Martyrdom of Saint Matthew" and "The Inspiration of Saint Matthew."[1]

Caravaggio was rumored to be quite a scoundrel in his public and private life, a notorious brawler and profligate. His subject, Matthew, was a tax collector, among the worst occupations in first-century Judea. Thus we have a sinner's portrait of a fellow sinner encountered by the Savior of sinners, only sinners. See Matthew to the left, hunched over his ill-gotten gain, so absorbed in his loot that he fails to notice the intruder who thrusts his hand into the dark room. Caravaggio required defense by his ecclesiastical patron Cardinal Francesco del Monte because he dared to portray the calling of Matthew as a contemporary event that happens now in a dark room in Rome. Matthew is surrounded by a group of Italian dandies in seventeenth-century fine attire. A bearded companion looks toward Christ and gestures toward Matthew, "Who? *Him?*"

The only light in the painting comes from behind Christ, possibly from the door he has opened when he disturbs the tax collector's den. Caravaggio has depicted the moment of vocation, the scandal of Christ selecting a scoundrel for discipleship. Christ's hand is thrust into the room, penetrating the group of preoccupied Roman money-grabbers. His outstretched hand is a quote from Michelangelo's "Creation of Adam" in the Sistine Chapel. Get it? We are witnessing not simply the vocation of an individual to discipleship. Vocation is repetition of Creation, a whole new world, light shining in the darkness in the election of an unlikely disciple.

Pope Frances came to Rome as a young man and often visited the chapel in order to contemplate the painting. The young priest in formation exclaimed, "This is me, a sinner on whom the Lord has turned his gaze." I first saw this painting as a twenty-year-old, similarly stunned by the thought that, wonder of wonders, Christ might be calling someone like me to become a preacher. I've never grown out of the wonder of that afternoon in Rome when I looked upon this painting and, as Christians so often do, shamelessly applied this Bible story to myself and switched places with Matthew, a sinner on whom the Lord had turned his searing, demanding, electing gaze.

Caravaggio has given more powerful testimony in paint than I can hope to do with words in a book. He has depicted the event of election, the outrage and mystery of a God who calls sinners, the wonder of a Savior who must keep reminding, "You didn't choose me; I chose you" (John 15:16).

The Election of God

I open my undergraduate class on Jesus by having students read Mark's Gospel, start to finish. The next session I say, "Mark gives away his point right at the beginning. 'This is a story about Jesus the Messiah, the Son of God.' Christ is God. God is Christ. Now, who can define *God* for me?"

The students call out various theistic conventions: God is omnipotent. Unlimited. Omniscient. God can do anything.

Then I ask, "Can you cite instances in Mark's Gospel that confirm your definitions of God?"

The students fall silent. Then one says, "I was bothered by the way Jesus began his work——calling twelve uneducated, untalented disciples. They are dumb at the beginning, dumber by the end. Like, if he is the Son of God and wants to change the world, how come he doesn't just change the world? Why does he need these guys to do it with him?"

It was for me a dramatic demonstration that Jesus Christ, as presented in the Gospels, provokes a crisis in our definitions of *God*. Would we really need theology were it not for Christ? God in Christ appeared, to our sensibilities, so odd that we were forced into theological rumination: "Who then is this, that even the wind and sea obey him?" (Mark 4:41); "Who is this who even forgives sin?" (Luke 7:49). Even more strange, "Why do you eat with tax collectors and sinners?" (Mark 2:16). This is the question that births all theologizing, *Who is God?*

The oddity of God in Christ accounts for why contemporary atheism is boring. At one time disbelief required intellectual stamina to devise a means for thinking without God (an undertaking that previous generations thought unthinkable), mustering the courage to reason, counter to established rationales. Today godlessness is the fallback position for anyone who thinks it is possible to think without help.

Modern atheism is itself an intellectual construction of the last three centuries. Atheism and secularism do not think by subtracting belief from thinking but rather by substituting one way of believing for another. James K. A. Smith, inspired by Charles Taylor, says that atheism is not *dis*belief; it is belief in gods that are required for the operation of the modern nation state.[2] The sovereignty of the nations as well as the globalism of a consumer economy required stifling the God who interfered with the aspirations of modernity. The West got to be secular by the same route that it became colonialist or enlightened. This is why atheistic culture is limited mainly to Northern Europe and some of its colonies.

American Christians deceived ourselves into thinking that we had at last helped create a society—American democracy—where no one could be hurt following Jesus. We could be American *and* Christian without the degradation of discipleship. That's why many Western liberals are so intolerant. Democracies get nervous when a significant portion of citizens answer to a sovereign other than the nation or who think that designations like *German* ought to be carefully qualified and sometimes disrespected by "Christian."

What to do about people who think Christ more worthy of the sacrifice of our children than Caesar?[3] Or, in the context of this book, what to do about odd people who think they have relinquished control of their lives to something other than the state? The state gave us freedom to be religious, making religion free—as long as religion promised to be personal and private, without public, political aspirations. American Christians woke up late to discover subtle forms of control and coercion hiding behind the Constitution's brand of religious "freedom."

As the story of modernity played out, it was easy for the state to manage the church. Christianity became personal, relinquishing its eschatological, cosmic, political claims. We eagerly transmogrified discipleship into an individual lifestyle choice. Pietism led the Christianity of the Reformation inward. People were urged to have a "personal relationship with Jesus Christ," which too often meant that they could make up God for themselves. Faith was rendered subjective and personal in order to defer to the sovereignty of the modern nation. The church produced thereby became the unwitting functionary of the state. Reinhold Niebuhr invited us to get in bed with Caesar, convincing us that consorting with the empire is not a problem since the imperial state is democratic. We hated ourselves in the morning.

Such an outcome would have horrified a pietist such as John Wesley. He knew that there was no way to practice holiness without the "people called Methodist" being odd. Still, the church Wesley produced, aspiring to thrive in America, has always had a tough time being much more than respectable: docile to the sovereign presumptions of the democratic, constitutional (i.e., godless) state. Sadly, American Christians do not feel threatened by the government, not because our government is tolerant of religious practice, but rather because our religious practice is unthreatening to the status quo.[4]

"Spirituality" is the latest, most widespread instance of nonthreatening Christianity. The "I'm not religious, but I am spiritual" crowd also construes religion as a human project by which we utilize God for private consumption and personal consolation. In North America, *spirituality* is unwittingly used to marginalize faith from political and economic life, confining the Holy Spirit to the individual self. This has made contemporary Christians vulnerable to the wiles of the state and the market.

In other words, religion has become a major means of trivializing God. Sadly, "religion" comes from the Latin *religio*, meaning a binding obligation. Yet binding obligations, particularly those that are externally imposed, are what modernity thinks it has risen above, blind to the restrictive obligations placed upon us by the state.

Schleiermacher sought to distinguish true religion from fake by making the mark of true religion to be sincerity, earnest interiority. Religion is to be judged by the intensity of the individual's experience, religion safely tucked into the realm of the tamed human heart. True religion, since Schleiermacher, "is only seen in secret by those who love it."[5] True religion is invisible.

Thereby the modern state secured for itself a sphere safe from divine interference. God became a private leisure activity, a notion that is constituted through human experience. Though at first glance it seems as if religion was made apolitical by being made private, there are few commitments without political consequences (and perhaps no politics today that does not assume for itself a religious aura). There was a time when Christianity colluded with imperialism, during the nineteenth-century age of foreign mission, for example. Today, Christianity becomes the unsuspecting handmaiden of imperialism, indeed of the totalitarian democratic state, by being willing to be private and normal.

American pietism slid into moralism. Rather than resist or challenge the world, let's improve it. My church talks so much about sex because sex is the last thing about which the state lets us care deeply. In my denomination's debate on God and sexual orientation, God is subordinate. The kingdom of the private and the personal is a small realm, to be sure, but through our preoccupation with sexuality, we shall rule as best we can and snatch for the church a modicum of social significance. It's difficult for us to focus on "God" alone; "God *and . . .*" makes talk about God intellectually acceptable.

William Placher noted that modernity attempts "to subject the divine to the structures of human reason."[6] "Before the seventeenth century, most Christian theologians were struck by the mystery, the wholly otherness of God, and the inadequacy of any human categories as applied to God."[7] Now, we subject God to our human judgments. Or as C. S. Lewis put it, the ancients "approached God . . . as the accused person approaches his judge." Now, "the roles are reversed. [Humanity] is the judge: God is in the dock. [God] is quite a kindly judge: if God should have a reasonable defense for being the god who permits war, poverty and disease, [humanity] is ready to listen to it. The trial may even end in God's acquittal. But the important thing is that [humanity] is on the bench and God in the dock."[8]

Or, under the guise of liberal modesty, incipient atheists in academia don't even mount an argument against the possibility of God; these agnostics simply assert that God, if there is one, is obscure, arcane, and unintelligible so nothing can be said for sure about God—other than what they say for sure about God's unintelligibility.

In a sermon, the late Marcus Borg ridicules dead Christians who overcomplicated the Christian faith by making Christianity mainly a matter of "getting our beliefs right."

What does it mean to be Christian? We have sometimes made the answer to that question very complicated, and that's because we Christians have often thought it means believing the right things, getting our beliefs right. A few examples. . . . For the first one, we go back in time almost a thousand years to the year 1054. This is the year of what is known as "The Great Schism." . . . The bishop of Rome excommunicated the bishop of Constantinople and the whole eastern church, and the bishop of Constantinople excommunicated the pope and the whole western church. The issue that led to this was a theological question concerning internal relationships within the godhead. More specifically, does the Holy Spirit proceed from the Father and the Son. . . . [Y]ou almost want to say, "How on earth could you ever know about internal relations within the godhead?" . . .

Another example. For this one, we go to the 1600s and the reformed church in the Netherlands. In the early part of that century, the Dutch Reform Church almost split over the issue of supralapsarianism versus infralapsarianism. . . . Did God decide to send a messiah before the fall—because God knew the fall would happen—or did God decide to send a messiah only after the fall. . . . [O]ne wants to say, "How could you know that?" . . .

The point of all these examples is that Christians, and maybe even Protestant Christians in particular, have been very concerned about believing the right things: infant baptism versus adult baptism and so forth. So that sometimes we have made being Christian very complex, as if it's about getting our doctrines right. But being Christian is actually very simple, even breathtakingly simple. . . .

. . . . [U]ltimately, being Christian is about loving God and changing the world. It's as simple and challenging as that.[9]

The preacher rightly asks, "How do they know" so much about God? As a perceptive, modern person, the preacher knows that God is humanly inexplicable. So far, so good. But then comes the brash assertion that "ultimately," even "actually," "being a Christian is about loving God and changing the world." Though the preacher knows for sure that God cannot be known by dead theologians, he is breathtakingly certain that thoughtful, modern people have now discovered that Christianity is about loving the God who isn't known for sure. Without a known God who does anything, it's up to us to "change the world."

Liberal theology has long been fond of God's otherness and transcendence—the old, "How do they know?" All we know of God is the vast difference between God and us. Barth suspected that transcendence can be but another way of denying that the Trinity is known to be charitably disposed toward us.[10] Liberal theologians apologetically defend God's existence by stressing God's distance but at the cost of God's immanence, which became a major path toward atheism.[11]

Our theological challenge is not that modern people are threatened by a God who exists. Whales exist, and though they are undeniably impressive creatures, we haven't let them hinder us from using and abusing their biosphere. With God, what we cannot abide is not just the possibility of a God but rather the existence of a God who speaks, who reveals and discloses; even more threatening, a God who for sure summons.[12]

A typically modern argument against revelation is merely to ask, "If what you claim about God is true, then why haven't I experienced it? After all," the questioner assumes, "I am an intelligent person and if there is a God, that God must be democratically accessible to me through universally shared rational capacity. Don't you agree that my personal thoughts and experience are the basis for all genuine knowledge?"[13]

"If there is a God, why hasn't God credibly presented him- or herself to me?"

"Why? Because *God is God*, for God's sake!" Surely it is the nature of any being worthy of being called *God* to choose to be God to whomever God chooses.

A more charitable response might be that the question, "If there is a God, why hasn't God credibly presented him- or herself to my reason?" ignores not only the past century of philosophical attacks upon the notion of universal rationality but also Wittgenstein's insights about the curious way in which (socially imposed) language tends to be prior to and formative of individual experience. I can only live in that world for which I have words. Human experience is subsequent to our words for the experience. Christians do not believe that we've had a prior, inner, individual experience of transcendence for which we have found Christianity to be an adequate linguistic vehicle for expressing that being's nature. Rather, in the preaching and liturgies of the church, we have had our lives encountered, named, shaped, and commandeered by One for whom we had neither reason nor name until it was graciously told to us—Father, Son, and Holy Spirit.

We owe new atheists a small debt of thanks. Secularism transformed God from something just about everyone believed into that which a few might choose to believe. God became an option, a contested idea that had to fight for itself in the marketplace of ideas, an idea, as Charles Taylor admits, that is "not the easiest to embrace."[14]

Contemporary Western atheists need to be asked, "Who is the God in whom you disbelieve?" An annoying aspect of the so-called New Atheists is their conceit that the god they shrilly dismiss is actually the same deity Christians serve.[15] We have no one but ourselves to blame for Dawkins and Hitchens. On the one hand, flaccid theists produced inconsequential, mentally flabby atheists. Our misguided, apologetic attempts to win the world have reconfigured the gospel in such a way that we have given the world little in which to disbelieve, presenting a "god" who is all too easy to denounce.[16] Or, as comedienne Tina Fey told a journalist who wrote that women can't be funny, "Hey, I don't like Chinese food, but I don't write articles attempting to prove that it doesn't exist."

On the other hand, the vehemence and the proliferation of New Atheist attacks suggest that God may be more actively revealing than even we believers thought. If God is so thoroughly ineffable, why these frantic efforts to silence an allegedly indescribable, unknowable nothing? If Nietzsche couldn't think God to death, well. . . .

Preachers do not enjoy the luxury of being intellectually coy about God. An apophatic God of whom nothing can be known is hardly a fit subject for public discussion. On a weekly basis, we preachers must stand up and overtly risk our sermons being used as weapon of choice in God's invasion of the world. To the chagrin of New Atheists (Dawkins, Hitchens) as well as Aging Agnostics (Ehrmann, Crossan), and blissful Panentheistic Gnostics (Borg, Spong) and all those attempting to cut God down to our size, we preachers ignore their breathless announcements. Give me Woody Allen rather than Dawkins any day. We have no stake in defending the "deceiving, dumb, dark thing that turns the handle of this idle show" (Thomas Hardy's bleak, transcendent "god"). Their pronouncements are rightly ignored by the church, except for a few self-designated "Progressive Christians," or determined disbelievers. Having had false gods widely dismissed, we preachers are now able boldly to speak afresh about the Trinity.

Talk about God

Speaking is more difficult for preachers, not for reasons that make fear of public speaking a number one phobia but rather because preachers must speak of a true, living, active God. What amazes faithful preachers is not that we have managed to come up with words about God but rather that God has come up with words for us.

Preaching's great challenge came into focus for me during a rereading of Barth's doctrine of election. Barth's fourth volume (II/2) has been called by his student, Eberhard Busch, "the highlight of the *Church Dogmatics*."[17] It is not insignificant that Barth wrote on election during 1940–1941, the apex of Hitler's power. When the sky turned dark, and it was very dark in the Third Reich *Hitlerzeit* of the early 1940s, "Barth believed that all our comfort and all our defiance depends on our understanding anew that . . . God bound himself to [humanity], and specifically to sinful [humanity]. . . . God determines himself free for fellowship with this [humanity] and thereby determines [humanity] to be in fellowship with him and with all whom [God] loves."[18] Barth could have spoken judgment and condemnation of Hitler; he chose instead not to mention Hitler and to speak with unreserved affirmation of the gracious, divine determination radiantly revealed in Christ. Thus is Barth's doctrine of election a comfort in the face of the pitiful and often deadly human efforts at self-determination that are at root of the bloody twentieth century.

In May of 1942, Dietrich Bonhoeffer visited Barth and received the proofs of Barth's unpublished *The Doctrine of Election*. (More Jews were murdered in 1942 than in any year of the *Hitlerzeit*.) The last part of Bonhoeffer's *Ethics*, written just before his arrest by the Nazis, shows Bonhoeffer's indebtedness to these pages. In a letter on the fourth Sunday of Advent, 1943, Bonhoeffer asked a friend for "something good to read over Christmas." In response, Bonhoeffer received more of Barth's work on election smuggled into jail—emergency theology composed for "evil times" as Barth said in the preface.[19] Not long before he was hung, Bonhoeffer praised Barth's doctrine of election as set, "Over against religious subjectivism, Barth here radically stresses the sovereignty of God . . ." but in a way that human beings "did not become puppets, but emerged with spontaneity, as self-acting agents."[20]

To a degree Bonhoeffer probably did not anticipate, contemporary servants of the Word in my branch of the North American church now wallow in a morass of "religious subjectivism," Arminianism gone limp. In the Reformed wing of the church, meanwhile, among resurging Neo-Calvinists, "the sovereignty of God" references the general, raw power of remote divinity. As Bonhoeffer predicted, our much-vaunted modern "freedom" and claims of free agency fail to acknowledge who pulls our strings, fictions whereby we console ourselves in our servitude to false gods.

What better time for preachers to have a fresh encounter with Barth's joyfully defiant doctrine of election?

Election in Scripture

The Hebrew *bahar* is most frequently used in the Old Testament in reference to human choosing. The verb becomes theologically interesting when God is the subject in God's choice of Israel for the purpose of being in covenant (see Deut. 7:6–7; 10:15). Barth rests much on this originating covenant with Israel, refusing throughout his career to sever one covenant into two—one with Israel, the other the "New Testament." There is only one covenant God has made with Israel: "I will be your God and you will be my people."[21] When Jeremiah speaks of a "new covenant" he is not speaking, says Barth, of any sort of negation or setting aside of the covenant with Israel but rather of an "*intensive* amplification"[22] of "the divine Yes to Israel" and not simply to Israel in the expectation of Israel's fidelity but yes to "the Israel which had crucified Christ."[23]

The rationale given for God's choice of Israel is "the LORD loved you" (Deut. 7:8). Election is love, God in relationship and partnership. In election, we have moved a long way from Aristotle's self-referential "unmoved mover" who neither needs nor wants us. This inert god, killed by Freud, Nietzsche, and the other masters of modern deicide, is ended in election. In Jesus Christ, God has turned to us and covenanted with us.[24]

In a sweeping survey, "The witness to Christ in the Old Testament," Barth surveys election as God in action. He considers the choice of Abel's offering over Cain's (Gen. 4) and notes that even Cain's fratricide does not lead to his abandonment by God; and though Abel's offering is accepted, his death is the first in the Bible. Cain and Able set off a series of "double" and "different" elections in which some are chosen for particular blessing and some are not; even those who are not chosen are not "utterly rejected" but "remain in a positive relation to the covenant of God."[25] In covenant, God promises to be God for us whether or not we are for God. Election is the plotline of the whole Bible.

These "double series" of elections "end with the patriarchal tales of Genesis." "Israel as a whole is now 'separated from all the people that are on the face of the earth' (Exod. 33:16)." Barth even sees in the ritual laws of Leviticus that declare "clean" and "unclean," "eloquent reminiscence" of the choices of God in Genesis. Election and rejection are two sides of the one God who makes one momentous choice to be Israel's God and to have Israel as God's people. Barth's interpretation is guided by Christology:

> the elect individual in the Old Testament, . . . in so many different ways distinguished, set apart and differentiated . . . is always a witness to Jesus Christ. . . . It is He, Jesus Christ, who is . . . the elect individual. All others can be this only as types of Him, . . . as prototypes or copies, only as those who belong to Him, . . . only as chastised or blessed, humiliated or exalted citizens of His community, only as in different ways His witnesses.[26]

In his creative exegesis of 1 Samuel 8, Barth eloquently compares and contrasts Saul and David, first kings of Israel. Rejecting the arguments of those who contend that the monarchy is Plan B, which God was forced to devise after God's original plans were thwarted, Barth says that the monarchy is part of the definite plan of God to achieve God's purposes. Saul is the "Lord's anointed," "One who is elect and marked by God," no matter how negatively or positively Saul responds. (We shall want to remember Barth's exposition on King Saul when we meet another outrageously elected Saul in the Acts of the Apostles.) David is "first secretly and then openly elected." Because "The Lord is with him," David is a first vivid embodiment of "Emmanuel" (Isa. 7:14). A "minstrel of God," who dances before the altar, David before Goliath is at the same time Israel's mighty "warrior *par excellence*, sent and equipped by God." In their differing lives and monarchies, David "represents the Divine Yes," while Saul embodies the "divine No."[27]

David, despite his undeniable messianic qualities, also demonstrates an eschatological "not yet." Barth notes that when the prophet Nathan condemns David for his sin, no emphasis is laid on David's adultery; his great sin is his betrayal of his selection. Thus David rightly says, "I have sinned against the LORD" (2 Sam. 12:13). David's life and death remind us that election is about that which "*God* purposes," not human virtues, failures, "gross or refined sins."[28]

Foreordination and predestination are English translations of the same Greek word (*Eklegomai, Eklektos, Eklogç*) found in Acts 4:28, Romans 8:28–29, 30, 1 Corinthians 2:7, and Ephesians 1:5, 11. In all these instances, election is a verb. "Elected" is interchangeable with "chosen." In Scripture, *election* is a name for what God *does* in history, God's peculiar way of intervening in and getting what God wants from human history. Jacob

(Israel) is loved; Esau is not chosen. God chooses Israel rather than Edom. Jeremiah's call is also Jeremiah's election (Jer. 1:4–5).

David Kelsey notes that "elected," "predestined," and "chosen" in the New Testament are mainly used in two different ways.[29] (1) The word can mean *a person or persons chosen for a particular mission*. In the Acts of the Apostles (9:15), the murderous persecutor Saul is chosen to take the gospel to Gentiles. Ephesians 1:1–10 testifies to the amazing reach of God's election in God's choice of not only Jews but also Gentiles as the church. This divine choice of pagans, so surprising to the first Christian preachers, is made from the beginning of history, though not manifest to us until Jesus. Jews and Gentiles are put (forced?) together in the church, not for privilege (privilege plays little role in God's electing), but for their participation in an earthly, historical mission to the world. Paul makes much of Israel's choice by God (Rom. 11:28) and God's election of Abraham (Rom. 9:6–13; 11:5, 7) as a predetermined move to the nations. Of all the peoples, Israel is chosen (Deut. 7:6, 7) for the mission of being a light to the Gentiles (Isa. 42:6). Out of all those whom he meets, Jesus chooses twelve to be apostles (John 15:19) to be sent forth in his name.[30] The very word *church*, *ecclesia*, "called out," denotes selection.

Colossians makes election the basis for Christian ethics (a connection that figures heavily in Bonhoeffer's *Ethics*, written after reading Barth on election): "As God's chosen ones, holy and beloved, clothe yourselves with compassion, kindness, humility, meekness, and patience" (3:12). The elect are elected to lead exemplary lives.[31]

Admittedly, there is exclusiveness in these instances of election, a mystery that God chose this people to do God's bidding and not another. Remarkably little interest is shown in the biblical narrative speculating on why God has chosen one and not another, and there is reiteration that the inscrutable divine choice is due to God's grace, never to the recipient's merit. What God decides, is decided in love; and love, as we humans know, is known for its particularity. For the Church and Israel to believe that our exclusive election is for the purpose of God's inclusive embrace of all does not lessen the partiality that is being ascribed to God in the idea of election, though we ought to be reticent to judge God by human standards of fairness.

(2.) Sometimes *election also means persons elected to be "in Christ"* rather than elected for a task, elected for participation in Jesus' unique relationship to God. In 1 Peter 1:2, the elect are "chosen and destined by God the Father and sanctified by the Spirit to be obedient to Jesus Christ and to be sprinkled with his blood." Sometimes the relationship that the elect have with God is a witness to the world of the nature of God, such as when Paul tells the Corinthians that, "God chose what is foolish in the world to shame the wise; God chose what is weak in the world to shame the strong; God chose what is low and despised in the world, things that are not, to reduce to nothing things that are" (1 Cor. 1:27–28).

Matthew and Mark use "elect" more specifically as those who, at the judgment, will be with God rather than estranged (Mark 13; Matt. 24). The Lord graciously forestalls the coming eschatological catastrophe "for the sake of the elect." Though false messiahs will try to "lead astray, if possible, the elect" (Mark 13:22; Matt. 24:24), at the last God promises to "gather God's elect" (Mark 13:27; Matt 24:31). Romans 8:29–30 portrays God's redemptive work as a series of elective acts: "For those whom [God] foreknew [God] also predestined . . . , in order that he might be the firstborn within a large family. And those whom he predestined he also called; and those whom he called he also justified; and those whom he justified he also glorified." The end result of this great chain of divine elective activity in history is eschatological glory with Christ.

> Presiding recently at a Service of Christian Marriage, it occurred to me how little the ritual speaks of "love." The couple thinks that they are having a wedding because they are in love, but the church speaks more about fidelity than love; the core of Holy Matrimony is not an expression of love but a *promise* unconditionally, exclusively and particularly to love. Is this countercultural definition of love—as promise to particularity, as the fruit rather than the cause of marriage, as something we elect to do—typical of a faith that is rooted in gracious election?

An influential biblical text on subsequent theologies of election is Ephesians 1:3–14, exuberant doxology rather than reasoned argument: "Blessed be the God and Father of our Lord Jesus Christ, who has blessed us in Christ with every spiritual blessing in the heavenly places, just as he chose us in Christ before the foundation of the world to be holy and blameless before him in love" (vv. 3–4). "Before the foundation of the world" figured heavily in later thought on election, some claiming that God's elective intent preceded God's actual creation—*supralapsarianism*. "[God] destined us for adoption as his children through Jesus Christ, according to the good pleasure of his will, to the praise of his glorious grace that he freely bestowed on us in the Beloved" (vv. 5–6). This election is part of the grand "mystery" (v. 9) of God's intention, a secret before Christ, in the "fullness of time, to gather up all things in [Christ], things in heaven and things on earth" (v. 10), an interpretive key to discerning God's future consummation of God's intent for the world.

Election in Theology and Preaching

"So, Reverend, I would like to hear your views on the doctrine of predestination."

"Now, that is probably my least favorite topic of conversation. . . . I have spent a great part of my life hearing that doctrine talked up and down, . . . I've seen grown men, God fearing men, come to blows over that doctrine. . . ."

"Do you believe some people are intentionally and irretrievably consigned to perdition?"

"Well," he said. "That may actually be the kind of simplification that raises more questions than it avoids."

—*Marilynne Robinson*, Gilead[32]

We study historical theology so that we'll know where the bodies are buried. Election by God for mission and for being "in Christ" became "predestination" in Augustine's thought, divine predetermination of human destiny. "Double predestination" is developed by Augustine in the heat of his second controversy with the Pelagians (418–430 CE).[33] To counter the Pelagian error of ascribing eternal merit to human striving, Augustine denigrates all human-divine synergism either at the beginning of faith (*initium fidei*) or in the perseverance of faith (*perseverantia*). Nothing in our relationship with God now or in the future is dependent upon human effort. Predestination became Augustine's bulwark of grace against Pelagian preaching of the need for meritorious human deeds.

Augustinian predestination—defended and modified by Aquinas and Duns Scotus—shows what happens when a theologian, amid theological argument, forces a doctrine to do work that Scripture did not intend.[34] Before the foundation of the world, taught Augustine, God has elected some for salvation, others for reprobation: *double predestination*. Election is God's decision concerning individual, eternal human destination, a decision made without knowledge of how we would live our lives.

Notwithstanding 1 Timothy 2:4, Augustine asserts that God did not want all people to be saved.[35] The Augustinian idea that some are elected for salvation, some for damnation, regardless of their merits, is defended almost always by quoting 1 Corinthians 2:7, where Paul speaks of "the secret wisdom of God decreed before the ages." Sadly, in the history of predestination after Augustine, election seems less about the gracious choice of God and more about some mysterious, decisive decree that excludes a portion of humanity, less about the calling of a few to earthly mission in Jesus' name and more a selection of a few for eternal salvation and many for damnation. Election becomes a matter of personal, individual eternal fate rather than corporate historical vocation and the outworking of divine providence.

For John Calvin, election guards salvation from being based upon any human contribution. Augustine, Luther, and Calvin are "monergists" in their rigid denial of the Pelagian notion that human beings have any means to cooperate with our salvation. These "predestinarians" hoped that election teaches humility by detaching my salvation from any of my godly deeds, thoughts, feelings, or the lack of them. Calvin's views on predestination are Augustinian, though Calvin stresses (overstresses?) the utterly secretive quality of this divine choice, calling it God's "arcane" decree, made for no better reason than "God's good pleasure."

Calvin wanted his rendition of election to engender gratitude for God's generosity; I am free from anxiety about my ultimate fate because my salvation rests in God and not in my frail powers.[36] Calvinistic understandings of election sought to give assurance and confidence to the faithful in times of distress and persecution. "I know my sheep and no one shall snatch them out of my hand" (John 10:28). In later editions of the *Institutes*, Calvin has an extended (laborious?) discussion of predestination for the apparently pastoral purpose of reassuring the elect of their sure salvation and to foster their gratitude for God's sovereign decrees. At the same time, Calvin warns that because the doctrine was apt to cause consternation among misunderstanding laity, the prudent course was to avoid preaching on predestination. (Barth smirked that any doctrine that can't be preached is questionable.)

All efforts to present Augustinian/Calvinist predestination as a cause for gratitude and encouragement failed. Since Calvin was unable to say for sure whom God has elected, his teaching tended to foster anxiety among some, smugness among others rather than humbling, comforting reassurance. God's sovereignty was cast in terms of an "eternal decree"—irrevocable, unchangeable—about which we can know nothing and (as John Wesley charged) encouraging us to do nothing. Calvin urged modesty and charity when it came to speculation on the eternal destination of our neighbors, and humble, grateful praise for assurance of our own eternal fate. Still, Calvin gave little basis for expecting charitable choices from God.[37]

As for Luther, who merely repeats Augustine's ideas on predestination almost as an aside (except for his ringing reassertion of Augustinian views in his *Bondage of the Will*), it is unclear what Calvin's ideas on predestination positively contributed to his overall theology; election by God doesn't seem to do much work in either Calvin's or Luther's theologies.[38]

Calvin's predestination, even if unintentionally, elevated to a theological virtue our ignorance of a great, arcane, sovereign God. Calvin's divine transcendence made it a short way from Calvinism to Unitarianism, then to Atheism, even to Richard Dawkins (who flatters himself as being more compassionate and gracious than the spiteful, prejudiced "god" in whom he doesn't believe).[39]

Fruitless, devilish speculation on the mysteries of predestination was mocked by Milton in *Paradise Lost* where he writes of a group of loitering devils who

> [R]easoned high
> Of Providence, Foreknowledge, Will and Fate—
> Fixed fate, free will, foreknowledge absolute,
> And found no end, in wandering mazes lost.[40]

Dutch theologian Jacob Arminius (1560–1609) opposed Calvin's double predestination by stressing divine foreknowledge. God created Adam free to decide for or against God; after Adam, human sin taints any assertions of human freedom of decision. Only God knows how we will use that God-given, depraved-by-sin freedom of choice, though God certainly wills that we will decide for God, even as God has decided for us in Christ. Arminians and Remonstrants believe in predestination and election but also affirm the power of God's prevenient grace working in us, thus advocating a kind of conditional predestination. Because of his stress on the power of grace to counteract our depravity, Arminius presented a form of *synergism* (divine-human cooperation in salvation). Arminianism rejects Calvinist unconditional election (especially unconditional reprobation) on the basis of God's character as revealed in Scripture; Jesus is compassionate, all-embracing, welcoming love. By the Synod of Dort (1618–1619), Arminianism had lost much of Arminius's dialectic of prevenient grace as powerful divine antidote to our sin and depravity.[41]

John Wesley, proudly Arminian, horrified both Lutherans and Calvinists with his enthusiastic preaching that God's Holy Spirit enables us synergistically to respond to God's gracious offer of salvation, God working in us to promote our sanctification. Wesley admired much of Calvin's thought, particularly Calvin's stress upon the "visible saints" and sanctification, but roundly condemned Calvin's double predestination. His objection was in great part based upon Wesley's contention that Calvin had ignored "the whole scope and tenor of scripture as well as the plain fact that in Christ, God is love."[42] Wesley's unabashed Arminian synergism was preserved from slippage into Pelagianism because of Wesley's stress on divine prevenient grace as necessary for salvation from our sin and efficacious even for full sanctification.[43] Jesus has not only done saving work for us in his cross and resurrection but also works in us through his grace. All this is from God said Arminius, and so said Wesley.[44]

Arminians fully agree with Calvin that all are born in depravity and sin, helpless without a massive, sustained infusion of God's grace. Christ's death on the cross is the remedy for the human condition, a redemption that (contra Calvin) is worked for all. With Calvinists, Arminians affirm prevenient grace—that grace of God that precedes our knowledge of the grace of God working in us. But Arminians stress the constant, usually victorious, working of prevenient grace that convicts, calls, illuminates, and enables, drawing us daily toward God in a way that we could not do on our own. Whereas Calvinists have traditionally taught that this prevenient grace is irresistible and always effective in provoking belief among the elect unto salvation, Arminians taught that this grace, though effective and expansive, is also resistible (as warned in Acts 7:51).[45] Still, Arminian strong stress on the special infusion of regenerating, renovating grace makes Arminian views of salvation seem naively optimistic when compared with Calvinism. Arminians such as Wesley combined utter pessimism about human nature with great confidence in God in Christ in the power of the Holy Spirit actively to save, though later Wesleyans all but lost Wesley's sense of human sin and finitude.

In comparing Calvinism and Arminianism, Roger Olson says, "Both believe God is supremely great and good. But one side starts with God's greatness and conditions God's goodness in that light; and the other side starts with God's goodness."[46] One sees God's sovereignty in terms of control; the other views sovereignty as love, one stresses majesty; the other mercy.

Many of the problems of Calvinist double predestination are displayed in John Piper's sermon, "Pastoral Thoughts on the Doctrine of Election."[47]

> As I pondered the pastoral implications of preaching through such a heavily doctrinal passage as Romans 11, it seemed good to me that . . . we should talk about some of the practical implications . . . of the biblical doctrine of unconditional election.
>
> This is the teaching that God chose, before the foundation of the world (Ephesians 1:4), who would believe and so be undeservingly saved in spite of their sin, and who would persist in rebellion and so deservingly perish . . . , on the one hand, God is sovereign, and

on the other hand, we are all accountable and guilty for our sin and deserving of wrath. If God chose us to come to faith and to be saved from this guilty condition, it is owing to nothing in us.

Piper extols the unknowability of our elected status:

> Not all things are good for us to know, and so God has not revealed them to us; and there are some things that are good for us to know, even when we can't explain them fully. . . . There are things God does not intend for us to know. . . . This is especially true of the doctrine of election. We are prone to ask more questions than God chooses to answer. There is a great danger that our questions will pass over into accusations. . . . The issue boils down to trust. Do we trust that God has revealed what is good for us to know?

Piper says that embracing this doctrine, even though we can't fully understand, has a salubrious effect upon the church's believing:

> The doctrine of election has a strong tendency to make a church rigorous about the truth and about the Scriptures, and so keep it from drifting into doctrinal indifference and conformity to culture. The doctrine of election tends to give firmness and fiber to flabby minds. . . . It has an amazing preservative power that works to keep other doctrines from being diluted and lost . . . to press onto our minds a God-centered worldview built out of real objective truth . . . the radical God-centeredness of the Bible . . . the doctrine of election is . . . one of the best ways to test whether we have reversed roles with God. . . .
>
> That's virtually what it means to be modern . . . for us to question and even judge God. The doctrine of election is one very effective test of whether you are being delivered from the indigenous ocean of arrogance in the modern world.

Piper then asserts that the doctrine produces some of the most radical, risky Christian mission.

> The humble embrace—not the discussion of, not even the intellectual belief in, but the humble embrace—of the precious truth of election and sovereign grace, produces radical, loving, risk—taking ministry and missions.

The preacher tells a couple of stirring stories of people within his congregation who have risked mission in dangerous places, attributing their bold missionary work to the doctrine of election. He asserts that believing that people are elected, regardless of their merits or demerits, elected solely on the basis of God's grace,

> produces that kind of radical, risk-taking sacrificial love; and then it humbles us to rejoice in the truth that we did not produce this beauty in ourselves, God did. . . . [God] expects us to feel assurance and joy and then be courageous and fearless.

After beginning his sermon by declaring that election predestines some for salvation, others for damnation, and that our eternal fate is unknowable, the preacher ends with the rather surprising (futile?) call for his congregation to "feel the assurance" that comes from embrace of God's gracious election:

> Do you feel the assurance-producing gospel force in the word "elect"? This is not mainly a doctrine to be argued about, but a doctrine to be enjoyed. It's not designed for disputes; it's designed for missions. It's not meant to divide people (though it will); it's meant to make them compassionate, kind, humble, meek, and forgiving.

Piper comes close to implying that congregational belief, feeling, and enactment of their election is validation of God's election:

> So in the name of Christ I call you: Come, take him as your Savior and your Lord and the Treasure of your life. He never casts out any who comes in faith. . . . "My sheep hear my voice, and I know them, and they follow me. I give them eternal life, and they will never perish, and no one will snatch them out of my hand" (John 10:27). Hear the voice of the good Shepherd and come.

Piper does a good job of boldly asserting traditional Calvinistic double predestination in a contemporary congregation. However (my Arminianism is showing) he fails to do so in a way that vindicates Calvinism from its Arminian critics.

"Arminianism," says Olson, "begins with God's goodness and ends by affirming free will. . . . God reveals himself as unequivocally and unconditionally good, which does not exclude justice and wrathful retribution.

It only excludes the possibility of God's sinning, willing others to sin, or causing sin."[48] At its best, the classical debate between Arminianism and Calvinism has been in terms not so much of free-will, foreknowledge, or predetermination but rather about the identity of God. One side sees election primarily in terms of a divine decision; the other in terms of a divine person.[49] Admittedly, Arminianism post Arminius has had its problems, tending to slide (in some North American theology) into liberalism with a non-biblical, Enlightenment-based emphasis on autonomous human free will paired with a sentimental, optimistic anthropology. (Much of Methodism, alas.) Pelagianism, universalism, and Arianism follow.

Efforts were made to defend what was left of Calvinistic predestination. Here's part of a sermon by Charles G. Finney on election. His text? Ephesians 1:4–5:

> According as he hath chosen us in him, before the foundation of the world, that we should be holy, and without blame before him in love, having predestinated us unto the adoption of children, by Jesus Christ, to himself, according to the good pleasure of his will.

Finney praises the doctrine of election as ground for "encouragement," but it is encouragement "in the use of means for the salvation of sinners." Anyone acquainted with Finney knows that phrase is tainted by utilitarianism.

> The doctrine of election affords the only ground for encouragement in the use of means for the salvation of sinners. Knowing as I do . . . that men are utterly opposed to the way of salvation; that they hate the Gospel, and all the efforts that are made to save them.

Finney says that the doctrine of election is his basis for preaching:

> What encouragement should I have to preach the Gospel, were it not that I know that God has chosen some to eternal life, and that many or all my hearers may be of this number, and that his providence has collected you here, with a design to reach you with the arrows of his truth. It is this consideration alone that can afford any ground for encouragement.

After his encomium to double predestination, Finney inserts what eventually became an innovative and influential "if," moving (perhaps unknowingly) toward conditional election:

If you will now submit yourselves to God, you may know that you are elected. But every hour you put off submission, increases the evidence that you are not elected.

"Evidence" of divine election is now situated in a human "submission."

[Election lays] a broad foundation for gratitude, both on the part of the elect and the non-elect. The elect certainly have great reason for thankfulness. . . . Oh what a thought, to have your name written in the book of life, to be chosen of God an heir of eternal salvation.

Now addressing the "non-elect" Finney finds a reason for even them to be grateful:

Nor are the non-elect without obligations of thankfulness. You ought to be grateful if any of your brethren of the human family are saved. If all were lost, God would be just. And if any of your neighbours or friends, or any of this dying world receive the gift of eternal life, you ought to be grateful and render everlasting thanks to God.

Before the sermon's end, Finney stresses that though election is up to God, much, very much, depends on our human election to be elected. Am I saved?

The question is as much open for your decision, that you are left as perfectly to the exercise of your freedom, as if God neither knew nor designed anything in regard to your salvation. Suppose there was a great famine in this city, and that John Jacob Astor alone had provisions in great abundance; that he was a benevolent and liberal-minded man, and willing to supply the whole city with provisions, free of expense; and suppose there existed a universal and most unreasonable prejudice against him. . . . Now, suppose that he should employ all the cartmen to carry provisions around the city, and stop at every door. But still they . . . would rather die than be indebted to him for food. Many had said so much against him that they were utterly ashamed to feel and acknowledge their dependence upon him. . . . Now, suppose that Mr. Astor knew beforehand the state of the public mind. . . . Suppose he also knew, from the beginning, that there were certain arguments that he could bring to bear upon certain individuals, that would change their minds, and that he should proceed to press them with these considerations, until they had given up their opposition, had most thankfully accepted his provisions, and were saved from death. Suppose he used all the arguments and means that he wisely could, to persuade the rest, but . . . they adhered to the resolution, and preferred death to submission to his proposals. Now, suppose he had perfect knowledge from the beginning, of the issue of this whole matter; would not the question of life and death be as entirely open for the decision of every individual as if he knew nothing about it?

God requires you to give all diligence to make your calling and election sure. In choosing his elect, you must understand that he has thrown the responsibility of their being saved, upon them; that the whole is suspended upon their consent to the terms; you are all perfectly able to give your consent, and this moment to lay hold on eternal life. Irrespective of your own choice, no election can save you, and no reprobation can damn you. . . . The responsibility is yours. . . . If you go to hell, you must go stained with your own blood.[50]

Finney seemed unaware that by putting people's relationship with God in terms of "the responsibility is yours," he had dramatically reworked the doctrine of election. The rest, as they say, is history.

In my experience, when contemporary Calvinists reject Arminianism it's the vulgarized, Pelagian form of Finney and his heirs. Salvation is made a matter of individual eternal destination based unashamedly upon human agency, individual decision, and the exercise of "free will."

Arminius acquitted himself well against the charges that he was a crypto-Pelagian; Christ comprehensively provides our salvation without our contribution. John Wesley's strong Christological stress on grace working in us helped to correct some of the errors of later Arminians.[51] North American Evangelical Christianity has not been so careful or successful in avoiding Pelagianism. Sydney A. Ahlstrom chronicles the defeat of Calvinistic double predestination in American churches in the nineteenth century:

As God's predestining decrees passed from favor, the floodgates of emotionalism and sentimentality in religion were opened, with the result that the doctrine of human depravity was also threatened with inundation. Because revivalists [like Finney] also addressed inter-denominational audiences, moreover, nearly all doctrinal emphases tended to be suppressed. . . . Revivalism, in other words, was a mighty engine of doctrinal destruction. "Are you saved?" became the central question of American Protestantism, and more and more it came to mean, "Have you decided to be saved?"[52]

In a sermon, Tim Keller admits that while the doctrine of election is not an essential Christian doctrine, it is still worth pondering. Keller explains that,

> the doctrine of election is . . . that all human beings, given . . . an infinite number of chances, will always—because their desires are such—will always choose to be their own lord and saviour and they'll never choose Jesus. And what God does, is he opens the eyes of some so they'll see the truth, but he doesn't open the eyes of everybody. . . . God doesn't want robots who follow him round, he wants people to choose him freely! . . . The doctrine of election only says God opens our eyes to be able to choose him freely. . . . [W]hy doesn't he do it for everybody? Well, *we don't know!*[53]

In closing, Keller says that, "The bible tells me that I am saved by grace, not by anything better, or good, in me," which means that if "my friends and relatives . . . aren't Christians—and I am . . . it has nothing to do with me being smarter or better at all."

While Keller's is an energetic contemporary rendition of what's left of Calvin's predestination teaching, note that some of the inherent problems in Calvin's election continue: Faced with the internal contradictions of double predestination, Keller says that "we don't know!" More troubling is his starting point—*the Calvinistic notion that predestination is about individual eternal destiny rather than about who God is and what God does.* Though he states, "I am saved by grace," the main consideration is the problem that "God wants people to choose him freely," and people don't. Human choice is the key; God's role is merely to "open the eyes of some."

American Christianity found Arminius's views, albeit in a degraded form, more compatible in a culture that so strongly stressed individual choice and freedom. (America is where even Catholics think they are Catholics because they chose to be.) To be sure, God's grace enables our choices, but still Arminius left the door open to what Calvin feared—a stress upon human rather than divine agency in our salvation.

We Methodists, when we once thought about predestination, modified Arminius so that salvation was dependent upon our faith—*contingent* predestination. Contingent predestination, which Calvin (with some justification) dismissed as mere Pelagianism, is now the prevalent American position. Human choice filled the vacuum left by God's arcane decree and trumped both divine foreknowledge and divine election.[54] Nowadays, who we are and where we are headed are up to us.

Combined with American democratic ideals and our optimism that we were shaping our own destiny and writing our own history, any vestiges of Calvin's predestination dissipated. A popularized, Americanized form of Pelagianism won the day. Arminian theologian Roger Olson says, "Today, semi-Pelagianism is the default theology of most American evangelical Christians."[55]

Chapter Two

Karl Barth and Election

From the Beginning, God with Us

Karl Barth is not like us. Barth thinks like a theologian, a person whose thought is utterly determined by its object, the unexpected God who comes to us as Jesus Christ and who is known to us only in Jesus Christ.[1] As a theologian, Barth not only uses words about God but also listens eagerly and receptively to words from the God who comes to us as the Word, Jesus Christ.

Calvin begins his *Institutes* noting that human wisdom consists of "two parts: the knowledge of God and of ourselves." But then Calvin says "which one precedes and which brings forth the other is not easy to discern."[2] Barth was clear that anthropology (doctrine of humanity) follows theology. Barth accuses earlier theology of "negligence or arbitrariness" in attempting to "go beyond Jesus Christ in the consideration and conception and definition of God, and in speech about God." "God" became little more than "an hypostatized image" of humanity.[3] He calls what he was doing in sections such as *CD* II/2 "theoanthropology," an anthropology in which assertions about humanity are strictly tied to prior claims about God.[4]

Nowhere is Barth's Christocentric, constantly-disciplined-by-God thought more evident than in Barth's grand excursus on the history of the doctrine of election, found in small print in *CD* II/2.[5] Barth ranges from predestination in the Reformers (not quite getting Arminius right, I think), through election as an Old Testament theme, to Jesus as the elected, narrowing to the apostles whose unfaithfulness does not undo Jesus' election of them as witnesses, eloquently celebrating God's eternal election of Israel, opening up into a virtual hymn of the election of all, and, on the way, radically recasting the doctrine as articulated by Calvin.[6]

Beginning with John 1:1–2, Barth asserts that the Word "precedes all being and all time."[7] The first great work of God is not Creation but rather God's election to Incarnation before Creation.[8] Election is who God is from all eternity; not some later decision made by God after deliberation. The Word was from the beginning, with God, as God; there is no prior God to the omnipresent Word, no separation of the Word from God the Father. The "Word"? *Jesus Christ.*

That the Incarnate is called *Word* is for Barth an indication that God is a revealing God from start to finish. God is God in God's revealedness, that is, in God's relatedness. Incarnation *is* revelation by which God is revealed to be self-disclosing, self-giving, and thoroughly radiant. The veiling, unveiling voice of God is the voice of Christ. In Christ, God refuses to remain outside. We must open the door (Rev. 3:20), but even our opening is a work of Christ who stands outside, eager to come in. That we know anything of God is proof that the risen Christ passes through closed doors (John 20:19).[9]

Thus Barth reads election not as an arcane grouping of humanity into the saved and the damned, not as futile speculation on human eternal destination; but rather election is disclosure that God is the One who elects "in the beginning" to be God for us.[10] In Christ we know: God is not obscure but revealing; not closed but open; not arcane, elusive, and reserved but ardently self-giving. God is not aloof from creation but constantly, providentially engaged in creativity that includes partnership with humanity.

When Emil Brunner charged that it was preposterous for Barth to teach that all human beings, "even those who lived thousands of years before Jesus" should be part of the history of Jesus, Barth gave the Trinitarian answer that in the history of Jesus we have to do with God's eternal being that underlies and precedes all other reality, including any reality we ascribe to human sin and even the reality of Creation itself.[11] Thus Barth's theology of election includes all species of humanity, in all of history, before and after Incarnation. God's being as God-With-Us is more decisive than anyone's placement in time. All.

As Barth preached to the prisoners in Basel on Romans 11:32, in any consideration of God, "We must start with the fact that God had mercy and will have mercy on *all.* . . . This is proved by Jesus Christ not only by words, but by the mightiest of his deeds. . . . [God] says 'yes' to us, [God] wills to be on our side, to be our God against all odds. . . . Since God's mercy is divine and not human, it is poured out on all."[12] Election is the "overflowing of God's inward being as the living God."[13] All.

In Dante's *Inferno,* as Virgil leads Dante through the circles of hell, showing the destination of various malefactors, Dante is given a glimpse of the bleak future that awaits humanity. This is a literary tradition that begins with Homer's *Odyssey,* in which a wandering Odysseus descends to Hades and sees the shadowy, meaningless, nonexistence after this life. Odysseus immediately turns back toward wife and son; make the most of this life since nothing is in the next. Dante and Homer imply that one can live this life well only if given a glimpse of the bleak next life; knowledge of the end determines how one lives today.

Barth's doctrine of election takes an opposite view: knowledge of the beginning that God has made with us leaves one free to live well in this world all the way to the end.

Barth's Rework of the Doctrine of Election

Though Reformed in many ways, Barth radically (he says "reluctantly") departed from Calvin, charging that Calvin's thought on election diverged from what we know for sure about the activity and identity of God in Christ. Barth admitted that his departure from Calvin, indeed his departure from the predestination teaching of most of Western theology, put him on a course that, "as far as I know, no previous dogmatician has adopted."[14] Barth replaced Calvin's double predestination—some elected to salvation, some to damnation—with *universal election of humanity to be with the Father by the Father's election of the Son to crucifixion and exaltation.*

God is triune in election. Election is not an afterthought of the Trinity. Election is one eternal act. God as Trinity is a single divine subject in three modes of being, God's divine self-repetition. The self-humiliation of God in the Incarnation is the act and being of a single divine subject, not the action of a subject who is subordinate to the divine subject. God as God-For-Us *is* God; these three are one. Christ is the eternal Trinity acting in history. We must therefore keep our talk about God closely tied to the event of Jesus Christ. Eberhard Jüngel stresses that "God is God's decision." God is God in relation, not in abstract freedom. "God's sovereignty is in God's electing." The Triune God is never God alone, God without a concrete relationship to the world God has created. It is the same God who acts, not God in two separate acts. "God does not will to be God and is not God, except as the One who elects."[15] The Trinity has determined not to be solitary, not to be God without us.

As Duns Scotus said, even if we had not sinned, God would still have come for us for it is of God's nature. God is already in eternity what God will be in time; there has never been God without incarnational intent, a God who revels in solitude. God elects to be the Reconciler who goes into the far country of sin and death to give life to sinners (*CD* IV).

In Barth's hands, election is first a doctrine about who God is and only secondarily about where the human race is headed. Calvin's obscure "arcane, eternal decree," Barth charged, reduced God into a dark, unknowable "shadow," hiding behind the God whom we know radiantly in Christ. Traditional predestinarianism acts as if God were holding back something of God's true identity and purpose, some essential though hidden secret that will eventually be made manifest only in eternity.

Fruitless predestinarian speculation goes against the facts of Scripture and everything we know of God in Jesus Christ. Barth rejects the idea that in an abstract decision in some primordial past the Creator predetermined the fate of all creatures, dividing the one humanity created in "the image of God" into two camps—elect and reprobate.[16]

Charles Taylor says that we in the West see ourselves as living in "closed world structures,"[17] a world without a beyond. Nothing is beyond our values, our words, or activities. There can therefore be no external word (Luther's characterization of gospel preaching), nothing arising from "beyond." Though we are imprisoned in this limited worldview, one of the conceits of modernity is to think that it is unbound. Election is therefore a great challenge for us moderns because it is a claim that the world is permeable and vulnerable to revelation from without; our lives are not our own.

Election is revelation, a means whereby, in Jesus Christ, God is self-disclosed. God's intentions for humanity and God's verdict upon humans are not hidden but graciously, fully divulged in Christ, the Elect who is "the will of God in action."[18] Election is gospel: "not something neutral on the yonder side of Yes and No; . . . but Yes . . . altogether Yes." The Eternal Word has become flesh and tented among us (John 1). Humanity is not some unspecified being whose destiny and significance are to be known only in some shadowy future. "In the mystery of election we have to do with light and not darkness" because election is first about "only one name and one person, the same name and the same person, Jesus Christ."[19] In Christ the God of Scripture is a revealed, revealing God, God who leaves nothing necessary in obscurity and refuses to leave us alone with a "mysterious shrug of the shoulders."[20]

Barth doesn't base his view of election on pastoral compassion, though his is an eminently comforting doctrine. Nor does Barth base the doctrine on experiential awareness of or sentimental commendation of

Christ's love, though it matches the experience that many have with God. Above all, Barth's views on election do not rest upon an abstract idea of God as omnipotent, sovereign, and free to elect whomever God chooses. Abstract concepts and obscure ideas of "transcendence" are defeated in the Incarnation.

Barth grounds his thought on election—indeed his thought on everything—in Jesus Christ. Christ is God refusing to hide in obscurity. God is light.[21] In Christ we are given light really to know God, and in Christ's light we know God as the graciously electing, selecting, inviting, calling, commandeering, commissioning God. *Pace* Calvin, Barth's idea of election is not an eternal decree; it is a person. Thus Barth prefers to call election, "the election of grace" (*gnadenwahl*) rather than "predestination." Election is not so much a claim about our future destiny as about the primordial origin of God's history with us, that dynamic whereby God graciously, from the beginning, unreservedly engages our history and sets in motion our salvation, engaging and saving even to death. "*In the beginning* was the Word," a Word that was God, a Word eternally determined to be God *with us*.

Milton ends *Paradise Lost* with these somber, sad words on the fate of Adam and Eve after the Fall:

> They looking back, all th' Eastern side beheld
> Of Paradise, so late thir happie seat,
> Wav'd over by that flaming Brand, the Gate
> With dreadful Faces throng'd and fierie Armes:
> Som natural tears they drop'd, but wip'd them soon;
> The World was all before them, . . .
> They hand in hand with wandring steps and slow,
> Through EDEN took thir solitarie way.[22]

Adam and Eve, having forfeited God's intended good garden are expelled, condemned to "wandring steps and slow," alone, defenseless, voiceless and bereft on "thir solitarie way," God's intentions thwarted by human rebellion.

Milton was wrong.

The Sum of the Gospel

Barth opens *CD* II/2 with a ringing declaration that the election of grace is "the sum of Gospel. . . . [It is] the whole of the Gospel, the Gospel *in nuce* . . . the very essence of all good news."[23] His first question: "Who is the God who elects and what does a knowledge of this God tell us about election?" We cannot know God in any predetermined, abstract, idealistic, theoretical, or speculative way. Above all, knowledge of God is not had by an extension of our alleged self-knowledge.

We, who are conditioned by Calvin and his heirs to think of election in terms of "What about me?" must allow ourselves to be theologians rather than anthropologists and make our major question, "*Who is the God who meets us in Jesus Christ?*" Election is thus the earliest shape of Barth's doctrine of God: "*God is the God of the eternal election of His grace.*"[24]

Barth daringly portrays God as both the subject and the object of election. God not only elects sinners for communion but also self-elects to be God for sinners. God elects to be in relationship with us as the covenant-making God who partners with us and elects us to be partners.

The "sum of the gospel," "glad tidings, news that uplifts and comforts and sustains"[25] is not a theory, a possible yes or perhaps no. Election is an elected and electing *person*—Christ—who is, in word and action, always yes. (I am thus concerned that in much of contemporary preaching there is a process of "*ex*carnation," the faith presented as a set of disenchanted, depersonalized ideas in PowerPoint.) Christ not only does what is necessary to reconcile us to God but, all the way to eternity, actively pursues reconciliation at great cost. Thus Bonhoeffer, building upon Barth, says that joy characterizes the elect, "a high-spirited self-confidence" and "steadfast certainty" even in the face of the world's ignorance of or resistance to the witness of the elect,[26] even, in Bonhoeffer's case, in the face of the Nazi gallows.

Barth claims such joy, such resounding, indefatigable Yes! because of his stunning contention that, "In Jesus Christ God in [God's] free grace determines Himself for sinful [humanity] and sinful [humanity] for Himself. [God] therefore takes upon Himself the rejection of [humanity] with all its consequences and elects [humanity] to participation in [God's] own glory."[27] There is, in Barth, a "double predestination," but not that of Calvin. The electing God graciously elects Christ to be our vicarious substitution, to take our place as reprobate. In the cross, we witness the "severe self-commitment" of God to us for our salvation.[28] The cross is God's most eloquent, dramatic self-testimony as to how it is between God and us. Here is the Judge who, in love, is judged in our place. "God so loved the world, that he gave his only begotten Son" (John 3:16 KJV).

Church Dogmatics II/2 pulsates with this Barthian discovery that *Jesus Christ is both the subject of election, the Elector, and the object of election, the elect human*. All that we know of God comes from our knowledge of Jesus Christ in his twofold election and, in Christ, we know God to be gracious. That is, we know God's covenant of grace: God has elected to be God for us *and* has elected us to be for God.

Classical theology often starts with what we allegedly know of the world and then cautiously moves to implications for what we can know of God. In Barth, knowledge of election precedes knowledge of the world. In election, God self-determines to be love and mercy in Christ and chooses, in Christ, judgment and reprobation for himself. The Father chooses death and abandonment for the Son and life and fellowship in the Holy Spirit for us. In the cross, we witness the full significance of our eternal election. Here is truth we cannot know from observation of ourselves or of the world; it can only be revealed to us, and, in the cross of Christ, it is stunningly revealed. "In Christ God was reconciling the world" to God (2 Cor. 5:19). This verse is a key for understanding all things Barthian.

Later, Barth treats salvific matters of reconciliation, justification, and atonement in the context of his prior discussion of God's election of Christ to carry though God's elective intentions for humanity. While I'm not claiming that election is the essence of or the key to all of Barth's theology (though to say that election is the "sum of the gospel" comes close), Barth shows that in thinking Christian, everything connects with everything else.[29] I hope to repeat faithfully Barth on election so that we might again marvel at the way this doctrine relates to preaching. As Barth said, "We can only repeat ourselves," especially us preachers.

> "Reconciliation" in the Christian sense of the word . . . is the history in which God concludes and confirms [God's] covenant with [humanity], maintaining and carrying it to its goal in spite of every threat. It is the history in which God in [God's] own person and act takes to Himself the disobedient creature accursed in its disobedience. . . . "Reconciliation" thus means and signifies Emmanuel, God with us, namely God in the peace which [God] has made between Himself and us but also between us and Himself.[30]

The One Who Loves in Freedom

Election reveals God as agent and the peculiar nature of God's agency. God is "the one who loves in freedom." Much of traditional Christian theology presents Christ's atoning work as "Plan B" into which God is forced after humanity's sinful "fall": God set up a good and perfect world, giving humanity freedom and a few simple guidelines for flourishing, Plan A. But we sinned, defacing our relationship with God, and God resorted to Plan B—sending the Son to die for us. Barth thinks that this makes the Incarnation originate not in the nature of God but in the sin of humanity implying a non-Trinitarian subordination of the Son to the Father.

The starting point between God and humanity is not in God's attempt to make right that which we got wrong by sending the Son but rather in God's sovereign freedom as Father, Son, and Holy Spirit to be in covenant with *sinful* humanity. The making of the covenant is not God's reluctant *reaction* to sin but rather God's eternally, committed from the first, free *action* in Jesus Christ.[31] From the first, God loves in freedom, and the sign of who God is and the goal of God's actions is God's election in grace.

Not only did God not *have* to create the world, God did not *have* to speak to humanity. Nothing in God necessitated such relentlessly gracious revelation. God freely, revealingly loves and is willing to pay the price for loving a violent people.

And so John Calvin said that God's freedom to love is the explanation for humanity:

> For if it be asked, why the world has been created, why we have been placed in it to possess the dominion of the earth, why we are preserved in life to enjoy innumerable blessings, why we are endued with light and understanding, no other reason can be induced, except the gratuitous love of God.[32]

Bruce McCormack helped us to see how Barth moved the discussion of election away from Augustine to Athanasius, away from the forensic, justification concerns of Western Christianity toward the Eastern sense of the Incarnation as an originating, universally revealing Trinitarian event. Augustine made Matthew 25, Jesus' parable of the separation of the sheep from the goats, central to his argument for double predestination. For Barth, it's 2 Corinthians 5:19, God in Christ reconciling the world. Augustine begins with human sin and ends with God's predestination as a remedy; Barth begins with God, with the Trinity, the way of Athanasius.[33]

> We are convinced that one has died for all; therefore all have died. And he died for all, so that those who live might live no longer for themselves, but for him who died and was raised for them.

> From now on, therefore, we regard no one from a human point of view; . . . If anyone is in Christ, there is new creation. . . . All this is from God, who reconciled us to himself through Christ, and has given us the ministry of reconciliation. (2 Cor. 5:14–18)

Jesus Christ is not only the demonstration of God's electing love but also its active, personal, present agent.[34] Incarnation is not a divine strategy, an afterthought set somewhere in an unreachable past. Incarnation is who God is, God reaching to us, through election, in the present. Incarnation is understood neither as divine humiliation (Luther) nor as God's hiding in human flesh (Calvin) but rather as full revelation of God's condescension, the actual being of God.[35] God has refused to render us the violence we deserve, that is, God has refused to relate to us as we relate to others. At every turn God matches our blustering no with God's gracious yes.

The Word not only became flesh but also dwelt among us full of grace and truth, God eternally electing to be God for us here, now,

> so that at the name of Jesus
>   every knee should bend,
>   in heaven and on earth and under the earth,
> and every tongue confess
>   that Jesus Christ is Lord,
>   to the glory of God the Father. (Phil. 2:9–11)

Not everyone rejoiced at Barth's reformulation of election. Emil Brunner charged that Barth's take on election "is in opposition, not only to the whole ecclesiastical tradition, but—and this alone is the main objection to it—to the clear teaching of the New Testament. . . . Barth [has arrived at] a fundamental perversion of the Christian message of Salvation."[36] Barth's thought on election is a major reason why most North American Evangelicals fiercely rejected Barth.[37]

Barth responded to critics by saying simply that a God who is not gracious from the very first is not the God revealed in Jesus Christ. As to the criticism that Barth is unbiblical, admittedly Barth does not begin with historico-grammatical exegesis of specific texts. He attempts to derive doctrine through realistic, narrative theological exegesis in which he views the purposes of God primarily through the revelation of Jesus Christ in both Old and New Testaments.[38] Christ is the Word of God, not a book about Christ. Barth's exegesis constructs an overarching narrative of God based upon what we know of God's eternal purpose in Jesus Christ and then interprets individual texts in light of this narrative. In Christ God acted decisively; we are forever bound to that revelation as the source of our knowledge of God.

Human Choice

Bonhoeffer praised Barth's doctrine of election for asserting an objective, divine act and yet divine action in which humans "did not become puppets, but emerged with spontaneity, as self-acting agents."[39] God's election is to *covenant*. "Election" does not mean "fate."[40] While election is first of all who God is and what God is up to in human history, election is also divinely initiated and sustained partnership with humanity. Election is therefore *vocation*, God's assignment of something for us to do and be in history. In Jesus Christ we know God's intentions for us though we don't know what ultimate difference our acknowledgment, or failure to acknowledge, our yes or no, our belief or inability to believe, our choices or lack mean for our eschatological existence.[41]

Augustine and Calvin knew that to be "predestined" is first of all a statement about God's eternal choice rather than a final verdict on the significance of any of our choices. Our identities are constituted as those who have been, in Jesus Christ, predestined by God, for God, elected by God to be with God. While our human cross-purposed choices surely result in serious consequences, it is doubtful that our choices constitute or deface our God-given identities as God's own. Our baffling, pitiful human no is always in the face of God's indefatigable yes.

Many of us, so consumed by our social roles, jerked around by various ideologies, find ourselves hostage to the outcomes of human efforts. We fear ultimate divine judgment on how well we have performed our sometimes-conflicting roles of daughter, wife, mother, and pastor. It is therefore good news that we are first elected by God to be with God in covenanted discipleship, and that is how we have been and shall be judged. Our ultimate significance is God's election, not our success in fulfilling self-assumed and socially imposed subsidiary roles. Our lives are God's before they are our human project.

Without acknowledgment of election, we condemn ourselves to superficial, constantly disappointed optimism or else to bleak, inert pessimism, victims of humanity's pitifully limited resources to transform history. In bondage to our myopic ideologies, it's up to us to change the world since we are the only active agents. It's up to us to make something of our lives or our lives won't be worth living. Exhaustion results from failure to concede election.

There is no fear in Barth's predestination, no consternation; only responsive awe and gratitude. Christ accomplishes the reality of our reconciliation, not its possibility. Reconciliation is effective before our knowledge of it. Our assent is not the determinative factor. We need not wait for our damaged wills to be healed. The triumph of God's grace is assured despite our resistance or our ignorance—good news for modern people who have been deluded into thinking that it's all up to us. The two-thousand year battle against Pelagianism can cease because our efforts to make ourselves right with God are silly in the light of our being made right with God.

In my experience, nearly all recent converts to Christianity know the truth of election. Listening to their accounts of how they came to the Christian faith (as pastor I never tire of hearing such renditions), election figures heavily in testimonials of how they came lately to the church. It's Augustine's *Confessions* all over again. New Christians tend to believe in divine election because the recently arrived in the faith seem intuitively to know that there is no adequate anthropological, developmental, experiential, purely subjective explanation for their being positioned at a place where they are able to say, "I partner with the God who has partnered with me."[42]

Perhaps election receives little attention in mainline Protestantism because our churches have limited ourselves to second-hand believers, cradle Christians and those who cannot remember when they were not culturally Christian. By so limiting the scope of salvation to the heirs of the previously committed, we have confused people into thinking that they are in the church on the basis of their astute choices or as the beneficiaries of skilled parenting. Is much of mainline church life boring, are many of my sermons flat because we lack invigorating, empty-handed, grateful, recent converts whose presence among us is testimony to the reality of election?

I remember a conversation with a bishop in Southeast Asia who was raised Hindu. As he told the story of his conversion to Christianity as a young adult, recounting the hostile reaction of his family, the inexplicability of his path to faith in Christ, he said, "I am amazed why, of all my family, God spoke to me. Why was I chosen for the daunting errands God has given me? I have few natural inclinations that qualify me for such assignments. It's all a mystery, a miracle, but also a reality."

God has given us a will, but we ought not to exaggerate what our wills can do. (Augustine decisively discredited the human will as the instigator of goodness.) Why do we have trouble breaking self-destructive, hurtful habits? Why do we keep sinning? (see Rom. 7:15–20). Have I used my free will today? Did I debate whether or not to eat? Have I freely chosen to write this sentence? How many of my decisions are only unconscious habits in action? And what shaped those powerful habits? Think of someone you love. Now, just for a moment, decide with your free will not to love that person. As a campus pastor, watching students grow, I decided that maturity is in realizing, and perhaps making peace with, what has been done to us and for us that we once were deceived into thinking we had done ourselves.

Christians have an advantage over the average American in thinking about will and choice because we have had more experience living our lives out of our control, of waking up to the odd realization that the great decision we thought we had so astutely produced by ourselves was made under divine compulsion. The path we thought we had chosen was actually where God had drawn us. In spite of our sinful bondage, in ways we dimly perceive, "the love of Christ urges us on" (2 Cor. 5:14).

We are more adept at attributing the externally determined aspects of our lives psychologically, genetically, economically, and sociologically than we are at naming the Christological compulsions and persuasions under which we live. And yet, sometimes, by the grace of God, even modern attenuated imaginations have flashes of revelation in which we are able to exclaim with our ancestor Jacob, "Surely the LORD is in this place—and I did not know it!" (Gen. 28:16). In such moments the doctrine of election becomes drama.

Election and Revelation

In his first discussion of election in *CD*, in his volume on the Word of God, Barth notes that the call of Jeremiah (Jer. 1:5) is at God's initiative. Barth finds it remarkable that God elects an individual in much the same way that, up to this point, God corporately elected Israel. Barth then notes that election of individuals becomes common in the New Testament. The Word of God "is not universally present and ascertainable" but is an act of God made "in this way and not another, to this or that particular" person.[43]

In his classic, *Dogmatics in Outline*, Barth defines *faith* as "trust."[44] Then Barth says, "Christian faith is the gift of the meeting in which [humans] become free to hear the word of grace which God has spoken in Jesus Christ." To say "I believe" is to say "I have been met by the God I had not expected to meet." "*Credo in* means that I am not alone."[45] Faith is relational and is determined by the One who meets us. Faith is therefore not so much when we freely assent to God but rather when we are "free to hear the word of grace" that is our election. Faith is the event that happens when we are encountered, when we hear God's word as address. Barth thus conceives of faith as an auditory event (Rom. 10:17).

Let preachers also note that God's gracious election is not only the source but also the agent in our knowledge of God. If we have anything to say in a sermon it is because God has mysteriously, graciously elected us to hear and then to speak, without our speculation or contribution. The issue is never, "Does God speak?"; we have ample evidence that God relentlessly reveals. The question is whether we hear the word as *address*.[46] Thus, Barthian theology is a form of prayer, the willingness to be met by God, to hear a word that is not self-derived. One reason why the *CD* is preoccupied with issues of epistemology and revelation is that Barth saw the modern world as an elaborate, but ultimately futile, mishmash of mechanisms of defense against hearing God. The modern world has multiple means of policing any word that appears to be inserted from outside into our closed system of exclusively naturalistic explanations.

The major excuse my people give for their reticence to speak of visionary experiences? "People would think I was crazy." That's rather brutal cultural policing of the possibility of divine address. We are schooled to be attentive only to self-initiated words.

One of the assignments of theology today is to cultivate receptivity to grace, not only to believe in God's existence but also to hear and be obedient to God's address (Acts 26:19). Fortunately, in election God, not only turns to us but also turns us to God: *sanctification*.[47] The disciplines required for the preparation of sermons are various forms of prayer, attempts to let God's revealing grace work in us to bring God's Word to human speech, to relent and let revelation control us, that is, to be sanctified.

Preachers take heart that Christ, in word and deed, is God's determination to be revealed. Christ is Revealed, Revealer, and Revelation of the One who is extravagantly known and unreservedly self-giving. There is no unknown God hiding behind Jesus, no God unlinked to this Jew from Nazareth who lived briefly, died violently, and rose unexpectedly. In him, "the fullness of God was pleased to dwell" (Col. 1:19). If the Son elects, calls, seeks, and saves in the power of the Holy Spirit, then so does the Father. If Christ talks, demonstrates, enacts, reaches out, judges, forgives, invites, and commissions, then so does the One who sent Christ.

Christ is the living God present, not confined to a dead past, not reified into a set of practical principles that provide guidance for how to live in the world as it is without having to live into Christ. Christ is present, not merely as potential for some future, eternal presence, but Christ shows up, speaks, commands, and summons *now*.[48]

God's word to us is God's will for us, and that word always remains God's. God's self-communication is not controlled by us and not available for our possession. The Word resists abstraction into three points in a sermon that enables the congregation to say, "I got it." The Word is not synonymous with human activity that is urged in the sermon. Jesus, so peripatetic in his historical ministry, stays on the move and will not be stabilized by our desire for balance and peace.[49] In being addressed in a sermon, it is more accurate for listeners to say, "He got me."

One of the challenges of the Christian life is to live with Christ's expansive election. Barth asserts, "God always takes [God's] stand unconditionally and passionately on this side and on this side alone. Against the lofty and on behalf of the lowly, against those who already enjoy right and privilege and on behalf of those who are denied it and are deprived of it." Election is the challenging self-assertion, self-definition of God that guards against our refashioning God into some manageable image of ourselves. I wonder how Prosperity Gospel preachers handle God's scandalous election of the lowly "against those who already enjoy right and privilege."[50]

Judas the Elect

Barth's stunning exemplar of the elect is none other than Judas Iscariot.[51] How odd. I remember, as if it were yesterday—when as a struggling seminarian attempting to fit myself for service to the church, wondering if I had what it takes to preach the gospel in South Carolina and if South Carolina had what it takes to take me as a preacher—I arrived at page 458 of *CD* II/2. Having sung of the gracious election of Jesus Christ as the one elected and rejected on our behalf, God's great yes, Barth finally considers the possibility of human rejection of God's election, our no to God's yes, and finds that best illustrated in *Judas*!

In Judas, we do not "find the rejected at a distance, but in the closest conceivable proximity to Jesus Christ . . . ," Judas of the inner circle, The Twelve. The rejected "cannot be so easily and simply recognized as if he were one who is wholly foreign to the kingdom of God. . . . Judas Iscariot is undoubtedly a disciple and apostle: no more so, but also no less so, than Peter and John."[52]

Barth marvels at the "remarkable calm" with which the Gospels speak of Judas. "Not a single stone is thrown at Judas. . . . The famous kiss, . . . simply shows again the proximity to Jesus. . . . The New Testament account of Judas does not say that among the genuine apostles there was one who was an apostle only in appearance. . . ." It says that "one of the genuine apostles, *one of the genuinely elect* [italics mine], . . . was at the same time rejected as the betrayer of Jesus." Barthian ecclesiology begins with Judas, this unexpected, proximate witness in which "his apostles, the Church and the elect is to be addressed."[53] We the church, the baptized, Jesus' current inner circle, find in Judas our precursor.

True, Judas' sin was of "the most atrocious character." Judas' peculiar atrocity was in judging Jesus to be less important than some other desirable good. "He is not opposed to Jesus," but Judas wants to *control* his relationship with Jesus: Judas "reserves to himself the right to decide for himself, in the face of Jesus, what the way of apostolic discipleship really involves," making faith a mere "means to some other end."[54]

"For Judas Jesus was for sale."[55] However, to tell the truth, any of the disciples "obviously could have done it."[56] "The New Testament does not see Judas and the other apostles apart, but together . . . ,"[57] together in election to be apostles, together in their misunderstandings and various attempts to control Jesus, together with Judas as recipients of Christ's body and blood at the Table. Our judgments of the disobedience of Judas have "no power to bring about a destruction or even a disturbance" in Jesus' selection of Judas as apostle.[58] Judas ought to be the epitome of the godless, lonely human being. Yet in Judas the electing grace of God, which we see in Israel, is all the more "unequivocal." Jesus Christ elected Judas to the Twelve. Even Judas, in his life and death, is enlisted as an unknowing witness, demonstrating to Barth that we can try to opt for godlessness, but when we do, we are not really "godless" because it is precisely the godless whom God elects![59] The *elect* and the *rejected* are two sides of the one human race whom God elects to love. The responsive, elected person is a justly rejected person who has "allowed himself to be loved by God."[60] All we can do is to be grateful,[61] say yes, relinquish control, and allow ourselves to be swept along in the machinations of God's grace.

If there is one sinner with whom we believe we have nothing in common, it is Judas. Yet Barth's treatment of the Betrayer reminds us that we can be at the Eucharist because Judas was welcomed to the Lord's Table. We meet no betrayal in the world that is not also witnessed in the inner circle—Jesus' good friends who are also his betrayers. Barth notes that

Judas "hands over Jesus" for thirty pieces of silver. Ironically, the apostles are sent to "hand over" the good news of Jesus to the world. Judas puts Jesus up for sale, an apostasy well known among us preachers who hand over Jesus for a salary.

Matthias is elected as a "witness . . . to [the] resurrection" (Acts 1:22), but Barth claims that whereas Matthias was a *de jure* replacement for Judas, compliant traitor Judas was *de facto* replaced by Saul, who "was like a ghost of Judas!"[62] While Judas's betrayal is serious, tragic, it does not negate the marvel of his election by Christ. Judas's betrayal and death open up a position among the Twelve that was filled by the murderous terrorist Saul. Even Judas's sin is woven into God's saving purposes all the way toward the Gentiles; the selection of sinners as apostles continues. Judas's great sin of "handing over" Jesus to the consortium of Gentile and Jewish authorities is miraculously used in the vocation of Saul as missionary to the Gentiles, Saul who "hands over" Jesus to the whole world. Judas's attempted no to Jesus becomes a mere "interruption" in God's determined yes in Christ. Barth warns that while we are not free to ascribe some "positive meaning to the act of Judas" ("veneration is as misplaced as contempt"[63]), we marvel at the way the devious "handing over" by Judas becomes yet another opportunity for divine "handing over" in Christ.[64]

The "conversion" of Saul-become-Paul in Acts 9 is thus a paradigmatic story of divine election. Counter to many sermons on this text, Saul was not on a spiritual search to find an alternative to Jewish "legalism." He was on a search-and-destroy mission against members of "The Way." His is a miraculous story about God's search for Saul, about Church Enemy Number One being confronted and disrupted, blinded on the Damascus Road by a God who made Saul the "chosen instrument" in God's move toward the Gentiles. It is not quite right to speak of this as Saul's "conversion"; he was already a faithful Jew. Acts 9 is the story of vocation, of the election of a religious terrorist to be the great missionary to the Gentiles. An implication of the story of Saul is that what we often speak of as "conversion" is better characterized as vocation, selection, summons, and partnership.

Romans 9–11 (the revolution began with Barth's confrontation with *Romans*) bases hope not in ourselves but in the perseverance of God's determination to stay with the covenant made to Israel. Barth notes that in the sweep of story that is Scripture, "everywhere we begin with human disobedience and everywhere we end with the divine mercy."[65] "The contentiousness of neither Israel nor the church can in any way alter the fact that objectively and effectively" God has sovereignly elected to be our God.[66] We humans are capable of many things, but we cannot "reverse what has been put right in Jesus Christ."[67] We can say no to the covenant summons, but our no achieves no higher status than that of an absurd, meaningless act of self-negation and annihilation. Sin is stupidity, lying about our true situation. "[Humanity] does not belong to [itself]. [Humanity] does not exist in a vacuum. [Humanity] is not given over to the caprice of an alien power, nor to [its] own self-will. [Humanity] may or may not know and will it, but because of Jesus Christ . . . [humanity] is inseparably linked with God and confronted by [God] . . . subjected to the divine will, Word and command."[68] In the case of Judas, the betrayer's "evil action is always relative to the saving action of Jesus."[69] Israel's or the church's rejection, "as the prophets continually testified, is absolutely serious, and has all the unqualified severity of the divine wrath, but all the same, it has no meaning independent of God's election."[70] In the face of any no we can mount, God counters with divine, triumphant, "Nevertheless!"[71]

We bafflingly pursue forms of existence that contradict God's intentions for us. That is, we refuse to live as creatures summoned, addressed, and loved, vainly attempting lonely self-determination. So we tirelessly cultivate and ceaselessly scan our subjectivity as if therein were to be found the truth of our existence. We listen to other words as if they were substitutes for the Word. We think about the truth as if it were neutral toward us rather than the gracious Word reaching out to us in order to use us and thereby give our lives meaning that they could not have without being part of the story of God's election. We attempt uncommitted, unconstrained listening, as if we were listening within a vacuum rather than listening to the One who has already addressed us. Such attempts are vain, not simply because we humans have limited capacity; more importantly, we cannot pull off godlessness because it is of the nature of God who elected Judas to be God for the presumptive godless.

Only a Savior like Jesus Could Love People like You[72]

Luke 16:1–13

I admit it: you know more about business than I. Unlike many of you, I've never actually held a real job where you had to get your hands dirty and do heavy lifting. (My only work experience is as a Methodist preacher and a Duke professor; I'm a business virgin.) Like many clergy and academics, I take a dim view of business ethics, informed by the movie *Wall Street*.

Stealing is wrong! Students write that down, so you'll remember. Stealing is wrong whether practiced by a shoplifting teenager or a commodity leveraging stock broker. Wrong!

Despite what Jesus says.

I stand before you forced to preach the most perplexing of Jesus' parables. Jesus told many strange stories; this, the oddest. Even the Jesus Seminar, that doesn't believe much about Jesus, believes Jesus told this shocking story.

Not to be critical, but it rather bothered me that, as this parable was being read, you acted as if this parable made perfect sense.

Made me wonder about your morality.

But to heck with morality. Jesus is on a roll: Hey kid, did you hear the one about the rich man (and you know how deeply we class-warfare-liberal democrats resent the rich!) who heard that his manager was stealing from the company? So he calls him in and says, "Show me the books, you, you alleged thief!"

And the manager responds, "The books? Sure Master. Just allow me a few . . . notations."

I'm too proud to beg and too lazy to do any honest labor, he says to himself.

Thus the swindle begins. The little crook calls in his master's debtors. "How much do you owe my master? A thousand? Let me drop a zero. How you like dem numbers?" To another: "Four million? Well look at this! Thanks to my efforts, you owe only four hundred!"

Huge sums are written off so that when the master sacks the little crook, he can go to these debtors and say, "Hey! Remember me? The guy who helped you jilt my former boss?"

Next day the boss calls in the little swindler, "OK, show me the books!"

The crook presents the ledger; you can see where he's thoroughly cooked the books.

And the master says . . . "You, you business genius you! I wish all these priggish sons-o-light in this company showed as much individual initiative, worldly wisdom, and commercial creativity! You are one shrewd operator! I'm moving you up to the front office! Even without a Duke MBA, you act as if you had one."

Jesus! There are young people here.

Jesus couldn't be serious in telling this story. Could he? Surely he must have delivered this parable with a wink. In the original, surely Jesus ended with, "Just kidding! It's a joke for God's sake! We all know that stealing is a no-no in the Commandments. Boys and girls, Martha Stewart could testify, model yourself on this story and the Feds will nail you!"

No. Though Jesus should have ended with a disclaimer, what he said was, "The master commended the dishonest manager . . . for the children of this age are more shrewd . . . than are the children of light. I tell you, make friends for yourselves by means of dishonest wealth."

Jesus!

What a burden for Jesus to force me, child of light, with a good deal of enlightened theological education, to tell this story (lauding the immoral children of this age) to fellow children of light like you! The majority of people on this campus remained abed this morning. That's why we good church-going Christians call them, among other things, "children of this age." Their morality is worldly wisdom, the grubby go-along-to-get-along values of this age.

But you, unlike them, got up, got dressed, and got to Duke Chapel—certifying you as the closest thing in Durham to "children of light."

And some of you are expecting that right now I'm going to say, "Relax. You can thank God that when faced with a perplexing parable you are in the hands of qualified, professional with an advanced degree in interpreting Jesus! He didn't really mean to commend the dishonest manager. It's first-century Semitic hyperbole. In the Greek, *kleptō* (for all you laypeople who don't know Greek) doesn't really mean 'steal,' it means 'borrow,' sort of."

Well, forget it. You children of light would love me to pull a little historical-critical slight-of-hand in order to get Jesus to say something other than what he clearly said. Believe me. If there were any way to get out of this outrageous, ill-considered, perplexing parable, the historical critics in the Department of Religion would have delivered us of it long ago.

Commending dishonesty? Praising thievery? Flinging back in our faces our enlightened, upstanding morality? Jesus!

I know that many of you—children of light—have come here this morning hoping to be the recipients of more light, hoping to engage in some fine moral tuning for your already well-burnished positive self-image. Some of you are young. You're students. You are trying to find the right way to walk in life. You want to be a better person, and you have come to church because, well, what better place to stiffen the old moral fiber than church?

While I hate to see Jesus disappoint, would you just consider the possibility that Jesus is about much more important matters than helping you to be a better person? Maybe Jesus is not going to wait until you get your books cleaned up and you are a certified "better person" before he loves you and takes delight in you, even when the best that can be said about your raunchy ethics is "shrewd."

Thomas Keneally studied to be a priest but dropped out just before ordination to become an author. His most famous book is *Schindler's Ark* (1982), the book on which the film *Schindler's List* was based. An opportunistic, alcoholic, womanizing German businessman, Oskar Schindler, bribes and cons Nazi officials into letting him open his own labor camp staffed by Jewish prisoners, thus rescuing hundreds from the concentration camps.[73]

Keneally told *Publishers Weekly*, "Stories of fallen people who stand out against the conditions that their betters succumb to are always fascinating. It was one of those times in history when saints are no good to you and only scoundrels who are pragmatic can save souls."[74]

"The master commended the dishonest manager . . . for the children of this age are more shrewd . . . than are the children of light" (v. 8). *Jesus.*

The last time I preached on this parable was in an affluent summer church in Southampton, Long Island. This tycoon (with Goldman Sachs, as I recall) took me to lunch so he could lambast me for preaching this text without saying for sure why Jesus told this parable. He called me "irresponsible." A guy at Goldman Sachs calls me irresponsible? *Jesus.*

Well, the best I could muster in defense was, "Look. I'm a good person; therefore I can't stand businesspeople who pay themselves big bonuses and walk away scot free. But Jesus? Jesus makes a guy like you the hero of his parable!"

With all of the serious, morally uplifting, important political, economic, and social issues before us, why would Jesus waste this holy day with his unholy, "Hey kid. Come over here. You hear the one about the boss who called in this little creep and . . ." How odd of Jesus to insult our goodness by commending this guy's badness?

But is there anyone here with the grace to love a Savior who would dare tell a story like this to children of light such as you and me?

James Joyce's story, "Grace," opens with a drunk businessman falling down stairs in a bar. Due to drink, the scoundrel has neglected his poor wife and family. After his near fatal, drunken plunge, a group of his bar friends scheme to reform him by getting him to a Jesuit, Father Purdon, who has a reputation for tough sermons that scare the hell out of sinners. That ought to sober him up and bring him to his senses!

To their dismay, that night the preacher preaches on this parable: "For the children of this age are wiser . . . than the children of light. . . ." Joyce says,

> Father Purdon developed the text with resonant assurance . . . one of the most difficult texts in all the Scriptures. . . . It was a text which might seem to the casual observer at variance with the lofty morality elsewhere preached by Jesus Christ. But, [the preacher] told his hearers, the text seemed to him specially adapted for the guidance of those whose lot it was to lead the life of the world . . . it was a text for business men and professional men. Jesus Christ with his divine understanding of every cranny of our human nature, understood that not all were called to the religious life.[75]

And Joyce names the story, "Grace."

Let's accept Jesus' invitation to be honest. Despite our earnest efforts and preening pretension, most of us are, more than we like to admit, "children of this age." We want to move toward the light, but then there are these shady urges, these secret habits, the things we think and do when nobody's looking. Some of the things we did last night after the party don't look so good in the light of Sunday in church. We pledge our allegiance to the Kingdom of Heaven, but the Kingdoms of this World own us. Look at our Master Card receipts, and you'll see where we really live.

You've got to love a Savior who doesn't mind getting mixed up with some of us low "children of this age," even to allow us to nail him to a cross; so determined was he to love us, as we are, rather than as who we wish we were. Only a Savior with a gentle, bemused appreciation for the antics of the "children of this age," could save sinners—like us.

Why did Jesus tell this parable? I don't know. Forty years thinking about this story, and I don't know! But then, I've had four decades of working for the "children of light," and something about church can mislead one into thinking that when Jesus says, "I've come to seek and save sinners!" Jesus isn't actually talking about me.

But if by chance, there's somebody here who is a card-carrying member of "the children of this age," somebody better at being shrewd than being good, then maybe you hear this story differently from the rest of us good ones. Maybe you thrill when the master calls in somebody who's a lot worse than you and says, with a smile, "Well done, shrewd servant. Sometimes I tire of these goody-goody children of light with their moral pretentions. I can use a shrewd wheeler dealer like you. And God knows you could use a savior like me who parties with whores and tax collectors."

How dare Jesus delight in forcing a preacher like *me* to make somebody like *you* his beloved hero of the story? *Jesus.*

Elected for Listening

After extended discussion of Judas, Barth's next section of *CD* (II/2, ch. 8) rather surprisingly takes up ethics, making ethics "a task of the doctrine of God" rather than (as we are accustomed to think) ethics as human discernment and action. Everything Barth says about ethics at this point in the *Dogmatics* arises in response to "the God who claims [humanity] for Himself" and takes responsibility for humanity in "saving engagement and commitment" with humanity.[76] A "free investigation of good and evil" in ethics is impossible for those who know their lives and thought are circumscribed by the choices of a freely loving, electing God.[77]

It is not simply that we are creatures who are the handiwork of a Creator; it is that we are engaged by covenant. Therefore, the first thing to be said about God is "the divine election of grace" (predestination), and now, in chapter 8, that God commands (obedience). As with Israel, God takes "original responsibility" for us by making us covenant partners, taking us into God's service, "for a share in [God's] own work," thereby to make even sinful humanity "a witness of Jesus Christ and therefore a witness of His own glory."[78]

Barth advocated a "purified supralapsarianism" in which he stressed election as God's gracious, eternal choice "preceding all [God's] other choices."[79] Christ's election and humanity's election are the same event. "In the beginning with God was this One, Jesus Christ. And that is predestination."[80]

"We have to realize how far-reaching is this change in the conception of ethics."[81] Humanity "is not a mere thing, a neuter, but a *person* . . . a partner in the covenant."[82] Thus even as Barth reformed the Reform idea of predestination, he modifies the Lutheran contrast of law and gospel. Law and gospel as well as justification and sanctification are inextricably linked. In Jesus Christ, "separation" is for the purpose of "subjection to the Lordship of Him who gave Himself for us."[83] Thus, what we call *law* is in the context of covenant with Christ, *gospel*, the good news that our humanity is not self-constituted.

What is our duty as creatures in the light of the identity and activity of our Creator? "Confronted with the mystery of God, the creature must be silent . . . for the sake of hearing . . . of obeying."[84] There is a "homiletic" at work here. Election is the content of proclamation; hearing is our fitting but modest human response. We are created, says Barth, for nothing more than "wonder, reverent astonishment," that we can "live this life affirmed by God."[85] God has not half-heartedly elected to be God for some and not for all (*pace* Calvin). Nor are God's intentions obscure and arcane. God is self-determined to be a redeeming, reconciling, and revealing God. We live and move and have our being under divine decision (Acts 17:28).[86]

Human happiness is to love the God who is determined to love us, listening and learning to live within the space delimited by the Triune God's redemptive purposes. This world is "the theater of [God's] glory."[87] True, we are notoriously unreliable, poor players in this grand pageant. Nevertheless, God will get what God wants and, in election, we are continuously surprised that God wants us. God does not need us, but God wills not to be without us.[88] God creates us for the grand purpose of listening "for His own Word,"[89] a thought that is both comfort and terror for servants of the word. The whole, wide world created in order to hear preaching!

The Life of the Elect

Colin Gunton says, "The people who have really moved history are those who believe that they are elected. . . . [W]hat we need is not absolute freedom but the confidence that what we are doing is actually worth doing."[90] Surely the most vivid (and funny) depiction of the bogus nature of American "freedom" is Jonathan Franzen's ironically titled novel *Freedom*.[91] America is where we are free to engage in unrestrained suburban sex, obsess over bird watching, and call it the pursuit of happiness. We are all dressed up in our overhyped "freedom" with nowhere interesting to go. This is the uncalled life.

Barth says that our modern "freedom" is perverted, Hercules at the crossroads.[92] Titanism. It is *freedom* defined as individual lust for independence combined with a drive to control and secure one's assets. Competitive by nature, our freedom turns our neighbor into a threat. We become "a marionette pulled by wires in a group of [people] who all share the same illusion of independence."[93] As the military billboards say, "freedom" isn't free—but not as they mean.

Gracious election is the basis for true freedom. "God has elected fellowship with [humanity] for Himself" and at the same time "fellowship

with Himself for [humanity]."[94] "[A person] is not nothing. [A person] is
. . . accepted by God, . . . recognized as . . . a free subject, a subject who
has been made free once and for all by restoration as the faithful covenant
partner of God."[95]

In God and humanity, there is real antithesis and real encounter. The
relationship between God's actions and humanity's is not symmetrical,
nor in "true continuity," nor "a static or permanently available one."[96]
"The free God elects and wills. The free [person] must elect and will what
God elects and wills. God is the giver and [humanity] is the recipient."[97]

Much later when Barth discusses baptism, he is reluctant to claim much
more for baptism than a modest human response to the majestic activity of divine grace. Yet this is not a denigration of baptism, because *all*
creaturely activity finds its significance within the arena of divine activity.
"If the Son makes you free, you will be free indeed" (John 8:36).[98] "The
truth will make you free" (John 8:32).

On December 10, 2009, President Obama received the Nobel Peace
Prize. In his speech he noted the irony of a president pursuing war receiving a prize for peace. After quoting Martin Luther King Jr. condemning
war, Obama said that we must "face the world as it is" (implying that
King did not) and proceeded to justify his Near Eastern wars and even
to announce additional military actions to make the world as it should be
under American rule. I am confident that King viewed the world "as it is"
now that Jesus Christ, the crucified and bloody lamb, rules. The pretentions of kings earn God's derisive laughter (Ps. 2:4) because there is a new
king (Ps. 2:5) who is the Lamb. That is what Christians see when we face
the world "as it is."

Modern Americans mistakenly make "freedom" the point of the United
States and the goal of our military ventures. "National security" is the sole
purpose of government. *Election* is permission to live freely as we are created to be, under the rule the Crucified rather than an attempt to secure
ourselves.

Election brings confidence that, by the grace of God, what we do matters. Only God knows the ultimate value of our little witness, but because
of Jesus Christ we know what God values, and that gives hope that our
obedience is worthwhile. We are free from attempting to make the world
turn out right because that's not what God has elected us to do. The destiny of the world is God's self-assigned task; our joy is to testify to what
God has already done in the crucifixion and resurrection of Jesus Christ.

With Augustine, Barth affirms that true autonomy lies in what Barth
called "theonomy." Obedience to God's call is our embrace of true

freedom from our enslavement to self-will, self-determination, and self-servitude so that we can be free to be who we were created to be.

A young man told me of the joy of his baptism into a Lutheran congregation in his mid-twenties, after his circuitous path. At his baptism, the church, "just flat out told me who I was and was meant to be," leaving him free "to relax, because now I don't have to make my life work on my own."

Election is counterintuitive for those of us who have been taught the fiction that our lives are self-constructed; God's election gives our lives purpose we could not have given ourselves.

David Kelsey says that we live on "borrowed breath." In contradistinction from modern views of the self, Kelsey says, "a human creature does not own her bodied personal life as though it were a piece of property . . . [T]he life of her living human body is borrowed in that her accountability to God for the way that life is lived as a response to God's creative relating to her puts her more in the position of a steward of a loan than that of an owner of a piece of property."[99]

The Christian life is not a laborious uphill climb but a responsive, downhill ride based upon a summons that is heard rather than upon the heroic exercise of our will to power. "Predestined [humanity] is [humanity] made useable to God by the Holy Spirit."[100] Election thus gives our lives an indelible, external determination in which we are free to risk discipleship because our lives, our choices and trajectories, are preceded by and circumscribed within God's risk to be God for us: "You shall be my people / and I will be your God" (Jer. 30:22); "I will walk among you, and will be your God, and you shall be my people" (Lev. 26:12).

Chapter Three

The Vocation of the Elect

We are heirs of the famous "turn to the subject," variously attributed to René Descartes or John Locke. Older anthropologies generally saw the human subject in substantialist categories as a work of God or as innately given. Modernity saw the human as a project of self-construction, self-actualization. We arrive in the world as humans with possibility and potentiality and struggle to self-constitute through our astute choices and decisions.

Charles Taylor says that we moderns moved in our minds from "the enchanted world, the world of spirits, demons, moral forces which our predecessors acknowledged," into a flat, interiorized, disenchanted world "in which the only locus of thoughts, feelings, spiritual elan is what we call minds, the only minds in the cosmos are those of humans; and these minds are bounded, so that these thoughts, feelings, etc. are situated 'within' them."[1] As detached, interiorized, unaddressed, disenchanted "minds" we are fated to the arduous task of living unsummoned, unaddressed lives.

Heidegger said that we are simply thrown into life, and it's up to us bravely to make sense of our random, directionless situation. Freud taught that we must grow up and get over our desire for extraordinary happiness, learning to live with ordinary unhappiness. The resulting world is characterized by vast loneliness. Marilynne Robinson takes us again to Gilead, Iowa, in *Lila*.[2] In this, Robinson's third Gilead novel, the town has lost its Midwestern, plain Protestant charm, and kindly, virtuous Reverend Ames becomes just another grief-stricken older man in a dusty, drab little place where everyone exists in isolation and numbing solitude. Robinson is unflinching in her descriptions of people who are disconnected, living in the same town but in different worlds, without bonds, comfort, or desire for more. There is no point in life other than what we make of it, and folks in Gilead know they are unequal to the task. In *Lila*, one suspects that Robinson believes that's all there is, and resigned, quiet, resignation is all that's to be done about it.

The doctrine of election is a stirring Christian protest against lonely, alienating interiorization and disenchantment that plague modernity. Barth characterizes deism's God (which is about as much of God as the modern, democratic state can tolerate) as an attempt to recast God as the non-electing, non-revealing, non-loving God who is detached from history.[3]

Though God's election is eternally determined in Jesus Christ, God's electing work is not concluded in us. We continue to be dependent upon God's address. There is no such thing as a fixed, self-defined "human being" in any abstract sense.[4] Our lives are not neutral. We cannot be defined by some alleged biological, intellectual, emotional "essence." Tragic or comedic events that occur in human history cannot define us. We are *persons* in that we are personally addressed by God's election, summoned by the person of Jesus Christ to enact our humanity as God's partner now, fresh every morning. Our chief duty, that which makes us human, is to allow ourselves to be loved by God[5] and enlisted for participation in God's ongoing pageant of salvation in a way that does not contradict God.

We are summoned to give thanks, that is, make Eucharist. Our thanksgiving is our responsive, small, but still significant yes that completes the circle of God's great Yes. We are free to be in covenant with the God who has freely determined to covenant with us. "In the New Testament election is the divine ordination to discipleship."[6] God has eternally determined to work with us in the world, to make our lives count by enlisting us as partners.

Fore-loved

David Kelsey ends his two-volume systematic theology with a coda on humanity as "image of God." After a close look at Romans 8:18–30, Kelsey says that we ought to render God's "foreknowing" as *fore-loving*. Rather than speaking of some eternal decision about who will be saved and who will be damned, Paul affirms God's constant, foreordained, loving determination to give faith to all. (How much closer Augustine and his heirs would have been to the tenor of the biblical witness if they had spoken of God's actions in terms of "love" rather than "decree" and "decision.") To be "fore-loved" is to affirm that God loves before the beloved respond.[7] Christ, the rejected, is not raised alone. We have hope, says Paul in Romans 8:23–39 because of the foretasted Holy Spirit (v. 23).[8]

A major aspect of the grand, eschatological, cosmic restoration that Paul foresees is the restoration of complete, intimate communication between Creator and Creation. The Spirit is power to speak and to hear. (Acts 2 is paired with Romans 8 in the Lectionary on Pentecost B.) One day, the occasional shall be forever; that done in us episodically by the power of the Spirit shall be us for eternity. (The Lectionary links Romans 8:22–27 on Pentecost B with John 15:26–27.) The Paraclete is promised for a purpose: *witness*. God restores divine/human communication by sending the Holy Spirit to heal our loss for words with God (John 15:26–27).

Election keeps our practice of the faith apocalyptic, leaning forward on the basis of divine promise to bring all things together, God's elective will consummate in heaven as on earth. Romans 8:28 is not cheery, sentimental glossing over present evil and suffering; it is an affirmation that we are now in God's hands; the sufferings of this present time are not the whole story. Without apocalyptic faith in the activity and ultimate triumph of God, optimism about human fate is dumb. Apocalyptic faith affirms that we are not, thank God, left to our own devices; the future is dependent neither upon us nor our fidelity. God promises never to allow us to snatch defeat from the jaws of victory.

In Romans 8:29–30, when Paul says "foreknow" or "predestine," we are free neither to speculate on our personal, individual destinies nor to interpret this foreknowledge as divine curtailment of human freedom. Paul is simply saying that, in Jesus Christ, God demonstrated a determination to be God for us; God foreknows the destiny of Creation. Because Christ is Redeemer, we are headed, in spite of occasional, egregious human detours, toward redemption; "pre-destined," "fore-loved" for God. Paul links predestination not with judgment but with hope. Hope is scarce in the modern world because we think we are trapped, fated within a world of cause/effect. In Romans 8, Paul proclaims that we are created not for naturalistic fate but rather for divine destiny.

Our experience of the redeeming work of the Holy Spirit, working even in flat, dull liturgies or in sorry, sad sermons is "first fruit" (v. 23), evidence of God raising the dead, making good on promises, redeeming our pitiful efforts to talk about God, and allowing us to say more than we could ever say on our own. One day, someday, we shall not only see clearly (1 Cor. 13) but our noisy gongs and clanging cymbals of sermons shall speak with faithful clarity.

Election and Vocation

Eugene Peterson, in his autobiographical *The Pastor: A Memoir*,[9] presents himself as an unintentional pastor. Peterson wandered into ministry, one day waking up, to his surprise, as a Presbyterian pastor, founding a thriving congregation that he didn't really intend, sharing with the church a rendition of Scripture that sprang spontaneously out of his personal love of the Bible. Peterson's account at first struck me as disingenuous. Come on now, Gene, you really are an amazingly competent, compelling linguist, skilled pastor, and eloquent writer. That just happened?

Then I realized that Peterson was pointing to a truth at the heart of all faithful ministry—*we are out of control.* Luck has little to do with it. It's not about our discernment of some alleged plan that God has mapped out for us, not about our skillful turning of our lives into our projects; it's about election. Providence. We cannot be certain, step-by-step, how the story of us and God will play out in each of our lives, but we can hope because our lives are not our own. A living God surprises, enjoys commissioning us for outrageous assignments, calls betrayers to be disciples, and likes nothing better than to create something out of nothing. By God's grace, we are out of control.

The first question of the Heidelberg Catechism is:

"What is your only comfort in life and in death?"

The answer:

That I am not my own,
but belong with body and soul,
both in life and in death,
to my faithful Saviour Jesus Christ.[10]

"I am not my own," because the reconciling, atoning Savior is also the calling, summoning, commissioning God. Paul, chastising the Corinthians for their sexual escapades, could have urged more responsible use of their bodies. Instead Paul asks, "Do you not know that your body is a temple of the Holy Spirit within you, which you have from God, and *that you are not your own*?" (1 Cor. 6:19, italics mine).

Losing control of our lives, "body and soul," due to divine, gracious election is a consolation of the Christian faith. When millions attempt uncalled lives, unaware of external authorization or commendation, it's a wonderful time to recover the vocational implications of election.

Rainer Maria Rilke was asked by an aspiring young poet for advice on success in the poetic arts.[11] Rilke advised, "turn inward"—don't listen to critics, introvert, develop your subjectivity, create from within. Look upon nature only after you have looked at yourself; study your perceptions of the world rather than the world.

The older poet seems unaware that his counsel to turn inward and listen to nothing external is advice arising from somewhere other than the young poet's subjectivity. Here is the modern way of knowing: Attend to no voice other than your own. Self-construct your life to avoid being claimed "body and soul" by anyone other than yourself. Was there ever a time when young people needed counsel to be self-centered?

In the history of Protestant theology, the conversation about election became sidetracked—whether among the Calvinists and their heirs who produced the Heidelberg Catechism or among the Arminians and their successors who spawned what's left of Methodism. Predestination, election, became a self-centered debate over individual human eternal destination. Karl Barth attempted to change the conversation by construing predestination as graciously given revelation about the eternal being of a gracious God, specifically about the eternal election of Jesus Christ as God for us.

When he arrives at a *Doctrine of Creation* (*CD* III) it is clear that Barth views creation as subsequent to, dependent upon, and arising out of his doctrine of election. Anthropology is subsequent to theology.[12] There is no existence for the human being outside the bounds of our relationship to God, no creation apart from that elected to be for God. Jesus Christ reveals that we are bound to God because God has freely bound to us. We have no independent reality apart from address by God.

In the modern age, theology has expended much energy in apologetic arguments (usually appealing to our subjectivity); the "god" who was advocated—often through sentimentality or abstraction—was rather inconsequential. The God who was (in Luther's words) "pushed out of the world on a cross" is now rendered innocuous by enlightened redefinition.

A more interesting assertion is that which cannot be known apart from Jesus Christ: God is God *pro nobis*. Against the modern conceit that we already know God, Barth alleged that knowledge of this "god" is merely the product human self-projection. By thundering, "God is God," Barth hoped to defeat our tendency, exposed by Feuerbach, for God talk to be about ourselves.[13] "God is God" means that God is singular, unknowable except through God's exclusive self-revelation. God is not us.

And yet, it is important for Barth not only to say "God is," but also to indicate the unique way that God is. God's irreplaceable, irreducible, full self-revelation is Jesus Christ. God has elected, before all time, to stand for us and thereby to enable us to stand before God, not only to stand but to be summoned. In all the Gospels, Jesus' ministry begins, not simply in his baptism in which he is openly designated as Son of God, but also in his calling and sending of his disciples.[14]

We have noted the importance of 2 Corinthians 5:19, "In Christ God was reconciling the world to himself." Now we must stress with equal intensity how that verse ends: *"entrusting the message of reconciliation to us"* (emphasis mine). The actions of God evoke, require, invite, entrust corresponding human responsive partnership. Therefore Barth taught that the church is elected and thereby called to the vocation of being the "mediate and mediating" community that exists for the witness to God-With-Us. The community is elected to be "a light of the Gentiles, the hope, the promise, the invitation and the summoning of all people and at the same time, of course, the question, the demand and the judgment set over the whole of humanity and every individual."[15] Should the community cease this mediatorial service of witness, Barth warns, it has "forgotten and forfeited" its election.[16] Election determines the life-content of those so distinguished. That life-content is the disciple-caller, Jesus Christ.[17]

Barth succeeded in transforming election from theories of how the elect finally "go to heaven" by arguing that,

> inwardly and inseparably bound up with that which God is for [humanity], is that which [humanity] may be for God; with [humanity's] deliverance, [comes humanity's] employment; with [humanity's] faith in the promise of God, [comes] responsibility for its further proclamation; with . . . blessedness, . . . obedience in [God's] service and commission as a witness of the divine election of grace [because] Jesus Christ . . . as elect person, is not only the ground and means of election, but also its pattern. It is here that we perceive the true telos of election as it applies to humanity. Election, in this 'second moment' in which the promise of election is heard, believed and received, is an election to authentic human existence as it is determined in Jesus Christ the elect person from all eternity, and as it was demonstrated in the earthly existence of Jesus of Nazareth. The elect are chosen in order to respond in gratitude to the gracious God and to become repetitions and representations of the

divine glory, replicating in their own lives that pattern of existence, wholehearted obedience and dependence on God that is exhibited in Jesus Christ.[18]

As Barth says, gratitude (*eucharistia*) follows grace (*charis*) as thunder follows lightening. Authentic human existence echoes the yes uttered by the Son to the Father from all eternity and replicates the pattern of humanity-for-others.[19] Vocation shows that election is a "completed work . . . [but] not an exhausted work, a work which is behind us. On the contrary, it is a work which still takes place in all its fullness today."[20]

Martin Luther King Jr. frequently told the African American church that it had a vocation to correct and to save the North American church from its racist sins. The election of the black church was to participate in God's redemption of the world. Vocation is to join in God's mission.

Chapter Four

Called for Mission

The French Roman-
esque tympanum
from the abbey at Véz-
elay, is unique iconog-
raphy. Worshipers are
greeted with a depic-
tion of Pentecost as the
sending of the apos-
tles to the ends of the
earth. Christ's hands are
thrown open as if casting

the apostles to the four winds. Those who have come toward Christ are
now sent out by Christ. Pentecostal fire descends upon the apostles, and
the Pentecostal wind blows them in centrifuge throughout the world.
Sending is an odd way to welcome entrants into the abbey. Those who
enter the church as the elect are also those commissioned, sent forth to
announce the outpouring of the Spirit on all flesh.[1] The word *Mass*, is
derived from *missio*, "sent." The church is "apostolic" when it allows itself
to be thrown out of the church into the world with news.

Elected for Mission

A primary way that God is for us is through elected people. Call is analogous to Creation. Israel begins with the calling of Abraham *ex nihilo*. Just
as God the Creator spoke a world into being out of nothing, so Israel
is created by vocation. John the Baptizer warns the crowds not to take

comfort, saying, "We have Abraham as our ancestor," for "God is able from these stones to raise up children to Abraham" (Luke 3:7–8). God's people are raised through vocation, rather than merely natural generation. The first Christians could be blasé about marriage and children because this kingdom grows not by children through coitus but rather by conversion through preaching.

Jesus, like David and his descendants, is God's "chosen" (Luke 9:35; 23:35), the "servant, whom I have chosen" (Matt. 12:18; related to Isa. 42:1). As "chosen one," Jesus chooses twelve whom he names "apostles" (Luke 6:13; Acts 1:2). Paul is "chosen" (Acts 22:14). The chosen choose others (Acts 15:22, 25). Thus the whole church is referred to as the "elect" (1 Cor. 1:27–28; Eph. 1:4; 2 Thess. 2:13).

To think about election as vocation we begin with the programmatic overview that opens the Acts of the Apostles: "But you will receive power when the Holy Spirit has come upon you, and you will be my witnesses in Jerusalem, in all Judea and Samaria and to the ends of the earth" (Acts 1:8).

This verse is the basis for the great missionary/theologian Bishop Lesslie Newbigin's claim that *the doctrine of election is the foundation for Christian mission.* Newbigin's groundbreaking work on mission and evangelism, *The Open Secret,* was inspired by his reading of Barth's *CD*/II, 2, upon his return to England from India in 1974.[2] Newbigin's is a fecund, missionary adaptation and vocational application of Barth's doctrine of election.[3]

Among Newbigin's insights on election are:

1. *In Scripture, election is corporate, the first case of election being God's choice of Israel.* The traditional Augustinian construal of election led to a highly individualistic, ahistorical (therefore unbiblical) idea of predestination. In the Old Testament, God chooses a particular community to accomplish God's purposes for the world. *Election* refers to the "chosenness" of those who comprise God's "people."[4] The people play no role in being designated as the "elect"; God has determined their identity, assignment, and destiny. Newbigin prefers to speak of the "electedness" of a people, whereas Barth focuses upon the "electing" choice of God. While Barth asserts the vocational quality of election, Newbigin gives major stress to particular vocational actions upon humanity whereby God's overall elective intent is realized.[5] Barth is amazed by election's revelation of the identity of God; Newbigin stresses election as the unique divine method through which the ultimate purposes of God are carried forward through God's utilization of Israel and the church. The church is necessary because it knows what the world does not yet know: God has reconciled the world to God, has reconciled not only those in the church but those without.

The church is those who have happily heard, who regularly pause to hear again and to listen more closely, then move into the world to witness to that which the world has not heard, thus widening the circle of those who hear—all the way to the end of the earth.

2. While Barth said that "the election of grace is the sum of the gospel,"[6] Newbigin stresses that *election is not only the gospel's singular content but also God's unique method.* For Barth, election is a divine decision (with continuing consequences) made for all eternity in Jesus Christ. Newbigin stresses election as God's acting personally and particularly in history by selecting and designating Israel and the church as God's own to do God's work. Election is less a "decree," or "decision," than *commission.* Hunsberger says, "Newbigin invariably takes Abraham as his point of departure while Barth begins emphatically from the election of Jesus." This Abrahamic point of departure enables Newbigin to portray the history of Israel as integrally connected to the church, defining election as missional in intent, universal in scope.[7]

Unlike Newbigin, many Missiologists see election as a negative, even dangerous idea.[8] Bryan Stone warns that there is a "temptation to turn election into . . . exclusion, nationalism, ethnocentrism, and self-trust . . . , [making] election, a precarious theological notion" that "plays out ambiguously in the story of the people of God . . . as true in the case of the church as of Israel."[9]

Newbigin audaciously makes election the basis of evangelism and mission:

> The Church is the bearer of the work of Christ through history, but not the exclusive beneficiary. God purposes the salvation of all. For this purpose [God] has chosen a people. Because that people have over and over again fallen into the sin of supposing that they have a claim upon God which others do not have, they have over and over again been punished and humiliated and have had to hear the word of God spoken to them from others. . . . Whenever the Church has imagined that it had a claim upon God which others did not have, it is already fallen away from grace. The church is servant and not master. It is appointed to a stewardship on behalf of all, not to a privilege from which others are excluded.[10]

3. Newbigin follows Barth in his opposition to a merely instrumental view of election. *Election is not only for service but also to sign, to signal, to witness, and to be a genuine, corporate, visible foretaste of what the kingdom of*

God looks like. The church is "not merely the instrument of the apostolic mission, it is also its end and purpose."[11] Election is an invitation not merely to a new concept of God but rather to participatory membership in the ongoing people of God. By God's sovereign call, the church is launched in mission. The church is a showcase of God's revelation in which the lowly and sinners are chosen as a sign of what God does now and of what God will do in the future. Election and revelation are corollaries. Israel and the church are chosen as object illustrations of God's glory. We can never talk about election in a way that is abstracted from the actual life of the elect community and its relationship with people around it. Nor can the church speak of election except in terms of a gracious invitation that extends beyond the church for all to join the church in living out the joy and the responsibility of election—now. This community has begun to taste, even if only foretaste, the reality of the kingdom. The church is the hermeneutic of its message.[12] Christians believe that God purposes the salvation of all, but that purpose will not be accomplished in a way that ignores or bypasses the historical events named *Israel* and *church* by which salvation is in fact visibly, institutionally revealed.

Newbigin says, "The church is a movement launched into the life of the world to bear in it God's own gift of peace for the life of the world. It is set, therefore, not only to proclaim the kingdom but to bear *in its own life* the presence of the kingdom."[13] This suggests that the greatest evangelistic, missionary need is not better arguments through which to appeal to the world but rather a better church that does not contradict Christ's appeal to the world.

4. *Salvation is from the Jews.* I infer that Newbigin would interpret the traditional Latin tag, *nulla salus extra ecclesiam*, "no salvation outside the church," to indicate that Christianity is training in humble receptivity of the gift of salvation from Israel and the church.[14] His reading of Romans 9–11 led Newbigin to state, "we are in a position of having to receive salvation from the hand of others, salvation can only be in mutual dependence and relatedness."[15] Salvation is not only intrinsically corporate but also a gift, first to Israel, then surprisingly to the Gentiles. The gratuitous nature of God's choice of the Jews induces humility in us Gentiles who can receive salvation only through the Jews.[16]

On December 10, 1933, Karl Barth preached in the *Schlosskirche* in the middle of the University of Bonn. (I preached from this pulpit sixty years later.) Only one year into his chancellorship of the Reich, the university had fallen willingly into the hands of Hitler, with many students and faculty embracing Nazi anti-Jewish laws. Barth stood in the university pulpit and, taking his text from Romans 15:5–13, preached on Christian indebtedness to God's election of Israel. Midway through his sermon, Barth reiterated:

> "Christ has received us," received us as a beggar is received off the street, received as people who did not even think it possible nor who could have thought it possible to receive him but rather as people who really could only have been received. We can even go so far as to say: accept[ed], like an orphan is accepted into an orphanage, accepted to be something that we innately are not, namely accepted as his brothers and children of his father. We could even say taken along or taken into the district where he, the Son of God, leads, governs, carries the responsibility and creates. . . . Based on our own will, we would never have been taken along and taken into this district. Yet he has taken us there. . . .
>
> [Christ] sees us as Jews in conflict with the true God and as Gentiles living peacefully with the false gods, but he sees us both united as "children of the living God" (Hos. 1:10).[17]

The resourceful university congregation—as well as the Nazis who fancied themselves as fully capable, strong saviors of the nation—received the sermon as an attack. A number of people walked out of the *Schlosskirche* before Barth finished.

Barth sent a copy of the sermon to Hitler. We have no record of Hitler's response.

Any attempt to detach our Christian electedness from Israel negates God's actions in history and leads to horribly unjustified Christian pride. The single nonbiblical example in Barth's sermon is the Marquis D'Argens who, when asked by Frederick the Great (Prussia's greatest ruler) for "a single irrefutable proof of God," replied, "Your Majesty, the Jews" (1779). The persistence of Israel against all odds is testimony to the faithfulness of God who keeps covenant. Israel and the Jews are at the heart of the wonder that is God's election of grace. How odd of God to choose the Jews, who, by their very existence, reveal and carry through God's electing intent for the world amid a world that has so many ways of rejecting the Jews.

The Jews are a visible, bodily present assertion that you can't be saved by yourself. You cannot think up the gospel on your own; we submit in empty-handed receptiveness to salvation at the hands of others.

A reiteration of the wonder of Israel's election is *church*. "Salvation is through this relatedness," says Newbigin.[18] This choice of God to work in, through, and in spite of the church in our election is the great scandal of gracious particularity that is at the heart of humanity's election. Newbigin describes the scandal as he has heard it from the lips of Hindu friends:

> Is it really credible that the Supreme Being whom I and my fore-fathers have loved and worshipped for 40 centuries is incapable of meeting my soul's need, and I must await the coming of an agent of another tradition from Europe or North America if I'm to receive his salvation? What kind of God are you asking me to believe in? Is this not simply the projection of your culture-bound prejudices? Let's be reasonable! Let us open our treasurers and put them side-by-side and we shall see that your symbols and mine are but the differing forms of one reality shaped according to the different histories and cultures. If God is truly the God of all peoples and all the earth, then surely God can and will save me, where I am and with the means God has provided for me in the long experience of my own people.[19]

Newbigin has heard similar outrage within the walls of his own church:

> Once I join with a sincere heart adherents of all religions, in seeking the fullness of truth to which they all aspire, is that not enough? Why not join all people of goodwill in tackling the real human problems of hunger, oppression, sickness, and alienation, instead of seeking mere adherence to your religious group? Is your missionary enterprise not an offense against the unity of humanity? Is not the just unity of all peoples a matter of such urgency that to propagate something so divisive as religion is almost a crime against humanity?[20]

Sentimentality of this sort is unsurprising in a world that considers "religion" (Hinduism, Christianity, and Islam have commonality as "religions"?) a threat to the global aspirations of democratic capitalism. Newbigin says such thinking plays into the hands of the modern tendency to universalize in order to suppress the particular. Universalizing and idealizing God's relation to humanity risks undercutting the uniquely historical claims of biblical faith. To reduce election to an inclination of generalized, vague, metaphysical divine love—rather than historically/

biblically grounded divine summons to membership in a peculiar people—detaches salvation from Israel and the church.[21]

Liberal Christianity's dis-ease with the election of Israel and the church is incipient anti-Jewishness. The peril of ignoring the election of Israel as revelatory of the truth about God is illustrated in an article by Joseph Webb (published *before* he was elected president of the Academy of Homiletics). Webb proclaimed a "revolution" in Christian preaching would occur when Christian preachers took their hands off exclusively Jewish Scriptures. Any attempt by Christians to see in Jews a precursor of Gentile Christian election is dismissed by Webb as a Christian perversion of the religious aspirations of Israel. In his attempt to defend Jews against anti-Jewish Christian preaching, Webb unwittingly dismisses the "Hebrew Bible" as a figment of religious imagination:

> What do we have, then, in the Hebrew Bible? We have a classic story of a people hammering out an identity for themselves and their families and clans . . . an identity that changed as their definitions of their God changed. So the questions for Christian preaching are not primarily . . . What did God do to these people? What claims did God make on them? . . . The questions center, instead, on . . . How did these historic religious people, at various times in their history and by their own telling, come to understand themselves as "children" of a supreme being for whom they had many names? How did they come to frame such odd ethical notions and define God as overlooking, if not blessing, those notions . . . ? How did they come to draft, and progressively refine, such a remarkable religious document as the Decalogue? Yes, of course, we can say that it came from God, was "given" to them by God; but that begs the question. These remarkable people created legends and stories to frame where those "laws" came from. They devised—someone in their past devised— vibrant myths to account for the origins of those priceless laws, but vibrant myths nevertheless. What remarkable religious imagination and ethical sensibility combined to create these great stories . . . of human and divine meeting in mortal flesh and flawed community? In Christian preaching, then, there is so much to draw on in the Hebrew Bible. . . . But it is not because the Hebrew Bible is about Christ—which it isn't; nor is it even because it is about God. . . . It is because it is about the human condition, about richly textured mythic stories of naming "God," . . . of coping with good and evil,

and of struggling to live together. . . . Thus, the stories of those
ancient peoples . . . whether we are Christian or Jew or Muslim . . .
still have power.[22]

Webb depicts the Old Testament, indeed the existence of Jews, as the
result of an overwrought human imagination. If you think Barth's polemic
against insidious "religion" too severe, Webb's thoughts on the "Hebrew
Scriptures" ought to give you pause.

Modernity's universal and democratic aspirations make anathema the
idea of divine choice of Jews. As Newbigin says, the gospel is "universal" but in a peculiar, counterintuitive way. Biblical universalism is that
dynamic whereby God provides that each receives Christ from another.[23]
The Christian life is training in receptivity and gratitude that "salvation is
from the Jews" (John 4:22). The universal is achieved through missionary
particularism. God's elective work begins as Noah is chosen to preserve
all creatures. Then there is a narrowing to Abraham and Sarah and their
progeny, a further reduction to the family of Jacob, and then to one chosen
man, Christ, "who bears the whole purpose of cosmic salvation in his own
person." From there election broadens out again in Acts to "a few who are
called to be bearers of the secret,"[24] spectacularly broadening into the excla-
mation, "Has God's salvation gone even to the Gentiles?" (see Acts 11:18).

The biblical idea of election boldly asserts Kierkegaard's "scandal
of particularity," that odd way in which God achieves God's universal
intentions by electing particular people: "Many are called, but few are
chosen" (Matt. 22:14). Election is an awe-filled "mystery" (Rom. 11:25);
pride is inappropriate, "Do not become proud, but stand in awe" (Rom.
11:20). God chooses particular women and men, not for privilege, but for
responsibility. This is why Newbigin says, "The doctrine of election, so
central to the whole Bible, is necessarily central for a true understanding
of missions."[25] Newbigin marvels that the New Testament interweaves
themes of particularity and universality without any sense of incompat-
ibility, universal purpose carried out in a continuous series of particular
choices, one chosen for the sake of many.

The secret of who God is and where the world is being guided has
been entrusted to marginal communities scattered throughout Asia
Minor—the narrative of Acts. Why has God chosen a particular community among all the peoples to bear the secret? Indeed, *why has God chosen
you or me?* That is the open secret of God's expansive intention to bless
all the nations through the scandal of God's elect.

True, the idea of particular people chosen by God can be dangerous. We need only recall Ronald Reagan's purloining of the Puritan "city on a hill" and transposing it to the United States. The nefarious notion of the United States as a "chosen nation" and the persistent fiction of "American exceptionalism" are mutated, mutilated versions of "election."[26]

Barth moves from God's eternal, general "election" toward the particular "elect," in order to combat the notion of "double predestination"; Newbigin moves from the particular election of Israel in order to undergird mission. Barth is unwilling to make much distinction between the "elect" and the "rejected"—God's "primal decision" is "altogether yes" for all. Newbigin keeps God's determination (Barth's "election") and God's determining (Barth's "calling") together, stressing what God is actually doing in human history.

Newbigin, as "universalist" as Barth, grants a kind of dignity to the unbeliever's disbelief that Barth appears reluctant to recognize. I presume that Newbigin's willingness to contrast the "elect" and the "non-elect" is part of his deep missionary commitment. Those who do not know God's gracious election ought to be told.

5. Those who search backward from their presumption of election to a possible rationale for their election are told by Newbigin to "*press forward from their election to the purpose . . . , which is that they should be Christ's ambassadors and witnesses to the ends of the earth.*"[27] They are the ones, "by whom [God] purposes to save the world," by "choosing and calling a particular people."[28] Salvation is more than a matter of individual soul-destiny; salvation is the choice of some to live uniquely on behalf of others who do not yet know that they too have been "chosen." Whereas Calvinism made ignorance of God's choice into a theological virtue, Newbigin celebrates that we are chosen, "to be the bearers of his promise of blessing of all [humanity]."[29]

Newbigin notes that Barth said, in his *Doctrine of Reconciliation*, that "it is common to all the biblical accounts of calling that to be called means being given a task,"[30] and that the vocation of Christians, "is that God makes them [God's] witnesses . . . in [God's] past, present and future action in the world and in history, of [God's] being in [God's] acts among and upon [humanity]."[31] We are elected as "bearers" rather than "exclusive beneficiaries," elected as witnesses to the salvation of God. When I encounter someone who is not Christian, Newbigin says, "I meet [that person] simply as a witness, as one who is been laid hold of by Another and placed in a position where I can only point to Jesus as the one who can make sense of the whole human situation which my partner and I share as fellow human beings. This is the basis of our meeting."[32]

The particularism of Deuteronomy ought to be read in the context of Creation and God's covenantal desire to be related not only to Noah and his descendants (Gen. 6:18) but also to "every living creature" (Gen. 9:10, 12, 15) and even the whole "earth" (Gen. 9:13). The logic of election moves from choice of the particular for the purpose of the universal. "I will walk among you, and will be your God, and you shall be my people" (Lev. 26:12), which Barth says underscores the two-sided nature of the covenant. Just as there is "no God but the God of the Covenant," there is "no [person] but the [person] of the covenant."[33] God has elected to be our "companion."[34]

God could have chosen others, but oddly, God chose us. We cannot say why but we know wherefore: "The great joy of the Christian is that we have gotten the news. The great *responsibility* of the Christian is that we are to bear this news into the world."[35] The narrowing of covenant to Abraham (Gen. 15:18) is so that "in you all the families of the earth shall be blessed" (Gen. 12:3), and Genesis 18:19 describes Abraham's assignment as "doing righteousness and justice" before all the peoples of the earth. "You did not choose me, but I chose you. And I appointed you *to go and bear fruit*" (John 15:16, italics mine).

In his last segment of the *Dogmatics*, Barth describes *sanctification* as "the separation, claiming, commandeering, and preparation of a person," with a view to the purpose God destines for them, which is the service of God.[36] Our diverse ministries, particularly the ministry of proclamation, have no greater authorization. We have been miraculously, inexplicably chosen for service, elected to speak to the church, thereby enabling the church to speak to the world. Our authorization never exceeds that given in Acts 10:40–41: "[B]ut God raised him on the third day and allowed him to appear, not to all the people, but to us who were chosen by God as witnesses."

Here is a Newbigin summary of what we are to say:

> I make this confession—that Jesus Christ is Lord of all—only because I have been laid hold of by Another and commissioned to do so. It is not primarily or essentially my decision. By ways which are mysterious to me, which I can only faintly trace, I've been laid hold of by one greater than I can lead into a place where I must make this confession where I find a way of making sense of my own life or of the life of the world except by being obedient disciple of Jesus.[37]

A fully human being is one who is summoned. The world is created through address. After preaching to the "formless void," God addresses the earthlings: "Adam . . . where are you?" (Gen. 3:9). Barth says, "We know [life] because God addresses us and acknowledges that *we are alive*."[38] To be addressed is to be called; my life specified, given significance by God's imperatival presence. My life is given distinctiveness, not by my heroic efforts ("I've got to be me."), but rather because of my particular vocation ("What does God expect of me?). Scripture shows little interest in some human inner essence, no notion that I am most myself when I have shed my commitments and my externally imposed relationships. I exist because I have been called upon. The Greek *parakaleo* ought usually to be translated not only as "called" but "called *alongside*."

For Barth, the whole notion of external divine summons, in its sheer objectivity, is rebuke to what Barth calls "the great anthropological myth," the fiction that what we call "God" is but a symbolization of human self-assertion and self-security.[39]

Thus Barth dismisses biography (and especially autobiography) as "a very questionable undertaking . . . because it almost always presupposes that we occupy some seat from which we can see the sequence of moments which constitutes the life of someone, or even our own life, whereas in fact we do not occupy any such seat. What we are in the totality of our moments, God knows, we do not."[40]

Emily Dickinson lamented (I assume), "Christ is calling everyone here, all my companions have answered . . . and I am left standing alone."[41] A major task of Christian ministry is therefore helping our people be open to divine summons and then to have the guts to say yes. No small task in a culture that leads people to believe that they can live unsummoned lives.

"A Christian is a person who is grasped and held by God and cannot escape [God's] claim."[42]

The First of the Elect

Abraham was the first called individual and therefore first true personality. Genesis presents nothing about Abraham that is of great interest until on a starry night Abraham is called out of his tent and drawn into God's covenant, made a partner in God's continuing work in the world (Gen. 12).

And yet Abraham's call into covenant is not the end of God's elective work with him. Another story of God and Abraham is even more revealing. In Kierkegaard's *Fear and Trembling*, "John the Silent" delivers a tough sermon to Denmark. His text? One of the most disturbing instances of election: Genesis 22 (my paraphrase):

"God tested Abraham saying, "Abraham!" And he said, "Here I am.""

We are hearing a call story with the responsive, "Here I am."

"Take your son, your only son, Isaac, and go to the land of Mariah and offer him there as a burnt offering on one of the mountains that I will show you. So Abraham rose early in the morning, saddled his donkey, and took two of these young men with him, and his son, Isaac.

On the third day, Abraham looked up and saw the place far away. Then Abraham said to his young men, "Stay with the donkey. The boy and I will go over there; we will worship, and then we will come back to you." Abraham took the wood of the burnt offering and laid it on his only son, Isaac, and he himself carried the fire and the knife. So the two of them walked together.

Isaac said to his father, "Father," and he said, "Here I am, my son." He said, "The fire and the wood are here. But where is the lamb for the burnt offering?" Abraham said, "God himself will provide the lamb for a burnt offering, my son. When they came to the place that God had shown him, Abraham built an altar there and laid the wood. He bound his son, Isaac, and laid him on the altar, on top of the wood. Then Abraham reached out his hand and took the knife to kill his son. But the angel of the Lord called him from heaven and said, "Abraham, Abraham," and he said, "Here I am.""

Vocation is not once but is repeated, intensified, and further explicated along the way.

He said "Do not lay your hand on the boy or do anything to him for now I know that you fear God."

Hebrews makes Abraham the exemplar of Christian faith, even though Abraham never met Christ. Kierkegaard calls him the "knight of faith." "Faith" had become a problem in Denmark, according to Kierkegaard, because everybody, being inoculated in the state church by a small dose of false faith, was protected from the real thing. In making Abraham the knight of faith, Kierkegaard highlights faith as obedience to inexplicable divine summons. God commands; Abraham obeys without explanation or argument. The Sinai, covenanting God speaks apodictically: Take your only son; that is, take your future, relinquish control of the significance of your life, and give back to God who gave to you.

Abraham is justly called not only "man of faith" but also the first disciple, for he is analogous to the disciples whom Jesus called with a mere "Follow me." They must venture forth without knowledge of destination or assurance that Jesus will take them anywhere other than to the cross. In his longest discussion of "faith" in Romans, Paul talks about Abraham. It's a problematic passage if faith is something we do; who is able to do as Abraham has done? This story, as told by Paul, is the story of Jesus, says Douglas Campbell. Abraham ought to be read christologically. Indeed, in his analysis of Romans 6:8 Campbell (in his assault on the "contractual theory" of justification) says that Paul defines *faith* as "*the theological journey that Christians are meant to undertake in the light of the Christ event.*"[43]

Abraham's stereotypical "Here I am, Lord" indicates that someone is venturing forth into unknown terrain solely at the command of God, relinquishing control. Election is not only invitation; it is also fearful command.[44]

I was attempting to console a pastor in Alabama after Easter week tornadoes had virtually destroyed his church's buildings. He said, "We had our white congregation almost next door to an African American church. We talked about how we ought to be more cooperative. We worshiped together on Thanksgiving. Once had Easter Sunrise Service. That was it. The week after that tornado destroyed our church, well, I'm not saying God did it. Funny though, next week we merged our churches. We didn't know we loved that old building too much for our own good, till God ripped it off. Bible says, 'God is jealous.'"

Or as Karl Barth exclaimed in a letter to his brother, after commenting on his life turned upside down in parish ministry, "Don't things get dangerous when God is?"

I enjoy teaching in a seminary because it is humbling to be cast with people whose lives are out of control due the vocation of God. Though Schleiermacher said it was impossible to preach Genesis 22 to modern people come of age, I can testify that there are still those whose lives are analogous to Abraham, risking subordination of success, family, and future due to the conviction that God is, that God refuses to be God alone, that God not only loves but commands.

As Barth said, "Preachers dare." Preachers dare that silent, solitary Abrahamic walk every week when we trudge into our studies and open the book and lay all we have on the altar in faith that God will make of our sermons more than we could on our own, that God will provide. Preachers' lives are not so much out of control as under control.

When Albert Schweitzer finished off the liberal biblical critics of his age, deftly trashing their sentimental, romantic reconstructions of Jesus (Schweitzer, we need you now) with his reconstruction of Jesus as the wild-eyed, failed, eschatological prophet, Schweitzer had little of Jesus left. He knew who Jesus wasn't but little of who Jesus was, a problem that has plagued questers for the historical Jesus into the present day. Jesus comes to us "as one unknown," a stranger, a vague, voiceless, nameless apparition shrouded in obscurity with which Schweitzer so eloquently ended *The Search for the Historical Jesus.*

Election renders a very different Jesus. Christ is strange to us, to be sure, but not because he is inexpressible and unknown. Rather he is odd precisely in his revelation of the unexpected God who barges in, goes where he is not invited, and shows up unexpectedly when we are just reading Scripture or simply sharing a meal. We thought we were doing a ritual of only symbolic significance, gathering for cool, rational consideration of some spiritual ideas. Then comes the wild one. Not only does he come, Christ present *calls, sends.*

"Sent"

Service of Ordination, June 2012
Matthew 28:5–8, 16–20

These persons before you, our newest clergy, tonight pledge their lives to one of the most unusual practices in historic Methodism—*sent ministry*. No congregation can hire a United Methodist pastor; our pastors are sent. Just as your call into the ministry was God's notion before you thought of it, so in your sent ministry, your assignment in the kingdom is God's before it's yours (or the Bishop's!).

Like you, I am here because I was sent. And, when the time comes, you will leave, as I am leaving, because you have been sent. A sent ministry is a countercultural challenge. Subordination to the mission of the church of career, marriage, and family, and even the choice of where to sleep at night, is weirdly un-American. We are a people who have been deeply indoctrinated into the godless ideology that our lives are our possessions to do with as we please, that my life is the sum of my astute choices, and that the life I'm living is my own.

There are less demanding ways to serve Jesus. But forgive me for thinking few more adventuresome than a life commandeered by Jesus into sent ministry. Meeting awhile back with a young woman, attempting to help her discern what God wanted her to do—whether Methodism's sent ministry was for her or not—I concluded the conversation with, "Though I can't say for sure that God is calling you into the ministry, I urge to you to pray really, really hard that God will."

Few things are more sad than an unsent life. What a joy, in good times, but especially in bad, to believe that you are where you are because you have been put there; you are doing what you are doing because God means for this to be so. Every follower of Jesus Christ, clergy or not, is sent.

At age ten, I was minding my business, doing time in Miss McDaniel's sixth-grade class, dutifully copying words off the blackboard, when I got the call: "Willimon, Mr. Harrelson [the intimidating, ancient principal] says he wants to see you. Go to his office."

Shaking with trepidation, I trudged toward the principal's office. Passing an open door, I saw a classmate looking out at me with pity, saying a prayer of thanksgiving that I was summoned to the principal and not him. Ascending the gallows, I went over in my mind all the possible misunderstandings that could have led to this portentous subpoena. (I was only a distant witness to the rock through the gym window incident; in no way a perpetrator or even passive conspirator.)

"Listen clearly. I do not intend to repeat myself: You go down Tindal two blocks and turn left, go two more blocks, to number fifteen. I need a message delivered. You tell Jimmy Spain's mother if he's not in school by this afternoon I'm reporting her to the police for truancy."

So this wasn't about me. It was worse. God help me. Jimmy Spain, toughest thug of all the sixth grade. Sixth grader who should have been in the eighth. And what's "truancy"?

Pondering these somber thoughts, I journeyed down Tindal, bidding farewell to the safety of the schoolyard, turned left, walked two more blocks, marveling that the world actually went on about its business while we were doing time in school. The last two blocks were the toughest, descending into a not-at-all-nice part of town, terra incognita to me, what was left of a sad neighborhood hidden behind the school. Number 15 was a small house, peeling paint, disordered yard—just the sort of house you'd expect Jimmy Spain to be holed up in—rough looking, small, but sinister. There was a big blue Buick parked in front. As I fearfully approached the walk, a man emerged, letting the front door slam, stepped off the porch, and began adjusting his tie, putting on his coat.

I approached him with, "Are you, Mr. . . . Spain, sir?" Just then I remembered that everybody at school said that Jimmy was so mean because he didn't have a daddy. The man looked down at me, pulled his tie on tight, and guffawed. "Mr. Spain? Haw, haw, haw." Laughing, he left me standing there, got into his car, and sped off. (I had to wait until I was in the eighth grade before someone whispered to me the dirty word for what Jimmy's mother did for a living, and until my Boy Scout Court of Honor before I realized the man I met that day was a member of City Council.)

I stepped up on the rotten porch and knocked on the soiled screen door. My heart sank when it was opened by none other than Jimmy Spain, whose steely eyes enlarged when he saw me. Before Jimmy could say anything, the door was pulled open more widely, and a woman in a faded blue, terrycloth bathrobe looked down at me, over Jimmy's shoulder.

"What do you want?" she asked in a cold, threatening tone as I marveled at the sight of a mother in a bathrobe even though it was early afternoon.

"Er, I'm from the school. The principal sent me, to . . ."

"The principal! What does that old fool want?"

"Er, he sent me to say that we, er, that is, that everybody at school misses Jimmy and wishes he were there today."

"What?" she sneered, pulling Jimmy toward her just a bit.

"It's like a special day today, and everyone wants Jimmy there. I think that's what he said."

Jimmy—the feared thug who could beat up any kid at Donaldson Elementary, even ninth graders anytime he wanted, indeed had on multiple occasions—peered out at me in . . . wonderment. Suddenly this tough hood, feared by all, looked small, being clutched by his mother's protective arm, his eyes pleading, embarrassed, hanging on my every stammering word.

"Well, you tell that old man it's none of his business what I do with James. James," she said, looking down at him, "you want to go to that old school today or not?"

Jimmy looked at me as he wordlessly nodded assent.

"Well, go get your stuff. And take that dollar off the dresser to buy lunch. I ain't got nothing here."

In a flash he was away and back. His mother stood at the door, and after making the unimaginable gesture of giving Jimmy a peck on the cheek, stood staring at us as we walked off the porch, down the walk, and back toward Tindal Avenue. As we walked back toward the school, we said not a word to each other. I had previously lacked the courage to speak to Jimmy the Hood; and Jimmy the Tough had never had any reason, thank the Lord, to speak to me, and walking back to school that afternoon was certainly not the time to begin.

We walked up the steps to the school, took a right, and wordlessly turned toward the principal's office. I led him in, handed him off to the principal's secretary, who received my ward. For the first time, Jimmy seemed not mean and threatening at all, but very small. As the secretary led him away, Jimmy turned and looked at me with a look of . . . , I don't know, maybe regret, maybe embarrassment? But it could have also been thanks, gratitude.

That evening, when I narrated my day to my mother at supper, she said, "That is the most outrageous thing I've ever heard! Sending a young child out in the middle of the day to fetch a truant. And on that street! Mr. Harrelson ought to have his head examined. Don't you ever allow anyone to put you in that position again. Sending a child!"

But I knew that my mother was wrong. That day was the best day of my whole time at Donaldson Elementary, preparation for the rest of my life, my first experience of a God who thinks nothing of commandeering ordinary folk and handing them outrageous assignments. That day, walking down Tindal Avenue was dress rehearsal for a summer night two decades later, when I knelt before a bishop, and he laid on hands and pronounced, "You, go down Tindal two blocks and turn left, go to seminary, study hard, then go to a church where I'll send you. God has a message that needs to be delivered."

Out of Control

Barth began his preface to his first volume of *CD* (1932), "Human affairs—even those over which we think we have some control—often take a different course from the one planned."[45] This first sentence of Barth's massive theological work suggests that he knew firsthand what it means to have one's thought commandeered by God, *out of control*.[46]

As pastor, I often heard the expression, "God is in control," meant as a statement of faith after some tragedy or natural calamity. "God is in control" may be what's left of what was once called Providence. I do not know what a Calvinist in the sixteenth century meant if she ever spoke of God's "control," but I expect it is not what a twenty-first century North American Southern Baptist means. Facile assertions of God's "control" probably say more about a modern sense that our lives are careening out of control than they say about the nature of God.

Christians believe that God causes things to happen in human history, but once again, we must work from God's major event—the Incarnation—back to any claim of divine causality in time past or present. Nothing we know of God as Jesus Christ justifies the claim that God does evil; Jesus Christ shows that God brings good out of evil. A relentlessly redemptive God offers us not control but rather an active agent who is more than an impersonal cause for everything that happens. (How difficult it is to think of a loving person as controlling.)

The overriding promise of the modern world is the achievement of human control. This may account for why so many sermons today are offers of various techniques for how to have a happy family, how to achieve balance in your life, how to relieve stress—that is, how to handle a world that lurches out of control?

The expression "control freak" was invented in the sixties culture, whose mantra was "do your own thing." Psychologists say that control freaks are perfectionists who defend themselves against their perceived vulnerabilities—futilely trying to organize the world around themselves—to give themselves the illusion that they are managing disorder. In personality-type theory, control freaks are "Type A" personalities driven by the need to dominate.[47]

In his popular presentation of contemporary neuroscience, Daniel Goleman extols the governing aspects of the cerebral cortex, the so-called "higher brain functions" that control our desires. Indeed, Goleman says that humanity's superiority over other animals is due to our self-control. We can plan, practice self-restraint, and delay gratification. Our ability to govern ourselves, to set priorities, and to focus on the tasks at hand, says Goleman, is "the hidden driver of excellence," the best predictor of "success" in school, business, and life.[48] And yet, that some of us suffer from hyper-controlling desires and that many of us feel out of control is a possible indication that the modern world has not delivered on its promise.

Psychologists see a connection between control and narcissism. *Narcissism* is self-absorption that flirts with solipsism. The only voice the boy Narcissus hears is Echo, the nymph who chattered so much that Juno condemns Echo to say nothing on her own but only to repeat that which is said to her. This means that Narcissus hears nothing but the echo of his own voice, creating conversation in his head, imagining what someone else is saying. For the narcissist, it's all monologue. The conceited person is wrapped in a cocoon of self-esteem, hearing only positive comments. Narcissus eventually wastes away. Personhood is obliterated when the person is no longer addressed by any voice outside the self.

Thus Iris Murdoch condemns self-love as a cardinal sin, the sad result of the self-deceptive flight from the complexity of reality into the confines of the self.[49]

Societies of Control

Our pretentions toward greater control of ourselves and our world wilt before the grimness of the bureaucratic, technologically proficient, banal, oddly totalitarian modern state. Nobody has depicted this nightmare more ironically than Kafka in his parable *The Trial* (my paraphrase):

On his thirtieth birthday, the chief financial officer of a bank, Josef K., is unexpectedly arrested by two unidentified agents from an unnamed agency for an unspecified crime. The agents' boss arrives and holds a mini-tribunal in the room of K.'s neighbor, Fräulein Bürstner. K. is not arrested but is left "free" and told to wait for instructions from the Committee of Affairs.

K. receives a phone call summoning him to court on Sunday. No time is set, but an address is given that turns out to be a huge tenement building devoid of signs or directions. He follows a labyrinth that finally leads to the court in the attic of the building. The room is airless, shabby, and crowded, and although he has no idea what he is charged with, K. makes a long speech denigrating the whole process, including the unknown agents who arrested him; during this speech an attendant's wife and a man engage in sexual acts. K. returns home.

K. visits the court again, finding that it is not in session. He talks with the attendant's wife, who attempts to seduce him into taking her away. This sort of strange, nightmarish, inexplicable wandering goes on and on. Finally, on the eve of K.'s thirty-first birthday, two men arrive at his apartment. Tired of waiting, he offers little resistance, giving them direction through town, leading them to a quarry where the two place K's head on a discarded block. One of the men produces a double-edged butcher knife, and as the two men nonchalantly pass it back and forth between them, we are told that, "K. knew then precisely, that it would have been his duty to take the knife . . . and thrust it into himself." He doesn't take the knife. One of the men holds him while the other man stabs him in the heart and twists the knife twice.

K.'s last words are: "Like a dog!"

Kafka understood the peculiar way that the modern, faceless, name-less bureaucratic society of surveillance renders our lives out of control. People somewhere up there are pulling our strings. We attempt to gain power to bring things to a conclusion, plead our case, and be exonerated. Our name is never called. We are denied our day in court. Kafka's German title, *Der Prozess*, better characterizes the frustrating, endless maze of postponements and the baffling, unending process whereby the trial never happens and judgment occurs without reason. The prudent course is to relent, to cease our futile attempts to identify the perpetrators, go with the flow, die like a dog.

Kafka was among the first to understand control as turning people into statistics, when every move is watched and compiled as data. For Kafka, the problem was not the machine—bureaucracy is blameless, a faceless agent. The blame is ours. We check the boxes, share images of ourselves on the internet, click the keys, and thus voluntarily report our every move. Officially we have freedom to do as we please, and yet we are haunted by surveillance.

"So then you're free?" someone asks Karl, the protagonist of Kafka's *The Man Who Disappeared*: " 'Yes, I'm free,' said Karl, and nothing seemed more worthless than his freedom."[50]

In an influential essay, Gilles Deleuze used Foucault to characterize the contemporary world as *societies of control*.[51] In societies of control, the new Leviathan is not recognized as a threat because, unlike earlier *societies of sovereignty* (i.e., the modern nation state), the control over our lives is rapid, free-floating, and invisible. Deleuze says that the most menacing forms of control are not genetic engineering or the burgeoning pharmaceutical manipulation and modulation of the brain. Nor is there any point in asking which governmental regime is less controlling than another. Without armies or gulags, constant control of the populace is within reach of all cultures. Technologies that were heralded as freedom-producing are now, in practice, forms of enslavement. The older, inefficient gulag is now the university, the office, the web. Corporations have found ways of constantly collecting up-to-the-minute information about our every movement. With each click on the keyboard we are governed without anyone building a prison or mobilizing a platoon. The phone in my pocket, the GPS in my car, the dozens of CCTV cameras that film my every move are as efficient as a court-authorized house arrest bracelet. Like K. in *The Trial*, I've never been charged. It's judgment without being judged, imprisonment without our knowing that we are in jail.

Modern collectors and keepers of information are anonymous and faceless. Jeremy Bentham's Panopticon is now achieved by Google. The art of controlling people has been perfected by convincing us that we are free from control. (On his visit to America in the eighteenth century, De Tocqueville smirked that Americans are free to do whatever they want, but everyone wants the same thing.) I am under the illusion that I live in the most free of all possible worlds. Yet dozens of people somewhere know where I am, what I'm doing, and can predict what I'll buy this afternoon. Huge amounts of data are collected, more information than the keepers of data have the capacity to utilize. But soon they will. Based on their knowledge of my buying habits, marketers target their advertising to me with precision.

I just received an unsolicited message that, based on the books I have been reading, I'm only two clicks away from being among the first to read a new book written just for me and a couple of other select scholars. I clicked.

The purpose of collecting data is to predict patterns of behavior, and the purpose of prediction is control. I am free to purchase what I please, but with Amazon so closely predicting what I will choose, how do I know my choice is free?

We were told that by having omnipresent, omniscient surveillance we would be more secure. And yet being constantly watched suggests that I am suspect, that I may be guilty, or at least potentially guilty of perpetrating some illegal or immoral act. As I pay for my purchase, a camera is watching the cashier. I understand why the hardware store doesn't trust me; I'm a customer. But that the store also mistrusts its own employees suggests a paranoid level of suspicion. Who sits in front of the screen that's behind the camera that's monitoring me? The camera's omnipresence whispers that I am guilty; why else would I be watched? Knowledge that I am constantly watched puts me under control.

I've seen the meticulous, hand-written lists of the inmates at Dachau, kept by the Nazis. How horrifyingly banal is bureaucratic evil. Yet strangely humane are those lists compared with the impersonal mass of information held by the IRS. In societies of control, said Deleuze, there is just too much information. What we know explodes beyond our capacity to assimilate so we are doomed to frustration and futility in our attempt to master our world; mastery of a subject has been replaced by superficial surfing. Our agency is diminished because as soon as we decide to act, more information comes in that calls into question our actions.

The most dramatic deflation of our vaunted claims to be a free society is the U.S. rate of incarceration. Alice Goffman begins her disturbing book *On the Run* by noting:

> The number of people imprisoned in the United States remained fairly stable for most of the twentieth century . . . one person for every thousand in the population. . . . By the 2000s, the number of people behind bars stood at a rate never before seen in US history: about 1 for every 107 people in the adult population. The United States currently imprisons five to nine times more people than western European nations, and significantly more than China and Russia. Roughly 3 percent of adults in the nation are now under correctional supervision: 2.2 million people in prisons and jails, and an additional 4.8 million on probation or parole.
>
> In modern history, only the forced labor camps of the former USSR under Stalin approached these levels of penal confinement. The fivefold increase in the number of people sitting in US jails and prisons over the last forty years has prompted little public outcry . . . because the growing numbers of prisoners are drawn disproportionately from poor and segregated Black communities. Black people make up 13 percent of the US population, but account for 37 percent of the prison population. Among Black young men, one in nine are in prison.[52]

Is our high rate of incarceration related to our sense that we are out of control, that is, we are contingent creatures? Because I'm a relatively affluent, North American person, I'm not in jail; my time is my own. A home security system guards my stuff. Unconstrained in so many ways, I am tempted to believe that I might be a god, admittedly a god with a Southern accent who has urinary problems, but still, with the right health care and a positive psychological attitude, godliness may be within my reach.

Ah, the sentimentalities with which we try to hide our mortality from ourselves.

Because I cannot control being sixty-eight years old and one day having to die, because I cannot bring back the minutes lost writing this sentence, my illusions of control are delusions by which I lie to myself about my contingency. One might think that in a church like mine where sixty is the median age of membership, the careening-out-of-control, contingent quality of our lives would be self-evident. Perhaps our inchoate sense of vulnerability accounts for so many sermons that offer various techniques to achieve balance, control, peace, and stability.

Dying is about as out of control as one can get.

Is there a connection between my serving a church that has, in effect, limited church to people over sixty years of age and the boring stability of my preaching? People go to church for the same reason we go to a doctor, hoping to achieve some modicum of control of our contingent, transitory lives.

Marcus Aurelius, in his Stoic *Meditations*, says that one ought to have the courage to admit that one is growing old and that prospects for continuity are bleak. Life is short. Fame is fleeting, "and after fame, oblivion."[53] Don't look for help from the gods. They are eternal; you are not. "One thing and one thing only enables us to keep the demon at bay," says Marcus: *philosophy*. As the gods do us in, our finitude is inconsolable except by rising above our mortality through the nobility of thought. While Christians may be unimpressed by Stoicism, can we be sure that we are not enlisting theology for the same purpose? Thought about finitude can be a complex form of evasion of mortality. Our lives are more out of control than we admit.

Augustine did a beautiful job of presenting the instability that is inherent in the passing of time.[54] The "present" is never really present; the past seizes the present so fast that I don't even know it is gone. There is nowhere to stand, no place to rest. Time renders human life harried, insecure, and evanescent. Time is the arena of disorder because time is not ours. Or as Hebrews puts it, "Here we have no abiding city" (Heb. 13:14). Only God has a future. In truth, in time, we are out of control.

Commandeered by God

Naturalistic truisms about our mortality and contingency are not my main concern, however. My thesis is more countercultural, more biblical, and more specifically Christian. We are out of control because, as the psalmist affirms, "It is [God] that hath made us and not we ourselves" (Ps. 100:3 KJV). We are neither self-created nor self-preserved. To be even more specific about our contingency, *we are not self-directed*. We are out of control because we live in a realm circumscribed by an active, commanding, interventionist, summoning God. "All our steps are ordered by the LORD; / how then can we understand our own ways?" (Prov. 20:24). We cannot have balance, control, peace, and stability, not because we are overworked and mortal, but *because of God*.

After noting that a large forest is set ablaze by a small fire, the Letter of James notes the great damage done by a small organ when it is undisciplined:

> The tongue is a fire . . . it stains the whole body, sets on fire the cycle of nature, and is itself set on fire by hell. For every species of beast and bird, of reptile and sea creature, can be tamed . . . but no one can tame the tongue—a restless evil full of deadly poison. With it we bless the Lord and Father, and with it we curse those who are made in the likeness of God. (Jas. 3:6–9)

While James' warning about the destructiveness of undisciplined speech is true, I'm not talking about the trouble caused by untamed tongues but rather the trouble provoked by preachers' tongues unleashed to speak up for an untamed God.

Do Jews keep Sabbath or does the Sabbath keep Jews? Do we pastors perform a marriage or do the marriages in which we officiate perform us? A few years ago, my denomination celebrated the "Fiftieth Anniversary of Clergy Rights for Women." (Ordination is a "right"?) In actual practice, most of us clergy could testify that ordination feels more like being placed "under orders," not an inalienable right within us but an obligation imposed on us. By God, we are out of control. We should have called it the "Anniversary of the Church's Willingness at Last to Allow God to Choose Whomever God Chooses for Christian Ministry."

Much of theology has been an attempt to commandeer Jesus rather than having him capture us. A few philosophers tried to prove that we possessed "free will." Human free will wasn't easy to defend. (Spinoza said that if a rock were sentient, and if that rock were thrown across a river, the rock would think it is crossing the river because it wanted to.) Today, genetics, gender studies, chemistry, and psychology vividly demonstrate that we are determined by a host of masters over which we have little mastery.

We are out of control not only because we live in a transitory life-giving, always life-taking cosmos but also because it's more than cosmos; it's Creation. The moment God preached to the "formless void" saying, "Let there be light!" God demonstrated that the *tohu wa bohu* would be other than it could be on its own. All subsequent divine creativity suggests our lack of control. *God* is a name for whoever jerks about our lives, surprising us, frustrating our efforts to be gods unto ourselves.

A major reason why the modern, post-Enlightenment world is essentially a-theistic is that the modern world is dedicated to the enhancement of human control and the lessening of unpredictable disturbance.[55] The modern project is to protect us from having to be persons who pray, "Nevertheless, not my will but thine be done," or, "Thy kingdom come, thy will be done on earth as in heaven," that is, persons who acknowledge that our lives are out of our control.

"The Enlightenment project" (according to Alasdair MacIntyre) attempted an independent rational justification of morality. MacIntyre says it failed. Scholars debate the intent of the Enlightenment (Secularism? Humanism? Progress?) yet agree that the Enlightenment in its various forms was born of a desire for independent human control.[56] Barth ascribes the perverse invention of the "individual" to the Promethean aspirations of the "so-called modern age."[57]

Until modernity, the natural world was *semiotic*; the world pointed beyond itself to something that was more than the world, more than nature. In modernity, Charles Taylor says that "exclusive humanism" emerged in which there is no "other than," no "more than." Meaning is not something inherent but rather meaning and significance are devised by minds that make meaning internally. The external world is only a catalyst for the generation of meaning in the mind. One of the burdens of modernity's liberation from God is that the significance of the world and of our selves is no longer given or received. Meaning is manufactured. "The world" is the construction of personal agents who have causal power.[58] With the disenchantment of the world comes the conceit that we are the sole agents. This leads, says Taylor, to a "sense of vulnerability."[59] The world and its significance are up to us.

The premodern self was "porous," subject to discoveries, revelation, and surprise arising from outside the self. The modern self, says Taylor, is "buffered," a self that is isolated in interiority, condemned in all matters to be *homo fabricator*, anxiously engaged in "giving its own autonomous order to its life."[60]

Along with this burdensome "liberation" of the modern self comes what James K. A. Smith has called a "lowering of the bar" for our expectations of the "life well lived."[61] We no longer expect significance to be received from eternity, nor do we ask ultimate questions to be answered in eternity; meaning is self-produced by us here, now.

I'm sure that my three-decade stint preaching to Duke undergrads made me sensitive to the burdensome task of meaning-making placed on them by godless modernity. Now that I'm exclusively teaching Divinity School students, I'm delightfully surrounded by people whose lives are not their own. Theological education is three years of training people to embrace lives out of control. Why would they be studying for the ministry if their lives were theirs to live as they pleased?

I open my Introduction to the Theology and Practice of Ordained Leadership by having students write short papers on "My Call to the Pastoral Ministry." I love reading those papers because of their oddness—Jesus appearing to people on patios, decades of attempts to give God the slip, the sense of being stalked by a vocation one did not desire, and other similarly odd, wonderfully un-American stories. No one ought to attempt seminary without an odd story of God's gracious (and often unsought and unwanted) election. My reaction to these papers is not, "What a strange person to be cast into seminary," but rather, *Jesus is amazing!*

Perhaps I ought to stop having them write papers on, "My Call" and instead, "Describe the God Who Would Call Someone like You to the Pastoral Ministry."

Gregory of Nazianzen[62] says that no one ought to undertake pastoral ministry without being "in the order of the Spirit," *akolouthia pneumatike*, under orders by the Spirit. At his own ordination to the episcopate, Gregory dedicated himself to be "an instrument of the Word tuned and plucked by the Spirit," offering himself to be God's lyre whereupon God played sweet music to the people.[63] Out of control.

I'm sure that most of the church continues to practice the baptism of the infants of Christian parents (Barth disapproved) because of the church's unconscious sense that baptizing one who has no personal experience, who has exercised no choice in the matter of being under the covenant, radically enacts salvation as being out of control.

Wesley's Covenant Prayer, with origins in the late eighteenth century, is appropriately odd. Our church repeated these words at a "Covenant Service" every New Year's Eve. Methodists gleefully praying, "I am no longer my own, but yours" is Wesleyanism at its countercultural best:

> I am no longer my own, but thine.
> Put me to what thou wilt, rank me with whom thou wilt.
> Put me to doing, put me to suffering.
> Let me be employed for thee, or laid aside for thee,
> exalted for thee or brought low for thee.
> Let me be full, let me be empty.
> Let me have all things, let me have nothing.

I freely and heartedly yield all things
to thy pleasure and disposal.
And now, O glorious and blessed God,
Father, Son and Holy Spirit,
thou art mine, and I am thine. So be it.
And the covenant which I have made on earth,
let it be ratified in heaven.
Amen.[64]

Out of control.

Church Out of Control

In the academy, much that passes for theology is a clever but vain attempt to stabilize (and thereby to control) a restless, living God. (Stabilization and mortification appear to be the unacknowledged intent of what has become the legalistic United Methodist *Book of Discipline*.) Issues related to the human desire for control were behind Barth's occasional invective against Roman Catholicism. While acknowledging that both Protestants and Catholics believe in "one, holy, catholic, and apostolic church," Barth thought Catholicism tried to stabilize the church's unity, holiness, catholicity, and apostleship through its teaching office and the church's authority. The Catholic Church acted as if it were the master—rather than the surprising beneficiary of grace—through the church's (biblically unsupported) ministry of priests and sacraments. For Barth, grace is more dynamic than any church—not something that could be assumed as a given. In short, the church in Barth's thought is a concrete, historical, daily, eventful demonstration of the doctrine of election. The church is what happens when the disturbance of God's election takes up room.

Catholicism saw the church as a divinely established institution in which Jesus Christ is "absorbed into the existence of the Church and is thus ultimately restricted and conditioned by certain concrete forms." What is meant to be a "personal act of address" becomes "a constantly available relationship." The church, argued Barth, is "an event of personal address" that "depends on God's ongoing act."[65] The church is significant only as evidence of God's turning toward humanity in election and of God's turning humanity toward God, God's bending of humanity toward its Creator.

For all its value, the church does not divest God of God's freedom to be for more than the church.[66] The church is not the normal, expected state of affairs between God and humanity but exists "only in the power of the divine decision, act, and revelation accomplished and effective in Jesus Christ."[67] That Catholic ecclesiology was too static for Barth can be attributed to Barth's doctrine of election.[68] As bishop in The United Methodist Church, I can say with some authority that the static, controlling, bureaucratic curia that Barth critiques in what he knew of Catholicism flourishes in the legalism, clericalism, and boring proceduralism of United Methodism.[69]

Still, the Christian life is warfare that is not waged alone. For all its limits, the church is a sign that our salvation is public, corporate, and communal. If we discover and live out our election, if we become more adept in our witness to the truth of Christ, God has elected for us to do that corporately, in Israel and the church. Surely a reason why Barth called his great work *Church Dogmatics* rather than *Theological Dogmatics* is that the church, within the limits of God's purposes, is material to and necessary for salvation in Christ. As Barth says, a Christian cannot sue for "a separate piece or wage a separate war for [God's] honor. [The individual Christian] stands or falls within the walls of the church."[70]

Reference to the continuing dynamic of election also informs Barth's criticism of the use of the "analogy of being" as a method of theology. Correlational thinking (Paul Tillich) assumes that there is something innate in the being of humankind that is an analogue to the being of God, a likeness so fitting that it stabilizes the idea of God long enough to tell us something we may grasp of the truth of God; for example, human beings are relational, so this tells us something about God being relational.

Barth denied that any such analogy resided intrinsically in the human person. Connections and correlations between us and God can be given only as a free gift of God in faith. Thus even the idea that we are created in the "image and likeness" of God is not a general human truth from which we can then discern who God is and what God is like. Christ's reference to God as "Father" is revelation that does not arise from human experience of paternity, but rather human fatherhood may be enlightened by Christ's designation of God as "Father."

Barth's criticisms of Catholicism's "analogy of being" can as easily be applied to the sentimental, inflated humanism at play in my own church: We are hungry for love, so God must be loving in ways we define as love. In our fragmentation and loneliness, God must produce community. We want someone to care about us, therefore we project a God who cares about that which obsesses us. I could go on.

Barth charged his teacher, Albert Ritschl, with having reformed Jesus to make him more acceptable to bourgeois culture. A chief promise of the Ritschlian Jesus was not only to make Jesus more relevant to German high-cultured despisers of Jesus but also to portray Jesus as a useful stabilizing influence on society. Christian vocation was presented as upright living within society; Jesus helps us do our bit to improve Germany. Christianity is justified by its social utility. It's the glue that holds society together, the cement of the social order.

Ritschl's son-in-law, Johannes Weiss, broke apart this pleasant synthesis before the end of the nineteenth century with his *Jesus' Proclamation of the Kingdom of God.*[71] Weiss said Jesus preached a message rather than launched a social program. The kingdom of God is not a moral kingdom; it is announcement of other-worldly, eschatological disruption of our social and moral order that makes Jesus more than a helpful moral teacher; he was an eschatological prophet. As Schweitzer showed six years later, Jesus was more a wild-eyed prophet of the end than a patient, reforming, gradually progressing leader of human improvement.[72] The carnage of the First World War ended the comfortable linkage of Jesus with European bourgeois culture.[73]

Preachers must resist our society's attempted domestication of faith in subservience to societal peace. Liberalism is the attempt to produce people for whom "religion" is something so flaccid that no one would think of dying for it and thereby challenge the state's monopoly on killing and dying. As the functional equivalent of God, the state is our major source of security. We have "rendered unto Caesar" sovereignty that once was God's. Christianity has been thrown into a ceaseless crisis of legitimation in which we are forced to justify the church as an aid in the achievement of allegedly "larger public good."

Kierkegaard attributed the boring, watered-down preaching in Denmark to the submission of clergy to control by culture so that tame, submissive drivel was "proclaimed as Christianity":

> As long as the clergy were exalted, sacrosanct in the eyes of [people], Christianity continued to be preached in all its severity. For even if the clergy did not take it too strictly, people dared not argue with the clergy, and they could quite well lay on the burden and dare to be severe. But gradually, as the nimbus faded . . . clergy got into the position of themselves being controlled. So there was nothing to do but to water down Christianity. And so they continued to water it

down till in the end they achieved perfect conformity with an ordinary worldly run of ideas—which were proclaimed as Christianity. That is more or less Protestantism as it is now.[74]

Lives out of control because of Christ are free of not just any control but specifically control by the state. In a sermon, Stanley Hauerwas speaks of the wisdom that comes from knowing that our lives are personally and politically out of control:

> It is one thing to acknowledge that we may not be in control of our personal lives, but it is quite another thing to recognize that our lack of control also applies to that larger world we call politics. We are told that if we do not infuse the economy, whatever that is, with stimulus money, then a depression cannot be avoided. We have not had a depression, so what we did must have worked. . . . [But] you cannot show a causal relation by something not happening. Yet, those we have endowed with authority have to claim they know what they are doing because if they did not know what they were doing, they should not be in positions of power.
>
> . . . [T]hink what the unpredictable character of life means in international affairs. Again, we are often told that we must continue this or that war because if we do not it will only invite our enemy to do X or Y, but because we continue the war, our enemy claims they must do X or Y. Yet lives are being sacrificed so those who make these decisions, because they are morally good people, must insist, . . . that they know what they are doing. [However] there is little evidence to support our presumption that we can be in control of our lives—much less the history of nations. Yet we are undeterred . . . determined to show that the contingent, the temporal, can be subject to our will. Whatever it may mean to be modern surely must, at the very least, entail our refusal to be determined, to be fated, by the past. We can make a difference. We can be in control. We can defeat contingency. . . .
>
> [Yet] to follow Jesus is ongoing training for learning to live out of control. Faith is but a word for letting go of our presumption that we have to make history come out right. History has come out right. We have seen the end in Jesus . . . through cross and resurrection, Jesus defeated the powers that deceptively promise to save us from death by our willingness to coerce and even kill our neighbors.[75]

Barth refused to enlist theology merely to sustain Western civilization. To make theology subservient to the state substitutes God's dealings with humanity for dominance over our neighbors. Religion becomes a way of better controlling our own unbridled desires as well as controlling the needs of others; a backhanded way of controlling God.[76] I suspect that the disappointing theodicy that preoccupied North American theology in the past century is a vain attempt to deal with the contingency of human existence and to insulate ourselves from the truth that God has no intention either of letting us get out of this alive or of allowing our lives to be our own.

In his last book, *Evangelical Theology: An Introduction,* Barth defines *temptation* as occurring when God withdraws from our theological ruminations. God "hides [God's] face" and denies the theologian the "presence and action of the Holy Spirit."[77] Temptation is the vain attempt to think about God without God's presence and action controlling our thinking. In the confrontation between Christ and the Grand Inquisitor in *The Brothers Karamazov,* Ivan tells a story in which Christ "decided to show Himself, if only for a moment, to his people."[78] The Cardinal has Jesus arrested. In the interrogation, the Inquisitor asks, "You? Is it really You? . . . You need not answer me. Say nothing. I know only too well what You could tell me now. Besides, You have no right to add anything to what You said before. Did You come here to interfere and make things difficult for us?" It takes a Cardinal of the church, the "Grand Inquisitor," to see how dangerous and unmanageable a contemporaneous Christ could be.

Barth's account of preaching in his *Homiletics* is mostly a commentary on how preachers must allow the Bible to control our speech: "Preaching must be exposition of holy scripture. I have not to talk *about* scripture but *from* it. I have not to say something, but merely repeat something . . . simply to follow the distinctive movement of thought in the text, to stay with this, and not with a plan that arises out of it."[79] Many of the interpretive issues that occupied biblical studies for over a century are negated by the simple fact that "[God] speaks for Himself whenever [God] is spoken of and [God's] story is told and heard."[80]

Biblical preachers must cultivate the art of relinquishment, letting go of our darling insights in deference to the Bible's words:

> The gospel is not in our thoughts or hearts; it is in scripture. The dearest habits and best insights that I have—I must give them all up before listening. I must not use them to protect myself against

the breakthrough of a knowledge that derives from scripture. . . . I must let myself be contradicted . . . loosened up . . . to surrender everything.[81]

At the same time that he speaks of preachers diligently disciplining ourselves to Scripture, Barth stresses *revelation as event*. Flexibility and humble receptivity are required:

The Bible is not God's Word in the sense of a state code that tells us precisely what the view of the state is. . . . [T]he Bible *becomes* God's Word. Whenever it *becomes* God's Word, it is God's Word. What we have here is an event. . . . Preachers are summoned to a life history with the Bible in which something constantly takes place between them and God's Word. Flexibility means, then, that we have to plunge into this movement, submit to it, and let it lead us.[82]

In the Bible, God refuses to submit to human control.

As to when, where, and how the Bible establishes itself for us as the Word of God . . . , we do not decide . . . the Word of God decides![83]

We should not try to master the text. The Bible will become more and more mysterious to real exegetes. They will see all the depths and distances. They will constantly run up against the mystery before which *theology* is like trying to drain the ocean with a spoon. The true exegete will face the text like an astonished child in a wonderful garden, not like an advocate of God who has seen all his files.[84]

At its best, the church trains us to live out of our control. Hauerwas, in a sermon for Good Friday, just before the rite of foot washing, witnesses to how liturgy renders him out of control:

I am more or less ready to wash someone's feet, but, like Peter, I discover I am not prepared to have my feet washed. I am willing to play like I am a servant and wash the feet of someone else. When I wash the feet of someone else I am still in control. But to have someone wash my feet makes me feel vulnerable . . . like I am being asked to expose myself. It makes me feel distinctly uncomfortable. . . .

   To have someone wash my feet, moreover, is an act of intimacy. . . . Who is this person willing to wash my feet? I may not even know their name. . . . Dear God, how did I get myself into this predicament? I did not come to church to be served, to be cared for, by someone else. Yet here I am, stuck in this communal rite that requires some acknowledgement on my part that this is a practice worth doing.

This is not going to be easy.

In *The Peaceable Kingdom*, Hauerwas finds it unsurprising that the church tends to be full of people who have experienced firsthand having their lives out of control:

> Perhaps that is why the church is so often constituted by those who have at some point lost control of their lives, who have faced the darkness of rejection and anarchy. For such a people know that there is no avoiding the tragedies that are part and parcel of our histories. . . . The church is thus those whose lives have been opened by God, often an opening that has extracted a great cost, and so are capable of being open to others without fear and resentment. Hospitality is part of their holiness, as they have learned to welcome the stranger as the very presence of God.[85]

Eusebius reports that some early Christians were hauled before the Emperor Domitian. Asked,

> concerning the Christ and his kingdom . . . [t]hey explained that Christ was neither of the world nor earthly, but heavenly and angelic, and it would be at the end of the world, when he would come in glory to judge the living and the dead and to reward every man according to his deeds.
>
> At this Domitian did not condemn them at all, but despised them as simple folk, released them, and decreed an end to the persecution against the church.[86]

How wrong was Domitian about the empire's ability to control "Christ and his kingdom."

Conflicted Truth

Once we introduce into the argument the possibility of counter kingdoms, truth/falsehood, or living/fake God, then we have Muslims, Catholics, Presbyterians, and Rotarians, and much conflict. Many have argued that it's fine for Americans to be religious, but religious freedom carries with it the responsibility to submit to democratically enforced order-liness. They assume (quite rightly, at least in the case of Christianity) that "religion" can be a cause of social instability, but they wrongly swallow the modern prejudice that religious disruption is the worst sort of commotion.

There have been unsuccessful attempts to end the intellectual conflict that arises from tension between truth/falsehood. Relativism, which is hard to take seriously, and versions of the "can't we all just get along" know-nothingism are two such attempts. Are truth claims simply a commentary on our various ethnocentricities? Is "truth" only a matter of who has the will and the power to force their truth on others? Barth mounted an early critique of liberal "tolerance" (which he saw as oppressive, "the worst form of intolerance in which the human subject attempts to lord over the truth, to make a separation from the truth, to stand above in some privileged position, to relativize all truths except the tolerating subject").[87]

Polytheism acknowledges a world full of gods, true and false. A primary modern way of dealing with polytheism is by constructing a metanarrative that presumes to take a superior, overarching view that stands above the fray and renders all gods into foolish, primitive human constructions. This is the old, "Convert to Western Enlightenment thinking and then we can stop the trouble caused by conversion to Judaism or Islam," the view that won the hearts and minds of the average undergraduate department of religious studies. The universalist claims of Christianity are judged to be intolerant and arrogant. Submission to "tolerance" and "diversity" become the doors through which truth must pass.[88] The lust for a metanarrative that silences all counter, particularistic, nonwestern narratives is a hard habit to break.

For Paul to admit, after giving his testimony, "I wish you all might become as I am" (Acts 26:29) makes Paul appear intolerant because of his attachment to a metanarrative that imperialistically challenges the myths that undergird the empire. The powers that be, whether Caesar, the Sanhedrin, or college religion departments cannot allow the assertion of counter metanarratives that endanger their power.

The Christian witness is "intolerant," if you mean, "Here is the truth about reality now that Jesus Christ has been crucified and risen; wouldn't you like to live according to the facts?"

A church removed the American flag from its sanctuary. The pastor explained the flag's removal: "There may have been a time when this national symbol, positioned so close to Christ's holy table, might have been innocent. But in our day, when it's becoming increasingly difficult for Christians to keep our symbols straight, and when we are asking too much of this flag, we don't want to confuse people about the dominant signifiers of Christian reality. As you know, our hope is not in the flag of any nation; our hope is in the cross, the broken bread and shared cup."

When, in *The Barmen Declaration*, Barth rejected any alliance between Nazi "truth" and any cooperative church support of Hitler's government, he was showing what the authorities surely considered to be a narrow, primitive intolerance or, "craziness" (*mania* in Acts 26:24). *Barmen* asserted that no one could constrict the church's proclamation. No one could control the free Word of God, which is superior to and therefore causes trouble for all other words. It's good to be reminded that *Barmen* said "No!" not to government power in general but specifically government power over *preaching*.

Christian truth covets more than intellectual agreement. Here is truth that can be known only by submitting to a way of life that confirms, validates, and makes possible its claims. Or as Hauerwas says, Christians ought to aspire not simply to win intellectual arguments but rather to live lives and to die deaths that make no sense if crucified Jesus has not been raised from the dead.

Conflict due to preaching the truth, ostracism of witnesses to the truth are, for Barth, the sole human confirmation of the truth: "Because the election of Jesus Christ is the truth, then the difference of those who are chosen in him [their calling] is *the* witness to the truth besides which there is no other . . . the difference of the elect from others, their isolation and foreignness among them, is *the* witness to the truth."[89]

Religion and Control

David Bentley Hart eloquently celebrates Christianity's culture-creating capacity. In just a few hundred years, the church recreated western European culture. Roman gods were difficult to renounce because, as is the case with all false gods, the gods were useful for social control. The church scandalized Greco-Roman sensibilities by granting "full humanity to persons of every class and condition, of either sex,"[90] by refusing to kill babies or to honor families and by staying in Rome to care for victims of the plague.

I wonder if Hart focuses too much on the culture-forming, culture-sustaining aspects of the Christian faith without also noting the culture-disrupting, dislocating qualities that come with service to a living God. Worship of the Trinity renders a world out of control.

My theme is not so much the cultural dislocation but rather the verbal, intellectual disturbance that comes with this faith. Can it be that Mark was forced to create a literary form (the first of the Gospels) that presents a life without reference to family of origin, human development, or historical precedents because the subject of Jesus required such rendition? Even as Christianity defeated and reconfigured the empire, Christianity also reworked classical literary genres so that they might do the work required to proclaim the Trinity.

We must resist the preacherly temptation toward reductionism (bane of modernist thought) to delude listeners into thinking that gospel truth is "breathtakingly simple." We cannot help preaching sermons as complex as the trinitarian God of whom we speak. Our task, as contemporary servants of the Word is not to simplify the gospel, cutting it down to our size, so that someone might say, "That's what I've always believed about God!" Reductionist, simplistic sermons in the interest of evangelism are the death throes of a Constantinian Christianity attempting to retain some shred of cultural respectability. Preachers ought not to simplify but rather to complicate people's inherited notions of God.

Attempts to control a living God assume many forms. My chief reservation about the two-decades-long enthusiasm for Christianity as a "practice" is based on my judgment that current commendations of Christianity as a "practice" tame the God who is determined, in election, to control us. The practices being commended and the reasons for the commendation of practices such as Sabbath or fasting boast that thereby life will be more manageable for harried members of a certain social class. We attempt to stabilize God, to lessen the stress on our lives produced by a living God and to "center" ourselves on ourselves, that is, to substitute predictable, patterned habits for the demands of divine-human encounter.

What we call *practice* is that which Barth dismissed as *religion*, "the attempted replacement of the divine work by a human manufacture."[91] In "religion" we "exchange the truth about God for a lie."[92] Barth calls "religion" a pitiful bid to protect ourselves "against revelation by providing a substitute for it."[93] Barth's opposition to "religion" was unrelenting throughout his career. His great concern was "*not* so-called 'religion' . . . but rather . . . *The Word of God* . . . which is the mystery of God in [God's] relation to [humanity] and not, as the term 'religion' seems to imply, the mystery of [humanity] in [its] relation to God."[94]

"Religion" vainly tries to know "apart from revelation,"[95] and assumes that we have within us capacity to grasp the divine through self-cultivation. ("It was the Church, not the world, which crucified Christ," Barth reminds us.[96]) Revelation attacks "religion" by contradicting us, stripping us of religious pretensions. "Religion's" fond wish is control of communication between us and God in order "to justify and sanctify" ourselves rather than to allow God to elect and love us.[97]

Yet God is great enough to meet us even in church, even in religion. We go to church, not knowing that our secret intent is there to make our last stand against God, only to be surprised by God coming and standing with us.

Karen Armstrong says that "Judaism is essentially about doing" and that Christianity has made the mistake of being too much about "believing."[98] Armstrong overlooks that both Judaism and Christianity are about "doing" and "believing" what has been revealed to us as the truth about what God is doing. Therefore, both make claims about where the world is headed, who is in charge, and why we are here. Whereas Armstrong argues that religious practices are "helpful," Christians believe that our beliefs and practices are *truthful*. Furthermore, the doctrine of election stands guard against anyone claiming that our faith is first of all about what we believe or what we do. It's about God.

The implication is that the construal of Christianity as a practice gives us a way around contemporary theological conflict. If we focus on practice, rather than conviction, we will avoid theological friction.[99]

One might think that a Wesleyan such as I might be enthusiastic about spiritual practices; John Wesley was high on spiritual "disciplines." From my reading of the spiritual practices literature, it is clear to me that Wesley was speaking about something other than helpful human activities. Wesley insisted that spiritual practices do not work from any inherent power, as if through them God's grace is conveyed.[100] While Wesley was equally critical of those who wanted the "end" (renewal by the Spirit) without the "means" (God's appointed means of grace),[101] Wesley always spoke of the spiritual disciplines urged by his movement as evidence of the miraculous grace of God working in the lives of ordinary people. In other words, Wesley's practices were not as interesting as Wesley's God.

Having heard Joseph Ratzinger's brilliant lecture in Tübingen, Barth asked the future Roman Catholic cardinal and pope whether Ratzinger's "magnificent church" and its glorious rites were not "a clever escape from the Holy Spirit?"[102]

Toward the end of his study of the book of Romans, Barth marvels at Paul's ability to overturn such deeply significant practices as circumcision by noting Paul's "relation to existing Christian practices is extremely uneasy. Even the most venerable traditions have for him no essential stability."[103] Since the resurrection of the crucified Lamb, we are compelled to regard all "venerable traditions" as having little "essential stability." We are out of control.

Christianity cast as a helpful set of practices risks making the church and its practices prior to Christ, who convenes and commands the church.[104] Kierkegaard's *Training in Christianity* (1850) advocates practices for the purpose of protecting us from seduction by the delusion that Danish Christendom has to do with Christ. Barth read Kierkegaard, nineteenth-century rebel thinker par excellence, in depth, resonating with Kierkegaard's persistent theme that Jesus is the only fully divine human, so there is never a comfortable alignment of our practice of religion with the life of a living God.

Kierkegaard wants readers who, in reading his pseudonymous authors, find that they have acquired a set of skills whereby even nineteenth-century Danes might gain the intellectual/moral ability to say no to facile, worldly surrogates for true faith. Lax official Danish Christianity was like a constipated person who took a half dose of laxative. Such a low dosage made the constipation worse. "So it is with today's Christianity. . . . The greatest danger to Christianity is, . . . not heresies, heterodoxies, not atheists, not profane secularism—no, but the kind of orthodoxy which is cordial drivel, mediocrity served up sweet . . . Nothing . . . so insidiously displaces the majestic as cordiality. . . . But the very essence of Christianity is utterly opposed to this mediocrity, in which it does not so much die as dwindle away." Domestication of the gospel is a greater danger to the faith than profligacy, said Kierkegaard:

> Today's orthodoxy essentially has its abode in the cordial drivel of family life. This is utterly dangerous to Christianity. Christianity does not oppose debauchery and uncontrollable passions and the like as much as it opposes this flat mediocrity, this nauseating atmosphere, this homey, civil togetherness . . . where God's unconditional demand has even greater difficulty in accomplishing what it requires: the majestic obedience of submission. . . . [We act as if Christianity] were for the betterment and enjoyment of temporal life. It is supposed to bring us meaning and fulfillment, happiness

and direction. This kind of religion is nothing but a deception. . . .
But this is precisely the way of mediocrity.[105]

The electing God is more than a helpmate "for the betterment and enjoyment of temporal life." The God who sovereignly choses to be for as and choses us to be for God requires "the majestic obedience of submission."

Kierkegaard is helpful in thinking about these matters because during his lifetime (1813–1855) Denmark was beginning to practice modern ways of thought. In Denmark's "Golden Age," theology was attempting confinement to the strictures of rationalism, romanticism, and the historical-critical method. Kierkegaard presciently saw that this led to misconstrued Christian faith. "No philosophy, no mythology and no historical knowledge" can attain the "Truth" disclosed in Jesus Christ.[106] The reality of the Son of God who comes to us as a lowly servant confounds our pretensions to know God because it is not possible to assimilate the Incarnate Son within modernity's "superior" worldview.[107]

In 1854, Bishop Mynster, the Danish primate, died and was succeeded in the episcopacy by Hans Martensen, one of Kierkegaard's tutors at the university. In his funeral oration, Martensen praised Mynster as "a witness to the truth." His sentimental characterization of the bishop enraged Kierkegaard (akin to Barth's ire after reading that his professors supported the German war effort?). Kierkegaard wrote a scornful article criticizing Mynster as a leading culprit in the transformation of Christianity into something any Dane could manage:

> Surely Christianity's intention is that a person use this life to venture out, to do so in such a way that God can get hold of him and that one gets to see whether or not he actually has faith.
>
> Is there anything more impractical than offering one's life for the truth? Is there anything more foolish than not looking to one's own advantage? Is there anything more ridiculous than making one's life difficult and strenuous and being rewarded with insults? We delude ourselves into thinking that to refrain from venturing is modesty, and that it must please God as humility. No, no! Not to venture means to make a fool of God—because all God is waiting for is that you go forth.[108]

Modern ways of understanding lord over the subject, attempting to grasp in order to control that which is being understood. Peculiarly

Christian understanding seeks to be in relationship with the subject, to risk embarkation on a life subordinated to the subject who is the Trinity. We understand not in order to formulate a proposition but in order to entrust ourselves to the Lordship of Christ.[109] Preachers, like all Christians, want to become that which we profess. That requires that we keep ourselves open to revelation, open to possibility and probability of being "re-called," that is to be out of control. Norms, concepts, principles can't surprise; only living persons shock. Revelation is always apocalyptic unveiling in which we discover that there is more than we can manage or master.

The distance between Barth's *Epistle to the Romans* and *The Humanity of God* is attributable to Barth's self-critique. He saw that to render God *ganz anders*, "wholly other" (*Romans*) is to isolate God as a vague, impersonal force over against humanity. This distant, wholly other God, Barth eventually concluded, is perilously close to the God of the philosophers who exists to be contemplated; not the God of Abraham, who shows up, makes covenant, and expects love and obedience. An indescribable God renders insignificant human life and activity and gives theological justification for the modern conceit of autonomous humanity.

The Humanity of God,[110] a work of the mature Barth, renders God as God of the covenant, God of Incarnation and reconciliation, God of love. In Jesus Christ, God not only becomes human but also partners with humanity. God's deity refuses to disconnect from the human. God's glory lies in God's speaking; humanity's in humble hearing.

Faithful speaking about God witnesses to our inability fully to do justice to the subject. Even with our limits, we can still tell the story of how God has dealt and is dealing with us in such a way that we, by God's grace, are able to say something truthful about God and therefore about ourselves.

Barth defines *real proclamation* as "human talk about God on the basis of the self-objectification of God which is not just there, which cannot be predicted, . . . does not fit any plan, which is real only in the freedom of [God's] grace, and in virtue of which [God] wills at specific times to be the object of this talk, and is so according to [God's] good pleasure. . . . [Preaching is] human talk about God . . . *[which] never passes under our control* " (italics mine).[111]

Faith is not just belief in something; it's also acknowledgment of our limits. Faith is not allowing God to give "Himself . . . into our hands but keeping us in [God's] hands."[112] All attempts to know God without God's grace are idolatrous efforts to "be as God" (Gen. 3:5). "We shall never be as God is. We can never put ourselves in God's place. It is to our shame that we continually want and try to do so."[113] Only God reveals God.[114]

And yet, God reveals God in the Word made flesh. "At no level or time can we have to do with God without having also to do with [Christ]. We cannot conceive ourselves and the world without first conceiving this man with God as the witness of the gracious purpose with which God willed and created ourselves and the world and in which we may exist in it and with it."[115] Revelation is truth about God that is not only out of our control but also reaching toward us.

The human creature has no "capacity to know God and the one Word of God or to produce true words corresponding to this knowledge. Even in the sphere of the Bible and the Church there can be no question of any such capacity. If there are true words of God, it is all miraculous,"[116] that is, out of our control, gift of God.

That's why Kierkegaard charged that attempts to make Christianity "plausible" necessarily led to a distortion of Christianity by domestication. We can understand God only by letting go of human epistemological resources, coming empty-handed to receive the gift of faith. Thus Kierkegaard ridiculed "admirers" of Christ who merely viewed Christ as the incarnation of our ideals, allowing us to keep our prerogative to judge Christ, our Judge.[117] Still, Kierkegaard would have been even more helpful if he had kept closer to the God who in Jesus Christ is not only concealed but also stunningly revealed.

More than fearing rejection by our hearers, Barth says we preachers ought to beware being enlisted by them for the purpose of "absorbing and domesticating . . . revelation, . . . making the gospel respectable. When the gospel is offered to [humanity], an acute danger arises which is greater than the danger that [humanity] may not understand it and angrily reject it. The danger is that [we] may accept it and peacefully atone, make [ourselves] its lord and possessor, thus rendering it innocuous, making that which chooses [us] something which [we have] chosen, which therefore comes to stand as such alongside all the other things that [we] can also choose, and therefore control."[118]

Sermons Interrupted

And yet, because of the free, sovereign Holy Spirit, there is hope for us preachers, even in our bondage to controlling listeners. This wonderfully disrupting, disarming Holy Spirit is seen most vividly in Acts. We marvel at the rapid, miraculous growth of Peter's homiletical ability. Peter was speechless before the serving woman in the courtyard (Luke 22:54–62). He weeps at his inability to witness, having denied that he even knew Christ. Which makes it all the more surprising when, on the Day of Pentecost, Peter moves from being the most notorious antiwitness to the chief spokesperson for the church. The first sermon (Acts 2) is Peter's rationale for the Pentecostal descent of the Holy Spirit. Short, poorly illustrated, and not too well constructed, Peter's sermon was one of the most effective in history—"three thousand persons were added" (v. 41).

Forty years I've preached and have never come close to such success. Since Pentecost, Peter has had the opportunity to preach in a variety of venues: Solomon's portico (Acts 3:11–26) and before the Council (Acts 4:1–12; 5:27–42). No sermons by Peter are then reported until chapter 10. One day, without preparation or predetermination, Peter has a vision while taking a noon nap, a vision in which all sorts of animals are let down a sheet. The voice says, "Kill and eat" (Acts 10:9–16). Three times the voice repeats the strange command.

While Peter puzzles over the vision's meaning, men appear, sent by Cornelius. At Caesarea, Peter enters the house of Cornelius, who is not only a Gentile but a member of Caesar's Finest, Roman overlords occupying Judea. Peter enters the house, unable to hide his annoyance that he has been thus directed: "You yourselves know that it is unlawful for a Jew to associate with or to visit a Gentile; but God has shown me that I should not call anyone profane or unclean. So when I was sent for, I came. . . . Now, may I ask why you sent for me?" (Acts 10:28–29). Not the most promising of sermon introductions.

"Peter began to speak to them . . ." (Acts 10:34), opening his sermon with a sentence that the church has repeated in order to correct itself throughout its history: "I truly understand that God shows no partiality, but in every nation anyone who fears [God] and does what is right is acceptable to [God]," (v. 35), a sweeping declaration of God's universal elective intent.

Peter manages only the first sentences of his sermon. "While Peter was still speaking, the Holy Spirit fell upon all who heard the word. The circumcised believers who had come with Peter were astounded that the gift of the Holy Spirit had been poured out even to Gentiles, for they heard them speaking in tongues and extolling God" (vv. 44–46). *Sermon interrupted*, ripped from the hands of the preacher and given to the listeners— *sermon out of control.*

Later, Peter recounts these strange events to the scandalized church leaders in Jerusalem: "And as I began to speak, the Holy Spirit fell upon them just as it had upon us at the beginning" (Acts 11:15). The Holy Spirit has not only instigated this strange evangelistic mission in this short but most effective of sermons but has now validated that the move to the Gentiles is of God.

This could have been Peter's best-formed sermon, beginning with a wonderfully concise summary of the history of salvation. The preacher manages only 175 words before the Holy Spirit breaks in, takes over, and Peter relinquishes control of communication.

The voice in the vision had told Peter to rise, kill, and eat the animals that drop down in the sheet. Peter refused a direct divine command. The Holy Spirit persisted, and only now what Peter misunderstood has been demonstrated in the surprising descent of the Spirit and the inclusion of even Gentiles into the gracious election of God. It has taken Peter ten chapters to see the expansive scope of God's salvation, the extravagant reach of the new community. God will have a family, and only God shall determine the borders of this new people by water and Spirit. The Holy Spirit will leap over boundaries, empower the telling of the mighty works of God, and surprise with the scope of election, even if sermons must be interrupted.

We who have generally been led to believe that the Holy Spirit is adjunct to baptism—the *epiclesis,* the laying-on-of-hands and prayer for the Holy Spirit predictably following the imposition of water—will be challenged by this account of the Spirit's descent preceding a baptism. Preachers who believe that our words precede and make way for revelation are challenged by this instance of a preacher's words post descent of the Spirit. We who act as if the church is the chief administrator of the Holy Spirit are challenged to hear that (at least in this case) the Holy Spirit precedes the church.[119]

Peter says 175 words, people hear, speak up, and we have the drama of the first Gentile convert. Before being so rudely interrupted, Peter notes that Jesus "went about doing good and healing all who were oppressed by the devil" and that Jesus did so, anointed with the Holy Spirit (Acts 10:38). It's an amazing claim: the same empowering Holy Spirit is now busy through the speech of once-denying, dumbfounded preachers such as Peter, reaching once-excluded people such as Cornelius. Acts portrays the Word of God as organic, growing, increasing, constantly expanding its reach (6:7; 12:24; 19:20). Indeed the whole of the New Testament, in one way or another, marvels that there is no controllable Word of God.

In my experience, our most effective sermons are the ones we don't finish. The Holy Spirit intrudes and takes over the sermon we thought we were preaching. Sometimes the true beginning of a sermon occurs when the preacher says the last words. The Holy Spirit romps in the congregation's imagination and the true proclamation occurs. That's why it is pointless for biblical interpreters to speculate on "What Peter really meant." Because of the uncontrollable, lively Holy Spirit, Peter doesn't know what his words will mean (nor do we) because preachers' words are constantly commandeered.

Just last Sunday, I preached as well as I knew how only to have a layperson accost me at the church door. "I thought what you said was right on. Except I wondered why you didn't use Romans 8." Amazing. My sermon was being enlarged, improved, engaged by the Holy Spirit thirty minutes after I thought I was done.

In such intrusive moments we are forced, like Peter in Acts 10, to expand our boundaries for the kingdom of God. Mission births theology; theological reflection is subsequent to the church's wonder at the work of the Holy Spirit in history. We do theology not to think our way toward God but rather to make sense out of the odd interruptions of the Holy Spirit as God moves toward us *and* beyond us.

Before he was interrupted by the descent of the Holy Spirit, Peter says of himself and the apostles, "We are witnesses to all that [Jesus] did both in Judea and in Jerusalem" (Acts 10:39). Peter becomes not only a witness of the things Jesus did and taught after resurrection but now a witness to this outbreak of Holy Spirit as the good news continues to leap over every boundary, out of our control.

In the university, we often practice what Hauerwas calls the "wink." We observe some phenomenon, or listen to some self-description of behavior, and we give a knowing wink to our intellectual colleagues. Social sciences such as psychology tell us what is "really going on." That which a less-informed observer describes as inexplicable and mysterious, those of us in the know understand to be only a matter of genetically determined behavior, social location, class, economic forces, et cetera. "What is to you a mystery," we imply, "has been revealed to us *cognoscenti* as only a matter of . . ." Wink, wink.

Christians also have a knowing "wink." When we hear someone describe a seemingly irredeemable tragedy, or we lament a life careening aimlessly into oblivion, or an odd person receives an unexpected, unearned insight, or we see empires rising or falling, we wink to one another. We know a secret. That public secret consists not in better explanations than those of the world but rather in our conviction of the near presence of the One who moves the sun, moon, and stars, a love that is rampant, invading the world, enlisting the oddest assortment of miscreants to tell the truth, a love determined to rule so that we don't have to. We are, by the odd grace of God, out of control.

"Waiting for God"[120]

John 11:1–45

Anybody still standing who worked with me at Duke Chapel (and there are only a few) will tell you: I'm not a patient person.

Today's Gospel—dead Lazarus raised by shouting Jesus—has an odd detail that affronts the impatient among us. Jesus is summoned by his buddies, Mary and Martha, to the bedside of their brother, Lazarus.

"Come quickly!" begs Martha, "Lazarus whom you love is ill." Jesus' response to Martha's plea for emergency medical assistance?

"Aw, Lazarus isn't terminal."

How does Jesus know that Lazarus isn't so sick? Three days later, when Jesus finally makes it to Mary and Martha's, Martha gives Jesus a piece of her mind.

"Don't rush right over Mr. Savior. It's too late for Lazarus. He's been entombed for three days," and, as she says it in the elegant King James' Version, "already he stinketh."

So Jesus wasn't great at remote diagnostics.

And thus my eye fell on an odd detail in an odd story in this oddest of Gospels. When Jesus is beseeched by Mary and Martha to rush over and heal his good friend Lazarus, John says, "Jesus waited two days."

Excuse me? Why didn't Mr. Compassion rush right over and save these sisters, and their brother, this grief? Isn't that your definition of friendship: a friend is someone who cares enough to drop everything and come when you call? What was Jesus doing that was more important than aiding a friend in dire need?

John just says, "Jesus waited two days."

Am I the only impatient person who finds this three-day lacuna, this insensitive seventy-two hour hiatus, odd?

True, when Jesus finally stops whatever he's doing (though whatever it is isn't significant enough for John to mention it) and gets to the cemetery, Jesus pulls off a spectacular resuscitation. At Jesus' cry, "Lazarus arise! Unbind him! Let him go!" Lazarus strides forth from the tomb! Impressive. All's well that ends well, you say.

But still, *a three-day delay?*

Church fathers speculated that this raising of Lazarus is a prefigurement of Jesus' resurrection. As dead Jesus lay in the tomb for three days, so Lazarus. Okay.

So . . . why did Jesus wait three days in the tomb before his resurrection? What was Jesus doing those three days?

Why did God make us wait from Good Friday to Easter for resurrection?

"He's back!" cried the women who ran from Jesus' tomb on Easter.

"Where has he been since Friday?" asks the church.

Maybe it takes an impatient person like me to settle on this detail in the raising of Lazarus. Why did Jesus delay?

In my first congregation, old folks sometimes said, "God is good, all the time. All the time, God is good." If that's true, why a three-day wait to do good?

Why can't we have God when we really, really need God? Why these empty spaces, this wasted time, hopeless despair, unanswered questions, and delayed salvation if God is God for us? What good is God's goodness if it is goodness postponed?

I remember the day that it occurred to me: From the time the Hebrews went into slavery to the day God delivered them was about four hundred years.

Exodus begins with God showing up to Moses in the burning bush, "I am the God of your forefathers. I have heard the cry of my people. I have come down to deliver them from the hand of Pharaoh." And though it is not found in your Bibles, Moses responded, "It's about time! We've been slaves for four hundred years. Don't rush right over!"

I know someone who has prayed to God every day for deliverance from the relentlessly painful arthritis that has plagued her since youth. And for six decades she has prayed to God for rescue from this hell and she has . . . heard nothing from God.

Stanley Hauerwas says that Israel's faith was "long training in being out of control" of its relationship with God, without despising God for our inability to control God.

That's not a bad definition of the training required for a faithful Christian life—learning the patience to live our lives out of control, vulnerable to the comings, goings, and tardiness of a living God whose ways among us are—in our self-concerned conceit—odd.

In my attempt to be bishop, my former flock in Alabama would tell you this was the major weakness of my leadership: I found it hard to wait for God.

I so wanted our efforts at church renewal to bear fruit. Now. I prayed for every pastor to be renewed in ministry. Now. I only had eight years as bishop. I couldn't wait for God to show up!

"It took the Lord four hundred years between God's last words of the Old Testament and God's first words of the New," they said. "We can wait eight years for you to leave Alabama."

Looking back, though I fancied myself as a decisive, timely leader, I made mistakes by rushing things, taking matters into my own hands, moving too quickly, not allowing a crisis to mature and ripen.

Grace is not *grace* (the word means "gift") if it's predictable, programmable, on demand.

Maybe that's why God sometimes takes God's own good time to show up, to reach out, to move, and to save.

"Sadly, my son, who grew up attending Duke Chapel, is not a Christian now," a mother said to me.

And I, having gained a healthy respect for God taking God's own good time, replied, " 'Not a Christian *yet*,' you should say. God's got ways of getting what God wants, but God takes God's own time. You tell your son to keep looking over his shoulder as he moves into his forties."

A cardinal Christian virtue is therefore patience: allowing God to be God in God's own good time. Our destiny is not under our sole control. We live on God's time, not ours.

It's conventional for Christians to say, at time of death, "I believe that my loved one is now in heaven with God." And perhaps that's the case.

Orthodox Christian belief has more typically said that when we die, we wait. The dead await the last trumpet, the general resurrection of the dead. In death, even as in life, we wait, utterly dependent on God to show up, to raise the dead, and to make our lives mean what they could not mean on our own. I believe that even in death we shall have a future; but our future, being totally in God's hands, will be, as our present, in God's own good time.

As the previous pope put it, "Only God has a future." Our sole hope is that the God who raised Lazarus, albeit three days after his death, shall raise us.

Maybe we are made to wait in order to purge us of our urge to make our lives turn out on our own, to be cured of ungodly impatience, to let God be God in time. Maybe we must wait because what God is up to is more than the righting of a few injustices, the soothing of some pain. If it's a new heaven and a new earth, creation brought to completion, total renovation, it may take a while.

I got sick. I was sure it was the dreaded swine flu, or bird flu, or some other bestial pestilence. It dragged on a week, then a month, two months. I was miserable. I had important things to do that can't be done while you are coughing up your guts and your nose is running.

When I was free of fever and finally on the mend, I was complaining to a friend about my suffering. He asked, "What did your illness teach you?"

What? I'm meant to grow in my relationship to God even during illness? You're not saying that God took two months to cure just to teach me about my finitude and my morality, are you? You're not saying that God has projects other than me?

One day, someday, we shall know. We are not in control of God's time. Jesus is God With Us, *though maybe not as soon as we'd like.*

Chapter Five

The Witness of Preaching

B arth famously kept the Crucifixion from the Isenheim Altarpiece over his desk as he worked, the only art so honored by him. This German Expressionist depiction of the lamentation for the dead Christ is somewhat surprising for a theologian who honors Bethlehem as highly as Golgotha. Barth treasured Grunewald's mas-terpiece chiefly for a detail that Barth noted in a number of places in his theology: the slender finger of John the Baptist.

The Fourth Gospel calls John a "witness to the light" (John 1:7). John is not the light but rather the one who holds an open Bible in one hand and points with the other toward the crucified God who is light. Positioned between his boney right finger and the open Bible are words from the Vulgate, "He must increase but I must decrease" (John 3:30). The Bible is thrust toward the viewer, whose eye travels up John's extended finger toward Christ as if to embody the text. The preacher does not possess light; the preacher is but an enlightening witness who points to a wonder too grand for words. Scripture, as revealing as it can be, needs a witness, someone to point toward the mystery of God For Us, pointing away from the book toward a man. The more revealing the preacher's witness, the greater the diminishment of the preacher before the awesome mystery of the Crucified.

> The Christian can confront the world only as a witness. [The preacher's] action is wholly dependent on the truth and reality of what [the preacher] attests. [The preacher] can only point [people] to the speaking of Jesus Christ, drawing attention to the fact that He speaks. . . . [The preacher] cannot . . . come and speak among them as a second Christ, as if Christ spoke. . . . [The preacher] can encounter them only as the friend of the Bridegroom. If Christ speaks through [the preacher], giving to [the preacher's] witness the power of His own self-witness, as He can and will, this is not in the Christian's hands and [the preacher] cannot boast of it to the world . . . even though [the preacher] may receive and have Him, [the preacher] does not control Him. Hence it does not stand in [the preacher's] own power to cause the Gospel so to shine that it must enlighten the world, to create and give [people] the freedom to grasp and appropriate the kingdom of God and therefore their reconciliation, to recognize and confess Jesus Christ as Lord. [A preacher] cannot convert anyone.[1]

And the sermon? The sermon aspires to be no more than the boney finger pointing to a miracle that has seized the preacher's attention.

Our preaching must be formed by its subject. Barth quotes Luther's lament that we lapsed into writing books about the gospel rather than preaching the gospel. Long before, Plato wondered if the written word would diminish the dynamic quality of dialectic argument and kill philosophy. Luther is wary of writing for christological reasons. He notes that in order to reveal the Christ child the angel merely pointed to the manger and the swaddling clothes rather than writing a guidebook. Likewise, the angel at the empty tomb invited the women to take a look at the grave cloths rather than offer them a book explaining the resurrection. The human need "to write books is a great injury and it is a violation of the Spirit . . . and is not the way of the New Testament." The gospel "should not really be written but put in the living voice, which then soundeth forth and is heard everywhere in the world," concludes Luther.[2]

A high school physics teacher explained why she preferred video and multimedia to physics textbooks. "Physics is the study of events—motion and mass—in the physical world. In attempting to understand an event in space and time, the printed word may not be the most helpful medium."

Preaching, not writing, is Christ's peculiar, elected means of communication and therefore—because Christian preaching is in service to a living God—preaching must be dynamic, vital, and willing to be out of control. Preaching is witness to the world of the possibility of speech that is tethered to something other than the world's means of control. Some of us preachers write out our sermons in manuscript before we preach, because words on the page give the illusion that we are actually in control of the sermon.[3] Our people delight in hearing a sermon preached without notes, full frontal, with the preacher looking them in the eye because a sermon thus delivered has more of the quality of witness—the preacher pointing toward something that the preacher has seen and heard so that others might hear.

Witness is a modest vocation. When I was summoned to testify in a child custody suit between two warring parents in my congregation, the court had little interest in my beliefs about parenthood, my professional opinion about either parent's spiritual depth. All the court wanted was testimony: *tell what you have seen and heard.*

John the Baptist's witness, as presented in the Fourth Gospel, lacks content and is repetitious: "Look! The Lamb of God!" (John 1:29, 36), whom he admits, "I did not know" (1:31, 33). Yet, on the basis of John's witness alone, two of his followers become Jesus' first disciples. They follow not by Jesus' direct invitation but because of John's testimony (1:37). Having seen, John testifies (1:34) so that others might also see; by God's grace, they do.

The significance of the witness is always other than the witness. "We do not proclaim [preach] ourselves" (2 Cor. 4:5). As Barth said, anybody who simply stops on the sidewalk, looks upward, and points, soon draws a crowd of onlookers, each one attempting to see what captures the gaze of another.

That's my theory for why people still gather on Sunday morning to hear a frail, fallible, modestly endowed preacher like me who is less attractive than Joel and less practical than Rick. Slick, pop TV preachers may have enabled the church again to marvel at the wonder of an artless human being standing up and witnessing to the truth. It is the truth that counts.

"Just hand people a plate of food," chided the urban missionary, "keep your church talk to yourself. We're not here to proselytize; we're here to help. We are not here to assert our privileged status over the marginalized." I assured the anxious activist that neither he nor the homeless had anything to fear—we are mainline Protestants who would rather hand the less fortunate a bowl of soup than risk telling them the truth. It's less disruptive to the powers-that-be to pacify the hungry by doing a little good than to testify to those in need that we wouldn't be standing with them, in the cold, on the sidewalk, if it were not for Jesus putting us here. More important, they are not here—out of work, hungry and unhoused—because of God. (Later, when the Baptist's voice is silenced by Herod, we learn how deeply threatening to the world is a preacher whose speech is out of control.)

The unwillingness of those who have heard to share good news with those who haven't heard is the worst form of priviledged smugness. Those who haven't heard the truth about God deserve to be told.

No one is born with this faith or stumbles on it after walks in the woods or by rummaging about in one's ego. Christians are recipients, never initiators. Here is truth that can be had only with receptive, empty, open hands. Someone had to love Jesus enough to talk about him. Someone had to love us enough to show and to tell the good news. We believe what we believe and know what we know only through witness, testimony.[4]

If I were made king of United Methodism, which may happen any day, I would ask only one question of candidates for ministry: *Have you seen or heard anything from God worth testimony to another?*

When Jesus calls himself the "light of the world," the prophet's promise is fulfilled: "I will give you as a light to the nations, / that my salvation may reach to the end of the earth" (Isa. 49:6b). Elsewhere Jesus turns to this ragtag group of disciples and dares call *them* the light of the world, God's elective answer to what's wrong with the world. The Light shines through witnesses.

The Witness of Israel

The first witness is Israel. Barth treats the Christian doctrine of election as an outworking or christological expansion of God's election of Israel:

> Now the LORD said to Abram, "Go from your country to your kindred and your father's house to the land that I will show you. I will make of you a great nation, and I will bless you, and make your name great. . . ."

The purpose of the gracious election of Abraham and his descendants?

"I will bless those who bless you, and the one who curses you I will curse; and in you all the families of the earth shall be blessed."

Election accounts for Israel's particularity, distinctiveness, and oddness.

Has any people ever heard the voice of a god speaking out of a fire, as you have heard, and lived? Or has any god ever attempted to go and take a nation for himself from the midst of another nation, by trials, by signs and wonders, by war, by a mighty hand and an outstretched arm, and by terrifying displays of power, as the LORD your God did for you in Egypt before your very eyes? (Deut. 4:33–34)

For you are a people holy to the LORD your God; the LORD your God has chosen you out of all the peoples on earth to be [God's] people, [God's] treasured possession. (Deut. 7:6)

No reason is given for God's choice of Abraham or for Abraham's response other than "the LORD loved you" (7:8).[5] Jewish theologians have struggled over the centuries with questions of election: Is Israel related to God because of God's election of Israel, or is Israel related to God because of the gift of Torah to Israel? Is Israel disjoined from the other nations because of God's election of Israel, or does Israel have a mission to other peoples because of election?[6] Many of these questions were dismissed by Baruch Spinoza, who disconnected historical revelation from philosophy in Jewish thought. Spinoza presented a secularized reconceptualization of election that, in his view, was a more modest claim of Jewish distinctiveness. Spinoza's enlightenment-produced God was an impersonal, abstract force, a metaphysical God fitted for the demands of Jewish participation in the Enlightenment. David Novak says that the problem created was that "the God of Spinoza cannot be attributed with the capacity for election in general and the actual election of Israel in particular."[7] Only a personal, active God who freely chooses, acts, and interacts in history is capable of election. An abstract force cannot be said to have "chosen" anything; only persons choose.

Novak says that Spinoza "inverted" the traditional Jewish divine election to mean that Israel elects to worship the one true God and to follow the Torah.[8] Election in Spinoza is human action; Torah an effective device for the ordering of society, no longer a sign of the purpose of Israel's peoplehood. By the time Spinoza and his heirs philosophically dismissed Israel's election, the matter was so abstract and generalized that Novak says, "[I]t is not really God who elects and it is not really Israel who is elected."[9]

The death of covenant as a choice of God became, after Spinoza, a powerful incentive for Jewish assimilation into secular European culture. In fact, Spinoza charged that the Jewish notion of an eternal election of Israel was a source of much Gentile hatred of Jews,[10] a premodern vestige that led to tribalism and chauvinism among those who presume to be elected and to resentment of the elect by the "unelect." More recently, some have argued that the Jewish idea of election led to genocidal actions by Israel in the conquest of non-Israelites,[11] and to justification for religious violence today.[12]

In opposition to Spinoza, a vibrant recovery of the conviction of Israel's election was achieved by Franz Rosenzweig (1886–1929), a contemporary of Barth. Dispose of election and the witness of Israel, said Rosenzweig, and one has lost the rationale for the continued existence of the Jews. Rosenzweig said that modern Jewish intellectuals robbed Israel of its witness because they could not make sense of election once modernity dismissed the possibility of divine revelation. Election is self-revelation of God. Once the Enlightenment's view of the world is accepted as the way things are and will always be, and all expectation of eschatological fulfillment of God's promises is lost, then election becomes unintelligible. The content of Israel's witness is lost; Israel is lost.

In Rosenzweig's luminous masterpiece, *The Star of Redemption*, he says that God construed as an absolute principle can never adequately account for a God who is in relationship to a people, or for a people who see themselves as chosen for relationship with God.[13] Like Barth, Rosenzweig was deeply impressed by the disaster of the Great War. And with the early Barth, Rosenzweig affirmed the wisdom that comes through honest confrontation with human finitude. Scripture teaches that the creature is created out of nothing and returns to nothing. The creature self-possesses nothing that establishes the creature's life as significant and can muster no philosophical protection against mortality.[14] The Great War ended the unjustified humanistic optimism of the Enlightenment and made possible a positive reassessment of the conviction of Israel's election.

Though many Christians have wrongly believed that the church has superseded Israel, replacing Israel in God's plan for the world's redemption, Barth (along with Calvin) stressed that God's covenant with Israel is unconditional and never annulled.[15] Rosenzweig mirrors Barth in his vigorous rejection of Spinoza's dismissal of election and the move of many Jewish thinkers toward bland assimilation.

God relates to all the nations by means of creation but only to Israel by means of election. God's means of the ultimate redemption of the nations is Israel and the Jewish people, reasserted Rosenzweig. Scripture insists that revelation is inextricably connected to the Jews, and the continuing life of the Jews as a distinctive people who are attached to the Torah reveals the truth of who God is and what God intends. Christianity is the only non-Jewish religion capable of comprehending the significance of Jewishness, says Rosenzweig, paying Christians a great compliment that we have not always deserved.

Rosenzweig presents Israel as a missionary community that is demanded by the revelation that Israel has received. Israel's mission is accomplished not through proselyting and witnessing but rather by God's mysterious showcasing of Israel for the sake of the whole world.[16] The star of Zion shines, not through its own light but rather in the light of the God who has chosen Israel to shine for the sake of the whole world.

Though God's choice of Israel is free and gratuitous, particular, and exclusive for Israel, Israel is the means of God's inclusion of the whole world into Israel's election. Israel is a "placeholder" to demonstrate the purposes of God until God brings all the nations to Israel's light. With most of the rabbis, Rosenzweig believed that in the eschaton there would be neither Jews nor Christians but all would be transformed by God.

God doesn't transfer the covenant; rather God promises to open the covenant to include all. The Jewish people would be redeemed when all humanity would be miraculously included in the covenant, mysteriously, wondrously Judaized by God's grace. This is how the Jew Paul could speak of Gentiles being "grafted" on to Israel (see Rom. 11). Jeremiah's "New Covenant" (31:31) does not supplant the "Old Covenant" but is covenant's new rendition.

David Novak, explicating Rosenzweig, says, "It is not that it is Israel's task to bring *her* light to the nations but, rather, that God will bring them to [*God's*] light that is to shine on Israel through the Torah and shines out from Israel as a beacon."[17] If, along the way, some convert to Judaism, it is assumed that God has been particularly gracious to those individuals: "for your light has come / and the glory of the LORD will rise upon you. . . . / Nations will come to your light" (Isa. 60:1–3).

Novak speaks to his fellow Jews of their elected purpose in the salvation of the world: "Our testimony to the nations . . . is to remind them by our very vulnerable and incomplete life that God is not present in the world, that redemption is not to be expected by human criteria, that redemption will only come when God decides by [God's] own mysterious criteria that the time is right for us and for them along with us. And so our testimony is to belie those [Christians?] who say that the world is redeemed and to insist that the world wait with Israel for her and its redeemer. 'I know my redeemer lives, even if He be the last to rise on earth' (Job 19:25)."[18]

Joel Kaminsky tells fellow Jews that the mystery of God's choice of Israel has continuing power, but he warns that the notion of the Jewish people as chosen by God becomes perverted and dangerous when it is conflated with "the Christian category of salvation, implying that the non-elect are damned."[19] I am hopeful that Kaminsky would be less fearful of linkage between Christian and Jewish ideas of election if he knew Barth's view of election and salvation.

Israel teaches the church the adventure of life out of control. Read any of the eighth-century prophets and you will hear speech out of the speaker's control, speech commandeered by a just God. The Psalms were sung by a people who had to learn through the ages to live out of control of their destiny, dependent on God's steadfast love to make their lives count. In the worst of times, even as victims of Gentile persecution, when Jews had children, Jews witnessed that they were not fated to be victims of Gentile hate, that their existence as Jews was not some kind of mistake, and God's choice of Israel was not stupid.

Election serves as a reminder that each of us Gentiles "is a guest in the house of Israel."[20] Post-Holocaust, Barth taught that evangelization of the Jews "is not the witness which [the church] owes to Israel." We have nothing to teach that the Jew "does not already know." Rather, as Christian witnesses, we have much to learn from Jews.[21] The church lives with the synagogue, therefore, not as with other faiths but rather as "the root from which it has itself sprung."[22]

The Jew witnesses that salvation is wholly from God and that Israel is God's providential means of saving God's world. The Christian witness is that the Incarnation is the climactic, singular event that takes place *within the history of God's election of Israel* for the redemption of the whole world. In Jesus Christ, son of Israel, God's elective intent is demonstrated to be more sweeping than even the most messianic of Israel's expectations. That is the wonder confronted by the Jewish members of The Way who populate the narrative of Acts, wonderment at the scope of God's elective intent. "God has given even to the Gentiles the repentance that leads to life" (Acts 11:18). Like Israel, the church does not effect divine election or produce salvation, but rather witnesses it and witnesses to it within its own life. The church, like Israel, is a tangible, bodily, concrete sign to the world of gracious election. "As election is the living ground of Israel, so it is the living ground of the community of Jesus Christ," says Barth.[23] It is through this minority, these resident "aliens and exiles" (1 Pet. 2:11) in diaspora that God means to bless the whole.[24] Salvation really is of the Jews (John 4:22).

The Witness of Israel and the Church

To Israel, God declared, "You are my witnesses, says the Lord, / and my servant whom I have chosen" (Isa. 43:10). In preaching the gospel to the man who would become the first Gentile convert (Acts 10:34–43), Peter says that, though Jesus was crucified, "God raised him up on the third day and allowed him to appear, not to all the people but to us *who were chosen by God as witnesses*" (vv. 40–41a, italics mine). Salvation rests on an accomplished act of God that lacks only witnesses, "who ate and drank with him after he rose from the dead" (v. 41b). In witnessing, the witness is validation of the claim of resurrection. Peter, who just a short time before lacked the courage to testify to a powerless serving woman (Luke 22:54–62), now speaks up and makes bold claims before one of Caesar's Finest. How to account for that miraculous change in Peter except through resurrection and election?

It is not by chance that Barth's first major discussion of ethics ("The Command of God," *CD* II/2, §§36–39) follows immediately after his discussion of election. Ethics is presented as a subspecies of election, what happens after God's command. "You will be my witnesses" (Acts 1:8). Scoffers would later call these first witnesses "ignorant and unlearned," as they might call us today, the mystery of God's gracious election in action.

The purpose of Christ's post-resurrection appearances is for mission, and that mission is *witness*. Witness, *martus*, is used in the Acts of the Apostles twenty-three times.[25] Indeed, *witness* is found in the opening programmatic summary of Acts 1:8: "you will be my witnesses in Jerusalem, in all Judea and Samaria, and to the ends of the earth." Paul is selected as the great witness to the Gentiles through the witness of Ananias (Acts 9:15). Acts 10:39 says that God has chosen us as "witnesses to all." The resurrection is an explosion that casts "witness . . . to his resurrection" beyond all boundaries (Acts 1:22). At Pentecost, Peter testifies before the scoffing mob in the street, "this Jesus God raised up, and of that all of us are witnesses" (2:32). Kavin Rowe demonstrates that the resurrection "is the fount of new reality out of which the *novum* that is Christian mission emerges."[26]

A dead man coming back to life could mean all sorts of things. In the case of Jesus, it confirms his identity as "Lord" (a bold political claim) and makes his identity effective now, in the present, and for the whole world. Some older interpreters of Luke/Acts accused Luke of toning down earlier Christian eschatology in order to make Christ a bit more palatable to the Roman world. My colleagues Kavin Rowe and Douglas Campbell (both of whom acknowledge their indebtedness to Barth) have amply demonstrated that the post-resurrection Christian witness is thoroughly eschatological—in Christ's resurrection an old world has ended and a new world has broken forth—and therefore very political.[27] We crucified Jesus, but "now" Paul tells the Athenians (Acts 17:30), God has decisively acted in raising crucified Jesus from the dead. Resurrection not only vindicates Christ's way but also inaugurates his rule. To be sure, the old regime doggedly holds on, but a new world has come, is coming, and the church is elected to be the first wave of that sweepingly cosmic, very political revolution.

Campbell urges us to begin our reading of Paul with God's appearance to Paul as the risen Christ. We do not start with self-assessment or self-discovery, nor do we begin with claims of alleged flaws in Judaism; we begin with God's beginning with us. A Christian, for Paul, is not someone who has been on a tortured journey of self-discovery; a Christian is simply someone to whom the risen Christ has shown up and given an assignment.

After a long discussion one evening in an Alabama church, of many of the deficiencies in United Methodism, a woman blurted out in frustration, "I spent thirty-eight years thinking God was mad at me. I tried this and that to get God to like me. When I came here, for the first time I heard about *grace*. This church, for all its problems, is the place where God finally brought me to my senses about what God really thinks of me."

The God of Jesus Christ is magnanimously disposed toward us. While we were hostile, ungodly, chaotic, and rebellious, Christ died for us, rose for us, and appears to us. God didn't wait for us to get our act together; in fact, our earnest efforts to do so were a kind of mockery of our true situation with God, a sad contradiction of who God is.

Justification is an unconditional, nonretributive act of God, not a forensic, contractual transaction. *Diakasune*, "righteousness," is best read in light of Romans 6 and 7, says Campbell. When we are baptized, we die and rise with Christ, set free from slavery to the present age, free to live on the basis of reality. As those who have been justified to God by God, we can joyfully live without insecurity, free of narcissistic self-concern and without worry about the behavior of everyone else, since neither our behavior nor theirs conditions our salvation.

World Upside Down through Witness

Because the Holy Spirit is the means and the manner in which God carries out God's elective intent among God's people and because the Holy Spirit seems, by nature, to be disruptive and discombobulating (Acts 2), Christians are predisposed to view historical change—social, economic, political change, ecclesiastical change too—as possibly meaningful indications of the activity of God, signs of the inbreaking of a new age. Death lost control in the resurrection. Real change is usually traumatic and often involves human pain. However, the apocalyptic nature of Christian thought leads Christians to be open to the possibility that God is with us even (perhaps especially) in times of dislocation, movement, and relinquishment.

Some revolt by marching on the Whitehouse or setting fire to City Hall, others by creative acts of nonviolent resistance. Christians understand such moves, and sometimes we find ourselves participating with them, even as did the young Barth (called "the Red Pastor" by some of his first parishioners). More typically we will be in the position, not of revolutionaries, but of witnesses—those who simply stand up and testify that the emperor has no clothes, thereby robbing the empire of ultimate validity or final dignity. The weapon God gives us to join in the fight for the liberation of humanity and the triumph of the kingdom is nonviolent words. In our verbal assault on the status quo and business as usual through announcement of the present and future reign of Christ, Christian preachers tend to be more radical and more critical than either conservatives or liberals.

That's what is lacking in James Davison Hunter's advocacy of "faithful presence" as the uniquely Christian way to change the world.[28] Presence, for any of its good effects, is not enough for the church. We have no biblical warrant for Hunter's quiet, humble presence in the face of the world's good and bad; we are called to *witness*. While presence may be a prelude, a necessary prerequisite to witness, it can never be a substitute for faithful testimony.

Acts depicts a church whose witness is beyond the control of the imperial authorities, out of bounds of established classes and socially assigned orders of classical Roman culture, a church out of control even of its own life and death as the gospel rips like wildfire through Asia Minor. People set free, let loose, saved—Roman army officers, sons and daughters, old women and men, upstart maids such as Rhoda (Acts 12)—people no one thought could be saved, whom few in power wanted free, nonentities who were never noticed, now being jailed, beaten, or worse in a vain attempt to shut them up. The church, fragile young thing, dragged all over the empire by the imperious Holy Spirit, hauled kicking and screaming into harm's way, even into Rome, where testimony would be given and, with nothing more forceful than speech, Caesar would be defeated without a platoon being raised or a shot fired, all done by a God who refuses to stay either dead or quiet, a God who makes revolution through the testimony of witnesses.

Thus the church is, through election, an inherently missionary community. "You are the light of the world. . . . [L]et your light shine before others, so that they may see your good works and give glory to your Father in heaven" (Matt. 5:14). Our good works do not bring glory to ourselves; we are not the source of light. Our witness is a reflection of the Light. When Jesus calls his disciples, he doesn't promise to make them Christians but to make them fishers of people, sent-out apostles, bearers of news who seek and who gather lost sheep, witnesses. Pray! Jesus urges, that God will send more workers for such a bountiful, expansive harvest (Luke 10:2).

A group of us gathers at the site of gun-related violence in our city. We have prayer and then simply stand silently with a sign, "Witness Against Gun Violence." The clergy wear their collars. At best, our witness merely points to some judgment, some reality beyond the present, a boney finger pointing to how God means it to be, a little light shining in the dark, anticipating Light.

Christian responsibility is the vocation to be a witness, a servant of the Word, elected to give the world the good news. Again, the key verses are Acts 10:40–41, "but God raised him on the third day and allowed him to appear, not to all the people, but to us who were chosen by God as witnesses." Here is a faith that is born not through introspection but rather by one person telling news to another, news that can't be known except through gift and reception. To be a Christian is to have received news from the outside, to know the eschatological truth of the end and beginning of the world, to be the spark that ignites a conflagration by the One who casts fire on the earth (Luke 12:49).

Jesus has now taken time for us and taken time from us. We live awkwardly between the dying of the old order and the birth of the new. In a Lenten sermon, Hauerwas witnesses that Christian life is living in an eschatological reality that is established in the cross and resurrection of Jesus:

> [T]hrough the cross and resurrection of Jesus, the powers of oppression and injustice have been defeated. The task for those who would follow Jesus is to live according to that reality. The powers of this age have been defeated. We do them no favor if we act in a manner that affirms their delusion that they are in control. Rather we should imitate God, who our psalm [Ps. 2] describes as laughing at those who think they are in control. The Son of Man has returned, restoring God's rule and thus humbling kings who would rule as if there is no God.
>
> I fear we, who never think of ourselves as kings but believe nonetheless that we rule ourselves and the world, are among those who should be so humbled. We live refusing to believe the Son of Man has come. We are pretty sure, if we are to get out of life alive, we are going to have [to] do what we fear God failed to do when he set Jesus on the road to Jerusalem. Cross and resurrection are all well and good, but someone has to do the things that need to be done to make history come out right. Thus the cleverly devised myth that America is the hope of the world. . . .
>
> But Lent beckons. Again we are forced to contemplate [that] we have not lived as those who believe that the Son of Man has come. We are desperate to be in control of our lives in a world in which we are not in control.[29]

Barth characterizes preaching as virtually impossible, not because our listeners are obtuse (many of them are) and not because we preachers must be courageous (few of us are) but because preaching is speech of and to God; therefore, preaching is *human speech out of our control*.

The Responsibility of Witness

Christians live as if the gospel were true. Preachers' lives must be at least in the process of becoming congruent with our sermons, or the world is right to question our testimony. Sadly, when the world rejects Christ, it's usually not Christ being rejected but the sorry performance of Christ's witnesses. We can't preach the ending of the old world and the advent of the new and at the same time take ease in and profit from old arrangements. We can't preach that God raised crucified Jesus from the dead and persist in honoring imperial mechanisms of control as if Caesar's ways have ultimate validity. As Cardinal Emmanuel Celestin Suhard put it, "To be a witness . . . means to live in such a way that one's life would not make sense if God did not exist."[30]

We don't devise the news, nor can we do much to make it more accessible. We're confident that God in the power of the Holy Spirit gains access to our listeners; we are no more than witnesses to an active, free subject. We cannot make Christ relevant; our listeners, through Christ's work in our preaching, are summoned to be relevant to him.

"A Christian is always 'a lonely bird on the house top' (Psalm 102:8) . . . this bird is finally and basically a contented one. Yet it is still a lonely bird," says Barth. "The song it has to sing is not an old, familiar and popular one, but a rather strange [odd] one in whose refrain no choirs can be expected to join. Christianity as a whole is a kind of 'forlorn hope,' finally and basically exulted, yet still a forlorn hope, with fewer chances to become someday the triumphant membership of a so-called world religion,"[31] the boney finger of the Baptist pointing to Christ.

In preaching, Christ not only turns to us but actively turns us to himself, beguiles us into fellowship with odd people whom we might avoid were it not for our election. Christ's presence does not await or require our actualization. Often, he shows up to people before we preachers do. That puts us in the same location as John the Baptist, pointing toward what Christ has already done. We would like for our words, if Christ chooses, to be transparent to him. It is his reality, his presence that generates preaching; he is preaching's resourceful Agent. "My Father is still working, and I also am working" (John 5:17).

Because we do not own, within the matrix of human experience, all that we need to be faithful as preachers, we preachers pray to be permeable to the work of the Spirit. Sermon preparation is the practice of various forms of begging; holding out empty hands, praying for the discipline to set no limits on what God can tell us to preach. Speaking as if this world really has been and is even now ending, being judged and redeemed by Christ, we witness to the "new normal."

During my annual physical, my doctor said, "Some of my friends are mad at you for what you and the Catholic bishop said about our legislature and governor" (referring to our suit against the ill-considered, draconian Alabama immigration law).

I told my doctor that I was sorry to have gotten him into hot water with cronies at the Country Club.

"Like I said to them," he continued, "what do you expect Willimon to say? He's a Methodist preacher; his options are limited."

My compromised witness is unworthy of such high praise. We won the suit, but even if we had not, we would still have had to say what was given.

We are witnesses, nothing more, tethered to an event we do not control. The church is not an extension of the Incarnation. We are not "the hands and the feet of Christ," Christ's presence in a world from which he is absent. We are not "the only Jesus most folks will ever see." We are not the content, goal, or agents of salvation. We don't "win people for Christ." We don't "make disciples for the transformation of the world" (current slogan of The United Methodist Church). We are not the key to God's will to be done on earth as it is in heaven. It is not up to us to speak for God or God will be unspoken. God is not predictably, constantly in us, reconciling the world; God is in Christ. We are not the world's hope, not even close.[32]

We are witnesses. We are spear carriers for the risen Christ's retake of the world. He makes us his Body, the way he takes up room. We are Christ's ambassadors, representing a disputed sovereignty we in no way control or limit. Wonder of wonders, Christ makes his appeal to the world through us (2 Cor. 5:20).

Barth calls the church the "inner circle" that exists constantly to open itself to the "outer circle," which is God's ultimate redemptive intent for all humankind. The church is elected by God for the sole purpose of "performing for the world the service which it most needs . . . giving testimony of Jesus Christ and summoning it to faith in him."[33] A preacher is lead witness to the witnesses on Sunday so that the whole church may be the joyful practitioners of testimony the rest of the week. "How shall they hear without a preacher?" (Rom. 9:14 KJV), a question asked during Paul's grand affirmation of the eternal, irrevocable election of Israel. "And how shall they preach except they be sent?" (v. 15).

"Each elect individual is as such a messenger of God," one who is "sent, . . . an apostle."[34] Our task as preachers is essential (because God has elected to speak through messengers such as us) but modest (because it is God who elects, not us). We are to witness, not to ensure the success of the witness.[35] Only God can do that.

In fact, "success" is qualified by the reality of a crucified God. There are all sorts of predictable human reasons why we ought to expect negative reaction to our witness. Jesus warned his disciples, "[T]hey will arrest you and persecute you; they will hand you over to synagogues and prisons, and you will be brought before kings and governors because of my name." In the same breath, he calls these persecutions "opportunity to testify" (Luke 21:12–13). Even the worst that happens to a Christian are opportunities to witness, to preach.

To prepare for such crucial speaking, Jesus commands avoidance of preparation. "So make up your minds not to prepare your defense in advance; for I will give you words and a wisdom that none of your opponents will be able to withstand or contradict" (vv. 14–15). I will give you words. We have something to say because God speaks. "I believed, and so I spoke," says Paul (2 Cor. 4:13). Or as Barth puts it, "Cognizance becomes knowledge when [one] becomes a responsible witness."[36] Christians think with our mouths open. We know, really know, that which we are able to speak, and we are able to speak only because God does. If our witness has never received rejection, ridicule, or even an apathetic yawn, we have good reason to question the content of our testimony.

We cannot force anyone into knowledge of election. God has given us no independent, knockdown, surefire arguments. All we can do is to "testify to the act and the revelation of divine grace."[37] Barth urges the church in its witness "to proclaim it loudly so that it may be heard and believed. It must be loud indeed," and we must refuse to let our proclamation be muffled or muted by the world's stupidity, ridicule, or rejection. Furthermore, we are not only to speak up and speak out, Barth says we are to speak "in the second person"[38]—singular and plural. Thus the primary mode of the church's peculiar speech is public speech, address, rather than introverted, in-house speech.

Preachers embody and exemplify the essential vocation of every Christian—election to be a witness. In preaching we attempt to give that which we do not control or possess, namely the good news of God's gracious control and possession of us. As witnesses we stand in solidarity with fellow sinners and preach in service to our fellow sinners, knowing that we have no differentiation from them other than our knowledge of our common election. Our election is only a fact to which we have modestly acquiesced, not an event we have effected or merited.[39]

We witness in confident conviction that God will use our witness, but our confidence "has nothing whatever to do with human presumption. . . . [God] still very definitely keeps the reins in [God's] own hands. As [witnesses] call upon [God] and with confidence, they do not gain the mastery over [God] or acquire control over [God's] gift or [God's] giving, let alone . . . the Giver."[40]

The ascription of any greater or more enduring purpose to the church and its witnesses Barth ridicules as "clerical fantasy and arrogance," a bogus attempt of the witness to attain significance detached from the One who is witnessed—Jesus Christ.

The composition of the church testifies to the oddness of the grace of God. In the church, we see dramatically reiterated the same scandal of election that is Israel. God elects "not an obedient but an obdurate people. . . . [God] does not choose a people which has something to give [God] but one which has everything to receive. . . . [God] chooses for Himself suffering under the obduracy of this people, and suffering under the curse and shame and death. . . . [God] burdens Himself with rebels and enemies."[41]

The church, by its existence, testifies to the scope of God's election; woe to the church whose composition delimits the breadth of God's elective intent. I find no biblical justification for a church (such as mine) with a median age of sixty and rising, a church where ninety-five percent of us are the same color and use the same language. The church, like Israel, ought to be constantly astounded by the scope of God's gracious election. In my experience, the scandal that is the church—the outrage that God Almighty should choose to make God's appeal to humanity through nothing better than the poor old church, Christ's bride who is also a compromised tart—is a chief evangelistic impediment. The world has difficulty comprehending that Christ attempts to retake all through nothing better than the church.

Such has it always been. Barth blames anti-Semitism on a truncated, parsimonious doctrine of election. Anti-Jewishness is a rejection of God's election of Israel as the particular, peculiar way God binds with all humanity.[42] The gracious election by God of Israel and the church is a scandal on par with that of a crucified God. "In order to be elect ourselves, for good or evil we must either be Jews or belong to this Jew."[43]

Baptist prophet Will Campbell used to tell us that in heaven Golda Meir will chase Adolf Hitler for a thousand years. When she finally nabs him, she'll pin a Star of David on his sleeve.

Witness, Not Explanation

The church bears witness to an active, busy Christ, and the best the church may hope for is that we are truthful witnesses, giving testimony to Christ's miraculous work, not surrogates for an active, living, presently working Christ. That's why Hauerwas urges us preachers not to *explain* the truth who is Jesus Christ, and why Richard Lischer says we shouldn't attempt *persuasion*.[44] As Hauerwas says, Barth understood that "explanation could not help but give the impression that the explanation is more important that the witness."[45] And as I think Lischer would say that to make persuasion the point of preaching is to give the listener too much power over preaching.

The highest (only?) compliment Hauerwas paid my preaching was to say that I rarely *explain*:

> [Willimon's sermons do not] help us to understand what is "really going on" in the text. He does not try to explain . . . because he does not think the text is really about "something else." . . . [H]e does not assume that there is a depth we need to discover that is more important than the text itself. . . . He has never invited his hearers to find something more basic or important than the stories we find in the Scripture. . . .
>
> [Will respects] the faith as a grammar of description . . . all the reading he has done in Barth over the years could not have hurt. The very character of Barth's *Dogmatics* is shaped by Barth's fundamental conviction that you cannot explain the Christian faith. . . . Barth . . . recognized that if God is God we cannot explain on grounds other than God's revelation who God is. Barth quite wonderfully imitates the character of the Bible by refusing to say more than can be said. . . .
>
> Will's sermons are his way of trying to help us resist the temptation to explain. We are not to speculate about what "must have really been going on" in Jesus' self-consciousness. Attempts to discern what Jesus must have been thinking in this or that circumstance fail to be disciplined by the silence of Scripture. Not only do attempts to "figure Jesus out" presuppose a quite misleading philosophical psychology, but they are sinful just to the extent that such attempts represent our attempt to make the Gospel fulfill our desires. The "search for the historical Jesus" . . . is but a symptom of our pride, a pride, moreover, that refuses to be humbled by the invitation to be a disciple. We try to substitute "trying to understand" for what it means to follow Jesus.
>
> Will's refusal to explain is a very effective mode of resistance to our endemic desire to make Jesus fit into our lives. To so preach risks "not being relevant to the real needs of people," but the whole point is to have our "real needs" transformed. Will's sermons . . . provide us with reminders that no explanation is required because it is not "all about us." . . .

[H]e also refuses to "translate" the Gospel into other registers such as existentialism, moral lessons, or psychological insights. . . . [Will] cannot explain the poem in words the poem does not use. Rather he must try to help us understand why it *has* to be in these words and not others. . . . The sermon is God's word just to the extent that the word does not replace the Word witnessed in Scripture. . . . [H]is stories rarely illustrate a more basic point. Rather his stories are the point, which means that he must often tell the story without saying why he is telling the story. . . . Will never explains because he is a preacher.[46]

I not only try to trust the text but also to distrust my ability adequately to control communication between God and my congregation. After one of my particularly obtuse sermons, Hauerwas told me that I showed unwarranted faith in my congregation to understand. I don't trust them further than I can throw them, but I do try to trust God.

Just last month a parishioner told me, "That was one of your best sermons" (it was not; the man knows little about good preaching), and "now I'm really convinced that God really wants me to quit my job and go do something more worthwhile for the kingdom."

I am not responsible for this response. Indeed I wonder if the man's insights, allegedly obtained through my sermon, had anything to do with me.

Here is a sermon that I preached on the Incarnation. Is this a product of a preacher out of control or a preacher controlled by revelation of a God who is beyond control?

God Is a Young Adult, Growing Younger

Hebrews 1:1–3

> "Long ago God spoke to our ancestors in many and various ways by the prophets, but in these last days he has spoken to us by a Son."

No one has ever seen God, say the Scriptures. We still want to. That's good, because God refuses to be obscure, arcane, ineffable. Jewish Kabbalists depicted Yahweh as a man, even going into detail about God's body parts. Kabbalah knew the peril of making God impersonal, abstract, and disembodied. Scripture dares metaphor—God the Rock, Mighty Warrior, Mother Hen, the pursuing, overwrought Lover in the evening in a fragrant garden, mighty wind making oaks to whirl, Good

Shepherd, King of Kings, Bloody Lamb, Woman tearing her house apart in her search for one lost coin.

Everyone knows not to take such poetry literally. These are metaphors, meant literally "to shine light" on a God who, in love, incarnates and still is God.

What if Plato, Freud, Marx, and the Jesus Seminar are wrong? What if these names, these metaphors are not solely constructed by us, not just our feeble human wish projection? What if (as Karl Barth said) some of these metaphors, maybe all of them for all we know, *are given by God*, gifts of God's relentless self-disclosure and tireless self-revelation?

This Advent morning, I invite you to see God through the metaphor that God gave us. Emmanuel. Joshua. In all sorts of ways God spoke to us, but now God has spoken to us as a young adult (Heb. 1:1).

All that we know of the Christ in action on earth is what we know of him as a young adult.

God is a young adult just getting started, in his early thirties, launched, but not quite, forever young. I can imagine that's a jarring, unwelcomed thought for many, particularly if you are a young woman who has had difficulty with immature men. And what about me—an aging male who feels a threat when around young adult males?

If you think you have come up with a comfortable, agreeable metaphor for God that works for you—think again. (We are inveterate idolaters.)

I've searched the Scriptures: Jesus says nothing to people my age. I'm offended. True, Luke begins with a couple of old people hanging out at church—Elizabeth, Zachariah—but then sends them back to the home after their bit parts, never to be heard from again. These Lukan seniors do what people my age ought to do for people under thirty—get out of their way!

God, the One who hung the heavens and flung the planets in their courses, has become a young man: barely adult, innocent, bright eyed, alert, nervous, edgy, and at the peak of his powers. He could do with a shave and a shower.

On Pentecost, the church's birthday, someone had too much to drink, according to the scoffing mob out in the street. Some of the furniture got tossed about in the upper room, there was the scent of smoke (is that burning hemp?), and everybody began to shout, shake, rattle, and roll—all against house regulations. That's what you sometimes get, I found as a college chaplain, when the kids plan the party.

God is a young adult who may be ADD in his inability to sit still. Watch his legs constantly bounce nervously when everyone else in the room is satisfied to just sit there. In his bounding and rocking, he has the demeanor of a twelve-year-old, not a person at thirty.

Eager, attentive, marveling as if everything is new and awesome, as if all the facts and figures of science, a tree full of figs, a seed germinating and taking root, and the poetry of Isaiah were fresh and for his joy alone. One of his best stories is about two boys his age who were both, though in different ways, a father's pain in the neck. Why am I unsurprised that so many of his stories end with parties, one a party with the lame, the maimed, and the blind—people with whom we wouldn't be caught dead on a Saturday night?

He walks too fast, this post-adolescent. He invites everybody to walk with him, to join him on a road trip to God knows where. We have trouble keeping up with his breathless pace. Along the way, he notices things we have, in our maturity and experience, stopped noticing: a poor beggar, a widow's coin, a wild lily, a disordered child. He also calls our attention, as people his age are wont to do, to the mistakes of pompous, self-important adults. He gets mad as hell over the injustices committed by the powerful. He once called the president a "fox." He said in public that no one goes in the kingdom of God but kids. Rich people are virtually impossible to be saved. But with God, well, anything's possible, he grinned.

With age and increasing experience, we thought, he will be just like us. He'll learn. He'll change his tune. He'll mature. Settle down.

We thought wrong.

Like all those who are beginning, he is obsessed with the future. With him, it's all tomorrow. Tradition plays not as large a role in his worldview as we would have liked.

God is a young adult for whom friends are everything. He invites, embraces even those whom he hardly knows, loves to hang out with his buddies, and tends to make most everyone his buddy, particularly those who are "buddy" to none. He loves to roam, careening from one party to the next where there is too much drinking and the wine runs out and miraculously overflows, and then to move on to the next place where he is uninvited.

Sometimes, at parties, random people come up to him, argue, insult him to his face. Not once did he turn anyone away or smack their face, but never once did he back down from an argument.

God is a young adult who spent more time with a crowd, a gang, out and about, than alone.

God is a young adult who knows us, wants to know us better than we want to know him. Unlike lots of other young adults, he puts himself out, gives an invitation to the big party, risks rejection. And most whom he invites reject him. Our refusal to let down our guard, get loose, and join the party must make him feel lousy.

Even though we said no to him in as nice a way as we knew how and even though we gave little encouragement, he will call in the morning. Then again, and again. We might as well relent and say yes.

God is a young adult—inexperienced, outspoken, rash, always in motion, having difficulty settling in, staying on the subject, moving in the same direction. He is almost nothing we expected in God.

Like many his age, he has yet to develop good self-defense mechanisms. He will probably be hurt. Whatever he thinks, he says. Idealistic, innocent, wise beyond his years, always reaching out, always desiring contact, wanting to touch, to risk relationship. Loves to stay out, engage in risky behavior, launch out on a trip in the middle of the night, middle of a storm, up all night until dawn.

God is a young adult in motion, tough to pin down, define, to fix. He is the polite kid next door who wants to be helpful, the guy on the make at the bar about whom your mother warned you, the belligerent, pushy, troublemaker itching for an argument. Everybody enjoys hanging out with him; nobody wants to follow him.

God is a young adult—intense, unbalanced, immoderate, passionate—but not as we usually use that word, oddly disinterested in sex, despite what you have heard from the Methodist General Conference. He may be a thirty-something, single male, but he doesn't act like most when it comes to sex, marriage, and family.

You suspect that he will ingratiate himself to you, tempt you to do things your father warned you never to do, ask you for money. It makes you nervous to be alone with him. Without encouragement, he will call you, maybe not tomorrow or the next day, but he will call. He will.

God is a young adult who constantly pushes the envelope, tests the bounds of propriety. He is the redneck, good old boy calling out, "Hey y'all! Watch this!" before he jumps. He is the unshaven, long-haired, Near Eastern-looking twenty something behind you in line at the airport, the one to whom you want TSA to give a close look.

Why couldn't God have matured, settled down, middle-aged, middle-class, via media, middle-of-the-road rather than God up close and personal? Why didn't God come to us building on the past, moderately? Why this lurch to the left, then to the right, careening into the future, all promise, potential and forward movement? Ever onward, vital, youthful, energy confined in a Jew. Why so few opportunities for quiet reflection, meditation, and rest? I didn't know I was aging, easily fatigued, winded, quickly tired until him and his relentless, unceasing forward movement. When will he settle down, get a minivan, vote Republican, develop spiritual disciplines, keep Sabbath, and act like the God we expected?

God is a young adult. This much motion, this much passion, this relentlessness of contact, intrusive, boundaryless intimacy, boundless energy, unarmed but dangerous.

Like many of his generation, he is slow to judge. Did I mention that he has trouble staying in one place long? Did you know he never had a job?

God is a young adult who will ask some outrageous favor, even before he knows you that well. Violator of boundaries, he touches, caresses, fondles feet, kisses men on the mouth, even those who betray him.

Unlike many his age, he was not in the military. But his "peace" is no peace as people my age define peace. While he never once raised his hand against anybody, something about him made us want him dead.

Hear me: I did not say we are free to picture God any way we like; I say that God is free to be God as God likes. God is not a sometimes helpful projection of all our aspirations of the God we thought we needed. God is the controversial, even offensive, projection of God upon us as scruffy, unshaven, Near Eastern young adult in whom "the fullness of God was pleased to dwell."

He wants you, comes to you, comes on to you, desires to get dangerous, causes you to be careless, outrageous. In many and various ways God has spoken to us. Now God speaks as a Son, a young adult, getting younger.

Chapter Six

Preaching as Public Truth

In preaching we publicly demonstrate that God still works by election of the foolish to shame the wise (1 Cor 1:27). Because the reality of election is known only through God's revelation, typically through proclamation, preaching trumps all pastoral duties in order of relevance. We need not preach or teach the doctrine of election; we are to enjoy preaching authorized, energized, and sustained by election. That we are compelled to speak to everyone the truth about God is itself a demonstration and validation of the scope of the odd truth that we speak.[1]

This past year I served a United Methodist congregation. In order to lead, I asked a church consultant for help. He spent a couple of days urging us to be honest about our huge challenges, trials shared by every mainline, aging church in an urban setting. Chief among our struggles is our relationship to our neighborhood and to a new generation of Christians. The consultant convinced us that getting out of our sanctuary and into mission, teaching church staff to lead toward the future rather than simply to care for the aging, expending less resources on internal maintenance and more on external witness were life and death matters.

On his way out I walked the consultant through our sanctuary with its century-old, odd, rather garish stained-glass windows. He stopped before our huge window that faces out toward the busy street, the window that we see as we exit church each Sunday. The window depicts a scene from Methodist lore; John Wesley preaching. Wesley was refused permission to preach in the Anglican parish that day. So he climbed atop his father's tomb in the churchyard and preached. The window shows Wesley outside the church, the closed church doors behind him, haranguing a group of eighteenth-century English people.

"Forget my report," said the awestruck consultant. "Gather your people every Sunday, at the close of the service, and make them stare at that. Everything required of this congregation is shown there. Maybe if they gawk at it long enough they will get the point and enact what that window preaches."

The point? *God's gracious election.*

He Went His Way[2]

Luke 4:30

> "[H]e passed through the midst of them and went on his way."

Our Scripture is the first sermon that Jesus preached (Luke 4:16–30). Jesus, hometown boy, has made it back to the synagogue in Nazareth where he grew up. The homefolks have heard amazing things about Jesus' work in Capernaum and elsewhere and are thrilled to have this celebrity back home.

They are not disappointed. He reads from the popular prophet Isaiah, beautiful words that promise "good news" when God returned as Anointed One, that is, "Messiah." "Good news to the poor, . . . / release to the captives" (v. 18).

That's good because who are more captive than they? Nazareth, like all of Judea, is occupied territory, the heel of the empire on their necks. How they have suffered at the cruel hands of pagans. Jesus tells them that this great promise of deliverance by God is being enacted as he speaks, "Today this scripture is fulfilled" (v. 21).

There had to be an exciting stirring in the congregation. Today! God had promised long ago to make of Israel a great nation that would be a blessing to all the peoples of the earth. And yet for centuries they had languished under Babylon, Assyria, and now the Romans. At last! God is coming for us.

And then Jesus begins to preach. Every eye is upon him. Here is Israel, a people elected to gather around scripture, a people birthed by the word, bending themselves to scripture. Jesus does not share his feelings with them, does not do autobiography or speak to them about current events—these are Jews, after all. People convened to submit to a book.

"God is coming for us! Today!" joyfully announces the preacher. But then, working exclusively from scripture—their own book of promises—Jesus preaches. "Now the last time God came for us, in the prophet Elijah, during the great famine, I'm sure there were many hungry women in Israel. Odd. God's prophet gave food only to one: an outsider, a pagan, a woman of Sidon" (see vv. 25–26).

One can almost feel the once-adoring congregation grow silent and uneasy.

The preacher continues, "Another time God came for us, in the great prophet Elisha, there had to be many sick Jews among us. Odd. God's prophet healed only a Syrian. A Syrian army officer, in fact" (see v. 27).

"Syrian army officer" meant the same then in Nazareth that it means today.

And with that, the congregation's shock turns to rage. They grab the young rabbi, hometown boy or not, and drag him out "that they might hurl him over a cliff" (v. 29).

What a reaction to a sermon! Of course some of us—even though we may have never reacted to a sermon by attempting murder of the preacher—know the shock of having our Scripture, our own comforting Bible, thrown back at us in a way that jolts. The good synagogue-going folk at Nazareth did not appreciate being reminded that many times when Israel's long-awaited God showed up—in the prophets Elijah and Elisha, for instance—God had shown mercy on those in need outside Israel. They were shocked and then enraged that the God who had shown "kindness and mercy" to Israel, as the prophets often said, showed mercy even to non-Israelites. Though they had prayed the great Shema, "Hear O Israel, the LORD your God is one . . ." (Deut. 6:4), to have their noses rubbed in the implications of that prayer, to hear that their one and only God was the God of pagan welfare widows in Sidon and militarists in Syria, well, it was a shock. They wanted to kill the preacher.

"I'm just quoting Scripture," the preacher must have said as they dragged him out of the pulpit.

"This is the first time I've seen this church united!" exclaimed one of the mob, I mean, congregation.

Later Jesus assaults the government, beats up the rich, and castigates the powerful. First he attacks the elect, God's chosen, using our own Scripture to unmask our perversion of scripture.

The faithful didn't succeed in killing Jesus. Not yet. Luke ends with a pregnant phrase: "But Jesus passed through the midst of them and went on his way"(v. 30).

Luke doesn't say that Jesus quieted them down; he doesn't say that Jesus miraculously landed safely at the bottom of the cliff. Luke says Jesus "passed through the midst of them and went on his way."

I daresay that we think of Sunday morning as when we—the Chosen—gather, and Jesus comes our way, opens the scriptures to us, confirms us as his own. Then we go our way. But that Sabbath at Nazareth, Jesus comes, opens the scriptures, and then departs on his way, leaving us to stew in our ways. Sometimes Jesus comes to church only to sovereignly pass through the church. Jesus called many to follow his way. A few did. They are called "disciples." But our Scripture implies that Jesus goes on his way whether we follow him or not. He comes to us, but he will not be bound by us.

And that's good news.

On one occasion we tried to crown him king; he went his own way to be Prince of Peace, King of the Jews, a king we did not want. Toward the end, we asked if we might sit next to him when he came into glory; he went his own way of suffering love. At the end, when we whipped out the sword to defend him, he rebuked us and went his own nonviolent way to the cross. Then, after his resurrection, when he appeared at Emmaus in the breaking of the bread, when the apostles pled, "Stay with us. We're scared. It's getting dark, after all, we are your beloved disciples, encamp here with us and make Eucharist," the risen Christ went his own way. His resurrection meant more than simply good news for his inner circle. When Mary came to the tomb on Easter, looking for Jesus' dead body, only to be surprised by his resurrected body, Mary attempted to hold him forever in her embrace. Christ went his own way into the world, unwilling to be captured even by those who most love him.

The good news is that though we try to silence him when he says things that jolt and anger us, he will not be silenced. He will go his own way.

Though we might try to hold him in our clutches in love—Jesus just for us and people just like us—he goes his own way. Then we are faced with a question: will we go with him?

He promised that when just two or three are gathered, he'll be in the midst of us. But he does not promise that he will settle in, be contained, constrained, or controlled by us. Having been in the midst of us, he also is able to pass through the midst of us and go his way rather than be trapped in our ways.

Dan Wakefield is a noted novelist and reporter. While Wakefield had youthful experience of the Christian faith, he was not a Christian as an adult. Then in midlife he found himself drawn back toward the faith. He began exploring his spiritual yearnings. At a fancy party in Boston, he was surprised to meet the great Christian writer Henri Nouwen. Nouwen was helping himself to refreshments, so Wakefield sidled up and said something like, "Father Nouwen, I've been on a journey back toward Christ. I have had some tough times in my life and felt the need for something more and I . . ."

With that Nouwen wheeled around and said bluntly, "Jesus is about more than helping you get your life together"; then he walked away.

Wakefield said that was the beginning of his journey back to true faith.[3] Jesus Christ is larger than our demands on Jesus Christ. We attempt to enlist him for our own ends, try to turn him into another technique for getting whatever it is that we think we just must have. The good news: Christ sovereignly passes through the midst of us and goes his own way whether we go his way or not.

At our men's prayer and Bible study breakfast (you know that we don't do much prayer or Bible study; we mostly discuss current events), the topic for the morning was gun control in America. We predictably split into two groups. Half said that guns are essential for self-defense. The other half said that guns give no adequate self-defense but actually make safely defending ourselves more difficult. We disagreed about guns, but we agreed on self-defense.

Then one of the men (an accountant!) asked, "Did Jesus ever urge self-defense? Preacher, I can't recall one instance of anybody practicing self-defense in the New Testament."

It was for us a moment when Jesus passed through our midst, bypassing our perfectly reasonable, widely held opinions, and went his way.

Shaking hands with folks at the church door after service one Sunday, a person said to me, "I have had a terrible week."

"I'm sorry to hear that," I responded. (I'm such a caring pastor.)

"Trouble at work, problems at home. I came here seeking consolation and help," she said.

"Well, I hope that you found my sermon helpful," I said sincerely.

"Not particularly," she responded even more sincerely. "I came here hurting and seeking comfort only to receive an assignment!" She came to get what she wanted out of God; God's getting what God wants out of her. Sometimes church becomes more than we asked for. Jesus passes through our often petty self-concern and goes his way, taking us with him.

Now I expect that there are folk here today who are seeking help and comfort. You are under stress; you have family problems that cause you pain. You are facing tough questions and are looking for right answers. Church is a reasonable place to come for help. You have been told that Jesus cares. Unfortunately, you have been led to believe that Jesus chiefly cares about that for which you care. It is only reasonable for you to regard Jesus as another helpful means to get what you think you must have.

But sometimes, by the grace of God, in the sovereignty of a resurrected, free Lord, you may receive more than personal assistance. Because you are unable to control a living God, you may receive Jesus Christ in all his uncontainable, unusable glory. God is greater, even than we supposed. Jesus passes through our clutches, refuses to be utilized by us for what we want, and instead uses us for what he wants. He goes his way into the world, unsatisfied with simply reigning inside the church. He goes his way and thereby provokes us to ask, "Will I go with him on his way, or will Jesus go without me?"

In preaching, we publicly demonstrate the reality of election. Our listeners need not believe in a doctrine of election to be elected. God does not await our fragile, humble human yes in order to—from all eternity—say yes to us. (Though it is very sad for people not to know the facts and therefore to live out of step with reality now that Jesus Christ has told us the truth about God. Thus we preach.)

Preachers are witnesses to the truth, mere witnesses, but by God's choice necessary.[4] How typical of an incarnate God to condescend to speak through a frail, Southern-accented voice such as mine. Preachers don't devise, serendipitously discover, much less possess or control this truth. In election, we are dependent on God to do for us what we cannot do, to say what we on our own cannot. Therefore the truth who is Jesus Christ must constantly open to us, must join with us in our attempts to preach the truth, or preaching is the most miserable of vocations. That we preachers feel anxiety in preparing sermons is weekly confirmation that we are empty-handed witnesses who require a loquacious God. That we preachers experience the wonder of being heard by our congregations is weekly validation that God is determined to reveal God's nature and purposes to humanity, even if God has to do it through our sorry sermons.

The best of our sermons are but the boney finger of the Baptist pointing to the truth as given. Like the Baptist, we are less significant than the truth that is granted us and may, in the course of witness, suffer decapitation.

One Sunday after service in Duke Chapel, amid the shaking of hands by well-wishers, one congregant loudly, angrily denounced my sermon. A crowd gathered to watch the pounding of the preacher. (Students tend to be anticlerical.) As my critic stormed out the door, a sophomore wise-cracked, "I guess somebody didn't want to be as close to Jesus as he first thought."

Why didn't I say that? What wonderful consolation for a preacher's failure to communicate. Or was the negative reaction confirmation that I indeed communicated?

The truth we preach is not residue after good exegesis or herme-neutics. Truth is gift, grace, the presence of a person. Every attempt to reduce the Christian faith to timeless ideals and disembodied founda-tional principles fails because here is personal truth that requires personal witness. Barth says that when preachers have something to say it is a sign of the freely given grace of God; not that they have, through hard work in preparation or in artful delivery, successfully attained the "object of their self-seeking."[5] Any availability of truth among deceitful sinners is a sign of the reality of God's election. "As witnesses [preachers] have to repeat what God . . . has first said to them."[6] Thank God that God doesn't first of all expect courage, boldness, or genius from preachers; God expects public repetition of what they have heard.[7]

The truth about God—revelation—is not the preacher but the cre-ative Father and the incarnate Son speaking in the power of the intru-sive Holy Spirit. It is difficult enough for preachers to have the guts to stand and deliver on a regular basis amid the wiles of American culture. Preachers take heart that the truth they preach is neither self-derived nor dependent on being communicated through a winning personality (*pace* Philips Brooks). The truth is true, not on the basis of being uttered by a duly consecrated clergyperson within church walls, not by who hears or who utters truth, but by the election of God. Speakers of the truth are "helpless and vulnerable," and yet our "witness . . . is the *only* instrument of justice and force."[8]

God elects to say more than God's witnesses can say. In election, we know that God's purposes are considerably larger than the constraints of the church's clergy. We therefore admit to witnesses to the truth outside the church in the so-called secular world whose unintended witness in a novel, a movie, or speech is more striking than our sermons. The testi-mony of these "secular parables," as Barth called them, is confirmation of our lack of control over the truth that is revealed in Jesus Christ. The church "must accept this fact that there are such words and that it must hear them too."[9] That we often discover witnesses where we least expect confirms that "there is no secular sphere abandoned by [God] or with-drawn from [God's] control, even where from the human standpoint it seems to approximate most dangerously to the pure and absolute form of utter godlessness."[10]

One Saturday I attended the film, *American Hustle*, a gritty, funny, and tragic tale of a couple of con-artists—one who had the worst comb-over ever—whose hustle eventually exposes the government agents plotting to nab them as hustlers too. America is where everyone has a con. All, even government agents, have "sinned and fall short of the glory of God" (Rom. 3:23). I left the theater embarrassed that Hollywood had told more truth in a movie—for which I paid ten dollars and was gratefully engaged for two hours—than I would tell in my meager message the next morning.

I should have rejoiced that Jesus Christ is the way, the truth, and the life who finds a way to reveal himself in spite of his limited professional witnesses.

I didn't.

For three decades I've labored through Proust's oceanic *Remembrance of Things Past*. I've wondered why I've given this massive, decadent, narcissistic, utterly unchristian novel so much time and effort, except the guilty pleasure derived from reading a book no Methodist preacher ought to read. Then in my third journey through, while thinking about election, I read the last hundred pages and knew why.

Marcel, the agonized protagonist, hears again a bell he had heard so long ago, considers his own mortality and the death of everyone he has so meticulously observed in the novel, and realizes his own vocation to be a writer. He will write, telling the truth about people, thus rescuing some shred of immortality from the ravages of forgetfulness, death, and decay.

And I, as a Christian, gave thanks to God that, unlike Proust, I did nothing to realize my vocation. I was not forced to write four thousand pages to discover the point of my life. All I had to do was to allow myself be loved, to hold out empty hands for a gift, to be elected, quietly to say yes.

Sometimes a preacher is tempted to despair by the refusal of our listeners to hear or by their outright hostility to our testimony. Barth says that we ought not be "troubled";[11] such affliction is "one of ministry."[12] We wouldn't be *faithful* witnesses if we were "absolutely secured."[13] Because the truth to which we witness is that of a crucified God who was driven out of the world on a cross, we preachers have reason to worry when our testimony is praised and perhaps reason to rejoice when it is refused. Two of my sermons in this book ("God Is a Young Adult" [see ch. 5] and "Waiting for God" [see ch. 4]) received negative responses—an angry letter from a pastor, pleading with the organizers of the homiletics conference never again to invite me; another saying that my sermon was blasphemy and urging the dean of the Chapel to strike me off his list. Though neither were the best I've preached, the negative responses suggested to my warped sensibilities that the sermons deserved wider distribution.

Against a modern, totalitarian, democratic state and a subservient church, Barth urges preachers not to go around with "clenched fists." We can wait. False gods are lies, and we need not fear lies. The defeat of lies is God's business. Our job, as witnesses, is not to testify against our opponents but rather to testify for the truth of Jesus Christ. Our Lord promises miraculously to make enemies our friends. All we must do is to speak obediently. Besides, every preacher is sooner or later an enemy of the truth of Jesus Christ because of our cowardice, ignorance, or sometimes just because we'd rather be circumspect than unemployed; we encounter among our listeners no enmity to the truth that is not within our own souls.

Chapter Seven

Homiletical Implications of Election

Betty Achtemeier, wonderful preacher of another time, told me that when she and her husband, Paul, were studying with Barth in Basel there was a dispute related to the stained-glass windows in the Basel Münster. The windows had been removed during the war and safely stored in case of bombing. Barth publicly stated that the windows ought not to be restored; the gospel came to the church by preaching, not through beautiful windows.

As someone who spent two decades attempting to preach the gospel in a church with over a million pieces of stained glass set in Duke Chapel's very-expensive-to-maintain windows, I would not so narrowly limit the gospel. Still, in encountering Barth, we preachers are in the hands of a theologian who esteems proclamation.

Of preaching, Barth said as early as 1922, "The whole situation in the church suddenly becomes intelligible if it is seen to be the framework of *this* event; the existence of the minister is justified if [the preacher is] the servant of this event; and the very act which in Protestantism should form the crux of the service, the sermon as the exposition of Scripture, becomes fraught with meaning when it is a preaching of the Word of God."[1]

If God has elected from eternity to be for us and for us to be for God, then we preachers know:[2]

1. God is the primary agent of preaching.
Election characterizes the work of an interventionist, active, initiating God. Our relationship with God is based on God's gracious choice to be for us and to speak with us through sermons of preachers. God's eternal decision to elect is not only revelation's substance but also its agent.

Preaching is not established by method or rhetorical technique but by the grace and mercy of God. Homiletical obsession with rhetoric appears to be waning; the best recent books on preaching are unashamedly theological.[3] Interesting sermons have something to say because an event of world-changing significance has happened; God is revealed to be other than we expected. God is Emmanuel, God reiterating God's eternal, gracious choice to be for us as Father, Son, and Holy Spirit. Our proclamation is driven, not by our desire to be heard, but rather by God's determination—testified throughout Scripture and fully revealed in Jesus Christ—to be God With Us. Our sermons ought to make no sense if election is untrue.

The continuing bodily presence of Jews is visible confirmation that God keeps promises, that God's yes is stronger than Gentile hatred and violence against Israel:

> The Jew, so miraculously preserved, . . . through the many calamities of this history, who as such is the natural historical monument to the love and faithfulness of God, who in concrete form is the epitome of the [one] chosen and blessed by God, . . . is the only convincing proof of God outside the Bible.[4]

The existence of the Jews is testimony to the reality of a certain sort of God; so is the existence of the church. As bishop, I experienced the depth and breadth of my own incompetence, ineptitude, and cowardice, to say nothing of observing these faults and more in my fellow clergy. Then there were compromised, limited congregations. Nevertheless, I took heart that for two millennia the church has not only persevered but even thrived, often thriving most vibrantly where it is least wanted. As Methodism fades in England, land of its nativity, Wesleyan Christianity explodes in Africa and Asia. More Muslims convert to Christianity today than at any point in history, though American churches, because of our government's unending wars in the Muslim world, will not be major participants in this remarkable evangelization.

I'll admit that the sheer persistence of the church is not the most invigorating argument for a living, resourceful, revealing God, *nevertheless* (how Barth loved that word) an incarnating God appeals to the world through us (2 Cor. 5:20). As with the Jews, so is the church a showcase for the outrageousness and dogged persistence of God's grace.[5]

Praise characterizes much of Christian worship because the Christian life is responsive to something good that God has done. One need not be able to report having had the experience of election to be elected. Pietism and liberalism find it tough to beat the rap that their theology is merely a subjective claim about us and only secondarily a claim about God. Election is so against our natural inclination that it is unlikely we could have thought it up ourselves.

Moralism, the bane of homiletics in my church family, is defeated by election as God's act to which we make little contribution. When the gospel is reduced to something that we must think, feel, believe, or do, the gospel is warped beyond recognition. Election is a constant reminder to us preachers that we preach not in order to take our listeners somewhere they aren't but to announce where, by God's grace, they are and shall be. All the difficult work between us and God has been done by God; all that is left for us is to allow ourselves to be "lost in wonder, love and praise" (Charles Wesley).

2. Our listeners have been graciously elected by God to be for God.

After Judas, we preachers ought never to be surprised that some obstinately refuse to listen or that others startlingly hear. It's easier to believe in our own election than to believe in that of others. Therefore a great challenge of ministry is indefatigably to believe that those to whom we speak are those whom God has elected to hear. They are not whom *I* would have called to be the Body of Christ were I doing the calling, any more than I am the one they would elect to preach if they were doing the election. They are God's idea of a fit kingdom, not mine. Part of the challenge of loving God is to love those whom God loves, trusting the God who elected Jacob, Abraham, Mary, Sarah, and even Judas and me to make wise choices in convening the church.

However, a joy of the preaching life is delight when someone hears, someone who, by all accounts, should not. It's then that we experience anew election, the inscrutable mystery of God's gracious choice, and exclaim with our ecclesiastical ancestors, "Has God's salvation gone even to the Gentiles?" (Acts 28:28).[6] To be honest, it is frustrating when an untrained layperson is elected for some stunning insight that God has not given me, the preacher who thinks I ought to be the custodian of theological discernment!

The best we can say about our Sunday morning listeners is that they are the recipients of God's gracious election, so, even though we are not the best of preachers and though they lack skills that would enable them to be the best of listeners, *they do hear*, and when they do, preaching becomes demonstration of the truth of God's miraculous agency and God's eternal election here and now.

If our people hear or refuse to hear, if they are docile and teachable or obstinate and resistant, if they applaud or hiss the sermon, they neither confirm nor negate God's determination to have them at all cost. Our listeners are a mixed bag, some of whom know the truth that "God so loved the world that God gave . . ." (John 3:16), and others continue to assume that the contest between them and God continues. If God the Father must sacrifice God the Son or make life unpleasant for us preachers through the prodding of God the Holy Spirit, God *will* be their God and they *will* be God's people, because God is determined to get back what by rights belongs to God. Let preachers pray for the courage to take our congregations' rejection less seriously than we take God's embrace of them in Jesus Christ. Their hostility to the truth who is Jesus Christ is no serious contender.

We preachers often complain that our hearers aren't sincerely listening or that they are biblically illiterate or theologically malformed. All of this is true, of course. However, such disparagement of our congregations is beside the point in light of the doctrine that by the sheer grace of God *they are elected:* "Christ died for the ungodly" (Rom. 5:6), not for those who are biblically informed and spiritually astute. Thus election disciplines our preaching to rejoice in what God has done and is doing rather than bemoan the inability and ineptitude of our congregations. We are not first of all to convince, persuade, or transform our hearers; we are to announce, proclaim, and herald the good news of God's gracious yes in Jesus Christ.

We ought to take the same posture toward our listeners that God has taken toward us in election. Barth was driven toward election's centrality through Paul. As Douglas Campbell shows, in the writings of Paul, "God's fundamental posture toward humanity, evident in Father, Son, and Spirit, is unconditionally benevolent. Despite human hostility, . . . those now involved in the ongoing mission of God to humanity—like Paul—share (or they *ought* to share) this basic disposition of benevolence toward humanity. . . . [M]oreover this may be strengthened by the experience of [their] having been part of hostile humanity originally and then saved by grace."[7]

By implication, if people do not hear, it may be because God has not (yet) gotten to them or (yet) given them grace to hear. Barth taught that the only difference between the Christian and the non-Christian was noetic. If we believe, it's grace, gift. We have received the news. When faced with rejection, we preachers will want to resist the temptation to lapse into apologetics—taking disbelief too seriously. We cannot manufacture more palatable revelation for those who have not (yet) received the real thing.

Rather than acting as if disbelief is decisive and conclusive, we will want to talk more of God's gracious election than of the disbeliever's rejection, humbly, patiently, expectantly to testify; convincing and converting them is God's self-assignment.

Election is a tremendous shove toward truly evangelical preaching. The sweeping scope of God's election could rescue evangelicals from the suffocating clutches of our culture's subjectivity and conditional salvation. Mark Galli, chiding fellow evangelicals for dismissing Barth because of his alleged "universalism," speaks of the evangelical joy arising from Barth's thought on election:

> Jeff McSwain was a Young Life leader for years before being forced to resign because of his Barthian views. But he remains in youth ministry, and continues to preach the gospel of God's universal redemption and the need for a response of repentance and faith.
>
> McSwain began rethinking his approach to ministry as a result of wrestling with the views of Arminians and Five-Point Calvinists. . . . For Calvinists, to say that it is our *faith* that makes Christ's death effectual is to say that salvation rests on our shoulders. It also smacks of relativism: Salvation is not true until we believe it.
>
> McSwain argues that like Arminians, Barthians believe that Jesus loves everyone he created and that he died on the cross for everyone. Like Calvinists, he says Barthians believe that the atoning work of Christ actually accomplished reconciliation and forgiveness for everyone for whom Christ died. He concludes:
>
>> Instead of dismissing Barth, it would behoove evangelicals to consider the possibility that Barth's theology is the most evangelical of all. . . . With a dynamic theology of the Holy Spirit to go along with his robust theology of the cross, Barth knifes through the Gordian Knot of Arminianism and five-point Calvinism, and encourages evangelists to consider a third way, a way of making bold and inclusive claims upon the life of every hearer. . . .
>
> McSwain notes a comment by Jim Rayburn, the founder of Young Life, . . . teaching on 2 Corinthians 5:19, . . . Rayburn said, "Every single person in the whole wide world is now reconciled to God. [. . .] It's been true for nearly two thousand years. *I wonder what they*

[high school kids] *would do if they knew it.* . . . God has reconciled us, all of us, it's already done." . . .

[W]hen it comes to presenting the gospel to those who don't believe, McSwain says, "Like Rayburn and the Apostle Paul, Barth's proclamation of the gospel began at the starting point of theological belonging for all."[8]

3. The gospel is apocalyptic speech.

Election is the eternal decision of God before time that has its consummation in eternity. All promises are in the future tense. Election is a promise that keeps the church eschatologically unsettled in the now, leaning into the not yet. The modern world thinks that what you see is what you get; this is all there is. People on top—well-fed, well-educated, and well-fixed—tend to disbelieve (and fear) the possibility of God's disruption of our present by a radically different future. That liberal theology has always been squeamish about both election and apocalyptic is proof of its bourgeois captivity. Preachers who are blessed with congregations of people who have been economically marginalized, educationally disadvantaged, and socially ostracized may have an advantage in this matter of apocalyptic proclamation since their congregations are likely not to place unwarranted faith in merely present arrangements.

A great recovery of apocalyptic preaching is under way in the Beecher Lectures of Tom Long, Richard Lischer, and, more recently, Brian Blount.[9] Hauerwas' latest book is *Approaching the End.*[10] If our sermons are only contemporaneous, stuck in the now, preoccupied with the defeats or victories of the moment, we do injustice to eschatological, whole-new-world-but-not-yet Christian expectation. In the end, God has promised to bring creation to fulfillment, to raise the dead, to let down New Jerusalem from heaven, to draw all peoples to God's holy mountain, to put down the high and mighty, to vindicate the meek and the marginalized, to make our little lights to shine radiantly, to unveil to all in undeniable reality what God has wanted all along.[11] In order for God's elective purposes to be consummated, heaven and earth will be shaken, the world as we know it destabilized, dismantled, and disrupted by God's promise to fulfill God's will on earth as in heaven. Whether that eschatological promise is received as good news or bad may depend on where one is standing when one receives the news. The doctrine of election says that at last the dwelling place of God will be with mortals, the great, grand, triumphant predestination that began in eternity. Everywhere eternity touches time, even in our sermons, there is disruption, wars and rumors of wars, death and birth, ending and beginning, relinquishment and homecoming that have always characterized apocalyptic literature. Our last hope is that the God who elected to be our God will bring us along into eternity.

Oh, the irony of white slaveholders teaching slaves the gospel hoping thereby to produce docility only to have their slaves hear the gospel more accurately than the masters. That which was intended to engender tractability was used by God to incite apocalyptically induced rebellion.

Barth's early discovery in his pastoral reading of Romans is that Paul is an eschatological preacher. Paul preached in a cross-and-resurrection-disrupted world. Influenced by Kierkegaard, Barth charged the theology of his day with bourgeois accommodation that trimmed the politically charged Christian faith to what an anxious middle class could bear.

Today, many of us preach to people who are well fixed in the now and are threatened by God talk that might disrupt present arrangements. Now is not that great, but it's all we have now that we have banished eschatology and no longer pray for, or even want, an intrusive Day of the Lord. We no longer expect judgment other than by the assessments of our own conscience. The words we hear are manageable because they arise internally.

Apocalyptic says that the death of Christ ends the world and decisively brings to a close all human aspiration (particularly that dubious undertaking, "religion") to put something in place of God's predetermination for the world. Crucified Jesus was not only raised from the dead but also returned to us, talked to us, and made us partners in his invasion of the old world.

Election keeps happening as God returns, calls, and draws us into the revolution begun in cross and resurrection. Christ has come, is coming, will come. We have certain hope on the basis of what we know of Christ, but even the longest sermons cannot with certainty provide an exhaustive account of God; we can only witness to the reality of the coming Christ and end with the prayer, "Maranatha!"

> So that at the name of Jesus
>   every knee should bend,
>   in heaven and on earth and under the earth,
>   and every tongue should confess
>   that Jesus Christ is Lord,
>   to the glory of God the Father. (Phil 2:10–11)

Every knee, every tongue. All.

Election renders human borders and barriers suspect, relativizing all human designations of race, class, nationality, and gender that in any way distrust God's overriding human designation: *the graciously elected*. American, Iranian, Rotarian, Presbyterian are secondary qualifiers to "the graciously elected." When American political leaders urged decades more of wars against Islam by the rationale that "We must secure ourselves and our borders from terrorism," American Christians ought to have had the theological chutzpa to ask, "Who is *we*?" When the errant governor of Alabama vowed, "we will protect our borders from illegals," thank God a few pastors and congregations had the grace to ask, "*Our*?"

A fellow divinity school professor, a Baptist, disallows his students from using the term "parish pastor." His rationale is that Baptists never had geographically limited parishes; Baptists expect their leaders to evangelize the whole world. All.

The *Book of Common Prayer* has a collect to be prayed at a funeral for someone who is not a member of the parish, quoting Jesus (John 10:16) that there are sheep not in this fold whom the Shepherd is actively seeking. We don't know them, but the Shepherd does, and he promises to have them as well. God's expansive, gracious election gives us a sure word of hope to speak over every life at the end. All. All those who do not know of their salvation in Christ do *not yet* know. That is, they are awaiting our next sermon.

A sermon is not ended until God says it's over. We preachers do well to preach in a way that does not demand or expect immediate impact. We also ought to preach in such a way as to make clear that God is not finished with Creation; there is more to come; the present age is not all there is.

"I don't see that your sermons have accomplished much in this congregation," said one of my critics after a year of my sermons.

With apocalyptically induced hopefulness, I replied, "Not yet."

Barth preached this sermon in 1941, at the funeral of his twenty-year-old son Matthias, who died in a climbing accident in the Swiss Alps. Barth took as his text 1 Corinthians 13:12, which, in idiomatic German, speaks of seeing an "enigmatic word." Barth affectionately admitted that Matthias was a son who was difficult to understand. Then Barth played off seeing "now" enigmatically (in English it's "through a mirror dimly") against "then" when all shall be light. Barth spoke of Matthias' (and our) "then" as in the hands of Christ who loves us into the future, giving us hope in this painfully enigmatic "now." Though Matthias was a mystery, Christ's intentions are not. Here are portions of the last half of the funeral sermon:

Who was Matthias, really, in life and in death? He was one "for whom the Son of God gave himself so that Matthias, the inexperienced one, would not perish but have everlasting life.

And now there is his sudden earthly end: once again . . . an enigmatic word . . . painful and terrifying . . . on that night, Matthias quietly left us. The rest of us then had to deal with the bitter hours . . . lingering questions . . . in the face of the great, inexorable mystery of death. . . .

Nevertheless: "The mystery of Good Friday . . . has been followed by the resolution of Easter day. Jesus now lives, reigns, and is victorious.

The Then has come so close to the Now so that this Now of death is no longer a realm of which we have to be afraid, or which we have to regard with questions and mourning, . . . death has power, terrifying and painful power. But we believe and we know that it does not have a deadly sting [1 Corinthians 15:55]. . . .

Matthias often seemed defenseless and helpless in the face of life. But even now we believe and know that there is One who long since took this strong one captive, . . . took away his power to kill, . . . This we shall see when we see him face to face. Therefore, in all our sorrow today, we cannot merely mourn.

Even if we cannot rejoice ourselves, we still hear an entirely different voice. . . . This voice speaks about the completion of even this incomplete one, . . . What else can we do as we hear this voice but thank our God—even if in tears—that he fulfilled his good will and purpose in the life and the death of our Matthias? And with us, too! "I am," Jesus says to us, "the resurrection and the life" [John 11:25].[12]

Hearing is a concrete, parochial demonstration of the mystery of God's election. It's a mystery that many listen but do not hear, analogous to the enigma that many are called but few chosen (Matt. 22:14). Jesus speaks in parables so that some may understand and others may not (Matt. 13:13). Why? I do not understand.

What preachers need in order to speak is to hear God. We need, in the words of the W. B. Yeats, "the falcon to hear the falconer," to be awakened "from centuries of stony sleep," and to make our way "towards Bethlehem to be born."[13] We are heralds.

Human rejection of God's truth in Christ is serious, but not ultimately decisive. Almost nothing about us humans has ultimate significance;

only God has eternity. When some, hearing such effusive praise for the reconciling intent of God, charged Barth with *apokatastasis*, the teaching of universal salvation, Barth replied that the question of whether in the end all shall be saved "remains open."[14] That some are saved does not necessarily necessitate that some not be saved. God is not forced to play a zero sum game. We must say nothing that implies constriction of divine intent. The ultimate significance of human sin, including the sin of rejecting God, has been conditioned by the gracious life, death, and resurrection of Christ. Even those who are determined to live against God have their human determination divinely determined by Jesus Christ.[15] The church's job is to testify to that reality still unfolding before us.

The difference between Christians and those who have not professed Christ is a thin line within the sure circle of God's determination to be God of all, of Christ's reconciliation of all to God.[16] By the grace of God, some know. We preach about, pray, work for, and live in anticipation of that time when all shall know and profess the reality of humanity's gracious election.[17] Our words are never the last. God has ways.

I asked a man in my church, a week before he died, if he felt fear. "Fear?" he replied. "No. As I've lain in this hospital bed these weeks, looked back on my life, I've recalled all the trouble God has gone to, showing up uninvited, pulling at me when I didn't ask. Well, I don't think God will let a thing like my death stump him. I expect God to do me in eternity like God has done me in life."

Therein is our hope.

4. Talk about the gospel tends to produce conflict.

Apocalyptic literature promises cosmic dismantling, disenfranchisement for those on top and restoration, redemption, and vindication for those on the bottom. Apocalyptic has therefore often incited revolutionary activity. We preachers like to think of ourselves as reconcilers and peacemakers. Many of our sermons seem designed to lessen the tension that is produced when a biblical text is dropped on a defensive congregation. Even to stand and say, after an outrageous text has been read, "I have three things I want to say about today's text," is to risk defusing the explosive encounter between God's chosen people and God's chosen word.

Too bad for our self-image as peacemakers; we must preach Jesus Christ and him crucified. The good news of God's gracious election is bad news for our cherished idolatries and self-deceptive ideals. Luke 4, Jesus' sermon in Nazareth with violent congregational response, displays the dynamic that typifies truthful proclamation. Presumably, if Jesus had not publicly preached, there would have been less trouble.[18] When Jesus read scripture, everyone smiled; when Jesus preached, hell broke loose. Personal, contemporary truth, affective truth uttered by the witness who is one of us and speaks to us is the most controversial. Preachers tend to have nervous stomachs; we know that we cannot control how God or our listeners will use our speech.

God is not a dim, distant, unknowable, alien force hiding in heaven.[19] God is a Jew from Nazareth who was tortured to death by a consortium of government and religious leaders and rejected by those whom he came to save, God's gracious yes followed by a baffling but determined human no. When Paul preached, there were riots. When I preach, I shake hands with the congregation, obtain an honorarium, and go home happy. Why?

Paul announced the good news that God had at last come back for us *and* for the Gentiles. Israel's exile is over, the lost sheep of Israel are being gathered, *and* God's elective intentions are greater than we thought. The "righteousness of God" has been unveiled. God intends to do right, not just to Israel, but to all.

Pastors, who spend so much of our time caring for and struggling with the congregation, ought to note that Paul not only preached; Paul also raced across Asia Minor founding new communities in opposition to the imperial "community" enforced by Caesar's legions. The "political" significance of Jesus is that he didn't write a book; Christ formed a community. Preacher/pastors stand in that fateful matrix where announcement is accompanied by visible congregational embodiment. If the gospel announcement were disembodied, without an accompanying institution in place and time, would Caesar have noticed? When the gospel word takes up room as a gospel people, the empire knows it has been invaded.

Yet caring for the congregation through our preaching is not enough. Faithful proclamation can never be merely parochial. Because of God's gracious election, Christian speech is public heralding rather than insider conversation. Proclamation's intent is missional rather than congregational. Any congregation that is merely a warm-hearted group of caring friends who is not actively, daringly crossing cultural, racial, ideological, national boundaries (mission) is not faithful. Thus Newbigin speaks of the congregation as the "hermeneutic of the gospel," God's means of interpreting to the world the visible, public truth of what the world looks like when the Lamb rules. The congregation is God's self-presentation.[20] If the doctrine of election is true, it is always demonstrated in mission.

Pastors cannot hunker down with the few faithful handed to us by hard-working pastors of a previous generation, those sweet older saints who have enough free time to hang out at church; election is inducement to mission.

My theory is that there is much conflict and quarreling in many congregations because they talk only to themselves. Boredom (and an uneasy sense that church is meant to be more than this cozy club) fosters congregational contentiousness. The conflict that validates a church as Christ's is not that of squabbling, miffed church members but the conflict between Christ and the world.

A church that is not restlessly probing the boundaries between insiders and outsiders, not regularly surprised by the expansive reach of God's saving actions is a church trying to be the elect of God without living the truth of election. God elects the church for the purpose of embodying God's gracious intent beyond the bounds of the church. Others may be enemies of our country or adversaries of the American way of life, but God is not their enemy. If the church condemns the lifestyle of a given group of people or the sinfulness of another culture or the foreign policy of some hostile nation, then we are under divine compulsion to do so in a way that makes clear that God has elected them to be our sisters and brothers through electing all for God's salvation. Pope Francis was right to chastise those Catholics who, in their condemnation of homosexual practice, appeared to have lapsed into impugning the ultimate worth and salvation of those whom they are criticizing. Mercy always trumps condemnation when the church turns from talking about Jesus to talk about sinners.

To criminals imprisoned in the Basel jail, Barth preached that the first Christian community was composed on Golgotha:

> "They crucified him with the criminals." Which is more amazing, to find Jesus in such bad company, or to find the criminals in such good company? . . . Like Jesus, these two criminals had been arrested . . . , locked up and sentenced. . . . And now they hang on their crosses with him and find themselves in solidarity and fellowship with him. They are linked in a common bondage never again to be broken . . . a point of no return for them as for him. There remained only the shameful, pain stricken present and the future of their approaching death. . . .
>
> They crucified him with the criminals. . . . This was the first Christian fellowship, the first certain, indissoluble and indestructible Christian community. Christian community is manifest wherever

there is a group of people close to Jesus who are with him in such a way that they are directly and unambiguously affected by his promise and assurance. These may hear that everything he is, he is for them, and everything he does, he does for them. To live by this promise is to be a Christian community. The two criminals were the first certain Christian community.[21]

Criminals hanging out with Jesus are the new normal, the first church. God has called us together into a new family that cannot live except as a growing family. The emperors tried but failed to achieve a unified empire. Cohesive, nonviolently united humanity is enabled because Jesus Christ is Lord (and the emperor is not).

Barth presciently saw that the liberalism of his day—with liberalism's plea for people of faith to be more moderate in their claims, not fanatically to say they have "the truth"—incipiently denies the possibility of truth. Such a plea is often made by "zealots," says Barth, who "can exercise self-control, because they have told themselves . . . [t]hat theirs is not the only faith, that fanaticism is a bad thing, that love must always have the first and last word." Theirs is "the clever aloofness of the rationalistic Know-All . . . , who thinks that he [or she] can deal comfortably and in the end successfully with all religions in the light of a concept of a perfect religion which is gradually evolving in history." The basis of the liberals' call to moderation is Hegelian skepticism about truth in general and the disparagement of religion in particular among those who say that "the truth can be known only in the form of doubt about all truth."[22]

The world puts pressure on the church's proclamation, coercing Christians to come up with provisional truth in a "diluted form," which leaves the world undisturbed.[23] Barth tells Christians that conflict comes with the territory; we cannot avoid the disturbance by "retreat into an island of inwardness."[24] Better that there be conflict in the congregation because it has been abruptly confronted with truth than for conflict to be in the preacher who is desperate to speak about Jesus without anyone discomforted.

In his discussion of ethics as command, Barth said that if "moral law is no more than natural law" then "all it needs is to be stated as that. . . . There is no need to preach it"; Christian ethical claims are "mere predication" based on human experience of the predictability of the world rather than on revelation.[25] If there is natural law, no need for preaching; Christians must simply act naturally rather than obediently. Being Christian is synonymous with being a caring human being. Preaching is required only when the truth is inaccessible except through grace, that is, revelation. "The Word of God, and in its faithful proclamation, . . . are always the aggressor in relation to everything else, to general human thinking and language." Preaching ought "not be surprised at the contradiction" between itself and what the world has to say any more than ancient Israel should have been surprised by the contradictions between the worship of Yahweh and Canaanite gods.[26] The "general religious self-consciousness" alleged by Schleiermacher's apologetics (beware, contemporary "spirituality"![27]) fails to do justice to the contradictions (and conflict) between Christian and worldly thought. Christian preaching is "the aggressor."[28]

Preaching is faithful when it is bound to its subject, when it is unashamedly partisan in behalf of the God who summons. God's gift is also an assignment. We do not belong to ourselves, do not exist in a vacuum, are not abandoned to our self-determination; by divine vocation, we are out of our control. God has made covenant with us so we are given a part to play, something to say in the grand pageant of God's salvation of all,[29] which is better than false, communicative peace.

5. Faithful preachers trust the God who has called us to preach.

"Is there any word from the Lord?" (Jer. 37:17) is the only good Sunday morning question, a question that is asked in trust that God speaks. Too much of contemporary preaching is anthropological, homespun wisdom for a purpose-driven life, common sense offered as if it were expert advice. Joel Osteen habitually ends many of his sentences with "Right?" or "Okay?" thus signifying the hearer's verdict as the final judge on the veracity of his sermons.

Trouble is, Scripture always and everywhere speaks about God and only secondarily or derivatively speaks about us. What God has accomplished and promised to fulfill in our election is more interesting than what we do, think, or feel about our future. Our great task is not to speak relevantly and comprehensibly to the world but rather to be the church that is not synonymous with the world. The odd doctrine of election is just one of the ways God helps the church not to disappear into the world.

Pelagianism comes naturally; we have an innate propensity to try to effect our own salvation. In all its forms, Pelagianism is fed by anxiety about God. It's up to us to set things right between us and God, to reform the church, to transform the world. An anxious church morphs into a poorly funded welfare agency, a gregarious club to remedy American loneliness, a handmaid for politicians of the right or the left rather than stick to its primary vocation—to be a people who show God's decision to be God for us and for us to be for God.

I experience the reality of election by using the Revised Common Lectionary as a source for sermon texts, thereby demonstrating to the congregation that I did not choose the text for my sermon; the text chose me, laid on me by the church. Neither the text nor those who hear my sermon are of my choosing; how appropriate for faith in a God we didn't choose.

To preachers who rely on their subjective experiences rather than attaching themselves to the objectivity of revelation, Barth said, "Against boredom the only defense is . . . being biblical."[30] Scripture stokes, funds, and fuels our imaginations with thoughts we could not have come up with on our own. "For what we preach is not ourselves, but the Jesus Christ as Lord" (2 Cor. 4:5).

Toward the end of *The Epistle to the Romans,* in his discussion of ethics, Barth turns to preaching. What's needed from preachers, says Barth, is a truly "radical word" that "points directly to the mercy of God." Radical preaching is with "Luther and Dostoevsky" and against "Tolstoy and the Franciscans"; preaching formed by radical mercy that lumps together "the Pharisee and the Publican" and sees no great difference between those within and those without, "even a Lenin"; preaching that judges even the most "dubious characters . . . to be no more than exaggerations of what we all are." Sermons that push human righteousness, commending merely human programs of social betterment are "raucous, croaking, and utterly unimpressive." Under the guise of being "prophetic," they are only "the cry of a Titan."[31]

6. Faithful preaching announces adoption into a new family, a holy people who are a showcase for what God intends to be one day for all.

Schleiermacher understood the church as "a community of those who share the Christian outlook."[32] Barth's church is where those who are surprised by their election gather to risk hearing and responding to the divine command. We listen not placidly but as those summoned to obedience, to partnership. Preaching is necessary because we can neither command ourselves nor be obedient by ourselves.[33]

Hauerwas says that when someone responds to his sermon with "You've given me some interesting things to think about," he hits back, "That's not good enough." Because of election, the sermon aims to be robustly vocational rather than merely intellectual.

Election is not a static past event; election is *pre*-destination. God in Christ is a living person who does not rest or halt at any point in time. As such, God's fore-loving demands, evokes, invites, and summons human choice. What do you think of Christ? Who do people say the Son of Man is? Who do *you* say I am? *Follow* me!

Summoning, vocational truth calls for response. So preaching must always move beyond the mere "Do you agree?" to the more active, corporeal, and responsive "Will you join in and join up?" Will you move in step with the truth about who God is and what God is doing to reconcile the world to God? If the truth we preach is not public, summoning truth, an odd divine event that is completed in odd human response, an invitation to all to become members of the Body, then we are preaching a static, abstract truth unworthy of a church driven by Christ's election. Faithful preaching is known by its fruit; a declining church is often indicative of a limited homiletic.

7. Our challenge, as preachers, is not to be true to ourselves, but true to the Elector, Jesus Christ.

News is not self-generated. Even as the Reformers used predestination as a bulwark against human contribution to our salvation, so Barth's take on election is a wonderfully objective corrective to our rampant subjectivity.

A few years ago, I was drawn to the reader-response literary criticism of Stanley Fish.[34] In dealing with a text, including the texts called Scripture, the reader intrudes powerfully on the text. However, as a preacher, I am regularly impressed by the sheer objectivity of the biblical text, the way the text says things that I would never say, the way the text stands against meaning which is my own sweet concoction. On Sundays, when the Scriptures are read and proclaimed, congregation and preacher bend under the weight of the otherness of the text.[35]

Though we preachers naturally bring presuppositions to our reading of Scripture, the text also brings something to us, resists easy accommodation, and refuses to be completely malleable. So as we are being honest about how our subjectivities intrude on our interpretation, let's be honest about how God has objectively intruded on us in Scripture.

In preparing to preach, the text unmasks us, stands against us, comes to us, and embraces us when we think we are simply reading inert words on a page. We have the joy of being able to deliver an odd word we did not come up with ourselves to congregations who did not ask for this message. Thus, the objectivity of the biblical text becomes an everyday demonstration of the objective reality of the election of God.

Philosopher Harry G. Frankfurt notes the way we moved, in public discourse, from concern for "correctness" to a demand for "sincerity."

We no longer demand that speakers accurately represent the truth of our world; we ask them candidly to present themselves. Don't talk facts, talk about you, revelation restricted to self-revelation.

Frankfurt says it is "preposterous" to believe that you know more truth about you than truth of the world. Nothing supports "the extraordinary judgment that it is the truth about himself that is the easiest for a person to know." The truth about ourselves is elusive, "sincerity is bullshit."[36]

I am concerned that when many young adults say they value a preacher's "authenticity" (sincerity), self-revelation trumps orthodox teaching, correct doctrine, or biblical fidelity. The sermon becomes a report on the preacher's interiority, an autobiographical exposé delivered while fighting back tears.

Before a guest preaching visit, I ask, "Do you use the Revised Common Lectionary? If you do, I'll base my sermon on the text assigned for Sunday." A typical response: "Bishop, just share what's on your heart." By inserting "just" the host acts as if he or she were making a modest request. Surely it's easier to be taken by a biblical text than to attempt to share "what's on your heart" without prevarication.

In an article on preaching, Paul Tillich called for heartfelt expression of things "transcendent" and "unconditional" in the pulpit. Barth responded that to think of preaching this way "can end only with its dissolution" and that "[p]roclamation as self-exposition must in the long run turn out to be a superfluous and impossible undertaking."[37]

The church is better served not by "sharing what's on your heart" or attempting to be "authentic" but rather by preachers praying for the courage to preach what we have heard God, through the Scriptures, tell us to preach, letting the chips fall where they may.[38]

"Whether proclaimed by the preaching of the Gospel or not, whether heard or not, . . . [God's] judgment issues always a call for faith. i.e., for our practical affirmation of the judgment fulfilled in our being and action. Faith is practical acknowledgment that right is done to us by God," says Barth.[39] We must speak of the "factuality" of our justification, that "in Jesus Christ we are accepted as holy by God . . . really accepted."[40]

Sin, on the other hand, "great or small, conscious or unconscious, flagrant or refined, consists in the fact that we don't believe, that we ignore in practice where we have our origin and what God has done in us and for us."[41] While unbelief is serious and sinful, because of the objective reality of God, unbelief never attains a higher status than "impotent action."[42]

"Conversion" (rarely mentioned by Barth) is discussed before he ends *CD* II/2 as that movement whereby "we confirm and accept the fact that we are placed before the divine *fait accompli*."[43] Preachers find comfort in this "objectivity." Knowing that we preach, not in hopeful expectation of some potentially saving act, we can preach in confidence of a decisive, accomplished work. We "preach not ourselves"; we preach Christ, what God has done and what God is doing and will do in Christ. As Kierkegaard said, the Truth who is Jesus Christ "does not arise in any human heart."[44]

Change *missionary* to *preacher* in the passage below (in which Barth speaks of mission as arising from the peculiar truth who is Jesus Christ) and you will have a Barthian basis for proclamation:

> The apostle of Jesus Christ not only can but must be a missionary. . . . It is not merely the formal necessity of proclaiming the Word of God, nor the humanitarian love which would rather not withhold this Word from others. . . . The determining factor is the concrete content of the Word itself. The truth . . . about Jesus Christ and human life compels . . . almost as if it were automatically to speak wherever it is not yet known. It is like air rushing into a vacuum, or water downhill, or fire to more fuel. [Human life] stands under the sign of God's judgment. This is not just a religious opinion. It is a universal truth. It applies to all. . . . It leaps all frontiers. It is more urgent and binding than any human insight, however clear and compelling, or any convictions, however enthusiastically embraced. This truth is the driving power behind the Christian mission . . . it bursts all barriers.[45]

8. Preachers need not worry much about being relevant to our listeners, but ought to concern ourselves with being true to the Elector, Jesus Christ.

Barth's theology was called "kerygmatic"—theology as restating, repeating, and proclaiming the gospel. Paul Tillich, in contrast, devised a "method of correlation" in which the message being proclaimed was shaped in response to the preacher's assessment of the existential situation of the listeners, correlating "the questions implied in the situation with the answers implied in the message. [Correlational preaching] does not derive the answers from the questions as a self-defying apologetic theology does. Nor does it elaborate answers without relating them to the questions as a self-defying kerygmatic [Barthian?] theology does. It correlates questions and answers, situations and message, human existence and divine manifestation."[46]

Among the dangers of this "method of correlation" are exaggerated confidence in the theologian's ability to define the questions and the actual situation of human existence and the pitfall that the theologian allows the questions subtly to determine the answers, thereby controlling and limiting what is revealed in the "divine manifestation."

North American mainline preachers seem to feel that the "human situation" is plagued by anxiety, stress, and personal concern. Sermons are full of reassuring, comforting words whereby Jesus helps us find more "balance" and less "stress" in life. (In my experience, people with big mortgages and inadequate governance on their acquisitiveness always feel stress. Jesus Christ may be more interested in relieving their sin than in ameliorating their anxiety.)

How do the sermons that I preach correlate with and take their cues from the median age, income, and social location of the aging "cultured despisers" of faith in my congregation rather than from the message of Jesus Christ?

Aristotle devised an elaborate typology of hearers so that the speech could be fashioned to fit the audience. Rhetoric tends to be greatly concerned with audience analysis, and rhetoricians are confident that they have privileged access to the minds and motivations of their listeners. Behind such rhetorical analysis and typology is the attempt to control communication by accurately pitching the speech to listeners.

As James Kay notes, what Barth rejected "is not rhetoric, as such, but an autonomous rhetoric, theologically ungoverned, that claims for its eloquence the power to make God real for people."[47]

"That preachers pay attention to the needs, interests, situation, and capacity of the public is no guarantee that they are really addressing [people]. . . . [The modern person] is arcane. Secret. Hidden. Sermons which should stir and edify and move . . . will probably leave this [person] empty, cold and untouched. By the high-angle fire of the heavy artillery directed above the head of the public, to the more distant entrenched position, this [listener] is perhaps better served in truth than by the all-too jealous pounding of the forward trenches, which [modern people have] long since derisively evacuated."[48] Having been conditioned to conceive of *God* as "Arcane. Secret. Hidden," Barth challenges us to think of God as fully revealed in Christ and of modern humanity as obscure, baffling, and slyly concealed.

Against the rage for "culturally sensitive preaching," Barth says, "Christian preaching . . . has met every culture, however supposedly rich and mature, with ultimate sharp skepticism."[49] The gospel need not be trimmed to the present cultural moment.

In 1933, as part of the Church Struggle, Barth founded a journal, *Theological Existence Today*,[50] for "preachers and teachers of the church" in which he defined "theological existence" as life bound to Scripture. In the church, "God is nowhere present for us, nowhere present in the world, nowhere present in our realm and in our time as in [God's] word; that this word has no other name and content than Jesus Christ and that Jesus Christ [is] for us nowhere in the world to be found as new every day except in the holy scriptures of the Old and New Testaments."[51]

Sometimes attachment to Scripture intensifies in proportion to the preacher's sense of crisis and threat. When the sky turns dark and our hearers bow to alien gods, flocking to false prophets who cry "peace" when there is none, it's then that we preachers are driven back to Scripture, tethering ourselves more tightly to the Trinity as our only relevant word. In *Karl Barth's Emergency Homiletic*, Angela Dienhart Hancock shows that Barth's homiletic, as displayed in his preaching lectures in Bonn, must be contextualized.[52] In disparaging sermon introductions, conclusions, illustrations, and sermonic appeals to the interests of the congregation, Hancock shows that Barth's homiletical tour de force makes sense in the setting of the German university of the 1930s. While Barth lectured, many university faculty (including the bumbling professor of homiletics) were becoming Nazis. In that context, only a homiletic that strictly focuses on Scripture and practices the free speech thereby evoked can match satanic rhetoric. Therefore Barth practiced an "emergency homiletic."

As bishop, a frequent congregational criticism of some of my best young preachers was, "Our new preacher is too biblical." *Too biblical?*

Congregations fed on mainline, liberal, experiential/expressive, therapeutic mush or fearful politics of the right or the left, choke on more solid biblical nourishment. To their credit, bright, young clergy realize that only by being biblical do they have anything significant to say.

Barth says he began *CD* in reaction to the scandal of German preachers who had discovered "deep religious significance in the intoxication of Nordic blood and their political *Führer*."[53] Preachers today throw our voices into a culture that is extensively militarized, incarcerated, and consumptive. We ought to be cautious of demands to tailor the gospel to the desires of our listeners. The gospel does more than speak to people's felt needs; the gospel is often judgment on and rearrangement of needs. Election by God gives us needs we would never have had if not for election—obediently to *testify*, to *witness*.

I have preached dozens of sermons when thousands of Americans are quietly deserting the church because they can hear worldly wisdom elsewhere. I preached in an age when our government pursued expensive, fruitless wars while defending the use of torture and deadly drones, with millions of Americans imprisoned and thousands of children shot to death in the streets around our churches and child refugees pursued and deported from our borders. Why did I not practice a more urgent "emergency homiletic"?

I have heard it said that the challenge is for pastors to "love your people." A greater test (after all, my people pay my salary and look a great deal like me) is to love the truth about God in Jesus Christ.

While human history is given meaning as the stage on which the electing God acts on us, history is not determinative of the address. Biblical narratives give scant attention to the historical, cultural, or geographical context where biblical characters are addressed. Why should we?[54] The cultural context is the space in which we find ourselves addressed, but hypothesized context has less significance for our hearing than divine address. Our relationship with and our knowledge of God is "not a beginning that *we* can make *with [God]*. It can be only the beginning *[God]* has made *with us*."[55]

The current rage for "Contextual Theology" is suspect. "Theologizing from experience," even from the illuminating experience of the poor and the oppressed, is not revelation. When even the great Calvin tried to talk about election on the basis of human standards of justice, the God revealed resembled "far too closely the electing, and more particularly the rejecting theologian"![56] Election teaches that in whatever situation we find ourselves, culture is significant mainly as "the place of responsibility."[57]

9. Preaching is witnessing to the graciously electing God.

"It is not you who speak, but the Spirit of your Father speaking through you" (Matt. 10:20). Bonhoeffer said there is only one preacher, Jesus Christ. The best we can hope in our sermons is that God may graciously use them. Early on, Barth noted a definite "one sidedness" in regard to God's Word.[58] Any "control" is in God's hands, not ours: "To have experience of God's word is to yield to its supremacy."[59] Sermon preparation is practice of the arts of submission, of taking God more seriously and ourselves (as well as our congregations) less so.

"Jesus Christ is the one and only Word of God. . . . He alone is the light of God and the revelation of God. [He] . . . delimits all other words, lights, revelations, prophecies and apostolates, whether of the Bible, the Church or the world, . . . biblical prophets and apostles are his servants, ambassadors and witnesses, so that even in their humanity the words spoken by them cannot fail to be words of great seriousness, profound comfort and supreme wisdom. And if the Church follows the biblical prophets and apostles, similar words are surely to be expected of it."[60] "So we are ambassadors for Christ, since God is making [God's] appeal through us" (2 Cor. 5:20).

Witness is not judged by social utility; the only Judge is Christ. There is no need to translate the biblical text into abstract terms, such as we once saw in the theology and preaching of Tillich and Bultmann and now in "Power Point Preachers" who render the gospel into principles for better living, timeless ideals, and helpful hints for homemakers. Witnesses require election; God's impersonating choice of certain words and phrases as God's revelation.

The metaphors for God in Scripture are self-depictions by a relentlessly self-revealing agent who elects to speak to us in ways that draw us more closely to the Elector. Much of modern theology stresses the dissimilarity of our words for God from the divine referent; for Barth, biblically given words for God are reliable depictions of the God to whom they refer because God elects to use these metaphors as self-offering. "God's true revelation comes to meet us by taking our human words and electing them to be revelation when we attach ourselves obediently to these words."[61] Biblical preachers can preach confidently because in the Incarnation God took definite form, located, and became concretely accessible though Israel and Church in a way that genuinely, accurately describes God.[62]

God's truth, while graciously given, is not at witnesses' disposal; our lives, our metaphors, are at God's elective service. When Jesus said, "This is my body," he was holding bread. God deals with us, not as if we were angels, said Calvin, but in ways creatures can comprehend. Atonement is too grand an idea for us creatures, but bread is well known and necessary to every animal. Luther said that when God speaks, God uses simple baby talk that even the least mature can understand.

Just as we are bound to receive our salvation through Israel and the Church, so witnesses are bound to the metaphors God has selected for us. Paul says that he forsook the lofty, pretty language of imperial rhetoric and instead said only "Cross," to the Corinthians. What Paul was compelled to preach could be said in no less scandalous and offensive way than the way the crucified God took toward us. When Barth says God is Wholly Other, he means that God is wholly incomprehensible in any way unfit to the God who is in Jesus Christ. The only way to God is provided by God, through the scandalous means of bread, wine, water, and the pitiful words of preachers.

The search for a way to translate Christian good news into more acceptable, easier-to-hear speech dead ends with the preacher saying other than the gospel, oftentimes what the world can hear without the inconvenience of sitting through a sermon. We have not said "salvation" when we say "transformation," or "discipleship" when we say "purpose-driven life." There is no adequate human analogical relation between human words and the divine referent; witnesses can only point to the mystery, speak as Scripture speaks, and enjoy revelation when it is given. "Whoever listens to you listens to me, and whoever rejects you rejects me, and whoever rejects me rejects the one who sent me" (Luke 10:16). It's a miracle.

Our sermons can't be bolstered apart from the revelation they seek to articulate. Barth says that when preaching rests on God-given analogies, "It will then have something definite to say, and that with a good conscience, with the promise of relevance, i.e. of standing in a real relationship to the reality proclaimed by it, and with the justified claim and well grounded prospect of obtaining a hearing."[63]

Our authority comes not from ourselves or even from our ordination by the church. We preach because of our odd, even embarrassing conviction that we have been elected by God to do so. Yet subservience to the Word can be liberating. When we encounter resistance, hostility, or zombie-like stares from our congregation, it is powerful freedom to know that our congregations are not the source of our authorization.

Election implies that, from the first, God has determined to be heard. As Kierkegaard said, "God did not assume the form of a servant to make a mockery of us," so it cannot be God's "intention to pass through the world in such a manner that no single human being becomes aware of [God's] presence."[64] Election gives confidence that God's word will not return empty (Isa. 55:11) and that our faith in God's faith in our preaching is not in vain (1 Cor. 15:14).

When we work conscientiously on a sermon and our congregations sincerely listen, yet strangely nothing is heard, we are thereby reminded of our dependence on God's grace and mercy. In preaching we witness to what makes us Christian—God's election to be our God from all eternity and, from eternity, God's choice of us to be for God. I have just heard a deeply introspective, shy, self-effacing, modest young man stand up and preach a stirring sermon with nothing to protect him from the congregation but a large open Bible. He is for me a witness to the truth of the doctrine of election.

Modern people assume that if God were really real, God wouldn't require witnesses in order to be manifest. Faith would come forth from within so we should not have humiliatingly to receive faith from the hands of Jews or anybody else. We wouldn't have to submit to a sermon that's hard to follow and to a preacher we dislike.

Think of the whole Christian life as lifelong training in how to receive faith from another. It's gift, grace, all the way down.

We are out of control.

How great a God to entrust God's work to thoroughly human, frail, witnesses; just the sort of God who would come to us as a Jew who lived briefly, died violently, and rose unexpectedly.

10. God weaves even our sermons into God's elective work.

The significance of our sermons is out of our control. All we know is that our future is determined by God's eternal decision to be God for us and for us to be for God, forever. A sermon is a supremely contemporaneous form of communication, an event in the present that can never be redone or reclaimed, a fragile art that is either taken up by the Holy Spirit or else sinks into silent oblivion.

Bonhoeffer said that sermons are twice born: once in the preacher's study and again when delivered from the pulpit. It's up to God either to make a sermon "work" in the power of the Holy Spirit, or the sermon is stillborn.

Even as God in Christ is fully human and fully divine, so Barth's theology of proclamation presents a provisional union between divine activity and human activity in the preaching event. Witnesses are elected to look forward to the next event of God's speaking, set free through this provisional union to move toward the time when all tears will be wiped away, the provisionality of God's promises shall be completed, we shall know as we have been known (1 Cor. 13:12), and God and God's people will live in full communion. Until that Second Advent, the suspect and conditional nature of proclamation continues. "[Preaching's] sheer impossibility," says Barth, "will always remain, but it has now pleased God to present himself in and in spite of this human action."[65] Wherever and whenever human speech and preaching become God's—in that place, to that particular people, in that dynamic moment—it is God's Word.[66]

Of course, our testimony to the truth who is Jesus Christ is partial, in process, incomplete, and sometimes wrong. We are sinners. And since the news we bear is not self-concocted but rather a gift, we never fully possess that of which we speak, nor are we fully possessed by it. We are unlike those witnesses who appear in a courtroom and pledge dispassionately, disinterestedly to testify to an event external to us—"The facts, ma'am, just the facts," as Officer Friday instructed on *Dragnet*. The news that has been given to us (quite unexpectedly and remarkably, quite inexplicably) has changed us. "You will be his witness to all of what you have seen and heard" (Acts 22:15). Indeed, a chief requirement to be a preacher is to be able to testify that the news we share is news that has happened to us, that the encounter with Christ we hope to precipitate among our hearers is one we are having. The gospel is affective truth. All our arguments are *ad hominem*. Paul never tires of commending Christ by marveling, "and last, as one untimely born, he appeared to me" (1 Cor.15:8; also see Gal. 1:1; 1 Cor. 9). No volunteer, Paul was elected.

Barth's "herald" image, his notion that the sermon should be just a polished pane of glass through which we see Christ, is not quite right. The witness is no disinterested courier. The truth preached is personal and personified. We are under a commission that we did not seek. Thus we witness with a tense mix of self-confidence and self-negation.

Good news rejected is a tragedy, a baffling refusal to accept a fact. Fortunately, the news we share is news that anticipates rejection; indeed, we ourselves reject the news in countless ways. And yet we take heart because even the strongest human rejection is circumscribed, relativized by the sweeping, divine yes of God's gracious election.

A non-Christian sociologist once said to me, when we were talking about the difficulty of Christians in the modern world, "Still, you Christians have never found a culture you couldn't crack. Even the most hostile. You've even got a mythology to explain why their rejection is validation of the truth of your assertions!" Odd to be told theological truth by a social scientist.

I remember the couple of negative comments from listeners and forget dozens of affirmative responses. I can recount stories of those who have rejected my sermons (indeed, I have done so in this book), while I am oddly dismissive of those who received my words as if they were God's address.

Many of my fellow preachers argue, "Preaching doesn't work." Odd, that those who are giving their lives to this vocation dismiss preaching as dumb and ineffective. Is it more fearful to fall into the hands of a living God (Heb. 10:31), more terrifying to admit that I and my poor sermons are actively used by God to invade the world than to admit that I often preach poorly?

Why am I so ambivalent about the significance of my own preaching? I doubt my difficulty is due to my humility. More than likely I am reluctant to take responsibility for the power of God working in me, in spite of me. It is scary that my sermons do more than I intend, unnerving to know that while I can construct a sermon, I cannot control or delimit the disruptive fecundity of the Word. Homiletical failure is easier to manage than success.

I take some comfort that I have been preceded in my reluctance gratefully to receive my election to preach by so able a preacher as Jeremiah. Any of my ambivalence about the preaching vocation pales before Jeremiah's periodic anger at being called *in utero* to be "a prophet to the nations" (Jer. 1:5).

When Jeremiah attempted to beg off and thereby regain some control of his life, God responded by invoking the power of election: "Do not say, 'I am only a boy'; / for you shall go to all to whom I send you, / and you shall speak whatever I command" (1:7). "See, today I appoint you over nations and over kingdoms, / to pluck up and to pull down, / to destroy and to overthrow, / to build and to plant" (1:10) with nothing more than words. A person would be a fool not to be intimidated by so apocalyptic a vocation. Still, it is greater foolishness to attempt to evade the long arm of God.

That's why every preacher's favorite Flannery O'Connor story is "Revelation":[67]

Ruby Turpin sat in a crowded doctor's waiting room. And as Ruby often did she spent her time looking around and one-by-one, in her mind, measuring herself by the people seated before her. As she evaluated herself on the social ladder, Ruby always came out more than a notch above everybody else—particularly that scowling teenage girl seated across from her, unkempt, sullen, and sour. She said to the girl's mother, after having tried vainly to illicit some response from the girl, "What is your daughter's name?"

The mother looked up and said, "Mary, her name is Mary Grace."

"Well Mary Grace" says Ruby, "I always think it is just great to sit up in your chair, and posture is so important, and er . . ." The girl sullenly glared at her. Ruby continued to chatter to herself—loud enough for everybody in the waiting room to hear. She talked about the relative goodness of poor black workers compared with "poor white trash." Lazy white workers had to be paid a full day's wage. And you had to pick them up and then take them home after work. Ruby said she knew white trash that lived worse than "our pigs that Claude and me has got."

She prattled on until the unkempt teenager fixed her eyes on her like "steely drills" and glared, making Ruby very uncomfortable. The girl had been reading a big book. Ruby squinted her eyes and saw that it was *Human Development*. She could only imagine the lurid things in that book. Suddenly the girl hurls the huge book across the waiting room, cold cocking Ruby across the forehead. Ruby sprawls in the middle of the floor. Mary Grace is on top of her hissing, "Go back to hell where you belong, you old wart hog."

It is for Ruby unexpected, undesired revelation, difficult grace. Before the story ends, she is given a vision of eternity. (In this faith, grace, revelation often come when a large book smacks you between the eyes.)

You can imagine with whom I most identity in the story. I am Mary Grace on a weekly basis. I'm a preacher; someone elected to whop a congregation upside the head with a great big book.

And yet in my sermon preparation, I'm more Ruby Turpin than Mary Grace. To be both the recipient and the donor of unsought, unexpected revelation isn't an easy job, God knows. But it is the vocation to which God has called Mary Grace, Ruby, and me.

As Ruby lies upon her bed at twilight, attempting to recover, she mutters, "I am not a wart hog. From hell." O'Connor says that her, "denial had no force."

"She had been singled out for the message, though there was trash in the room to whom it might justly have been applied. . . . There was a woman there who was neglecting her own child but she had been overlooked. The message had been given to Ruby Turpin, a respectable, hard-working, church-going woman. The tears dried. Her eyes began to burn instead with wrath."

To be "singled out for a message," when the news is meant not only for everyone but also aimed at you, a word that is death-dealing, life-giving, out-of-control gospel, well, that odd vocation elicits joy in the preacher and sometimes wrath. God only knows what good it does.

Ah, but what a wonderful way to go.

Notes

Introduction

1. Hauerwas says that "Barth's *Church Dogmatics* is best read as a training manual for Christian speech." Stanley M. Hauerwas, "New Afterword," *With the Grain of the Universe: The Church's Witness and Natural Theology* (Grand Rapids: Baker Academic, 2013), 244.

2. William H. Willimon, *Conversations with Barth on Preaching* (Nashville: Abingdon Press, 2006), 161–83. See also, Thomas Christian Currie, *The Only Sacrament Left to Us: The Threefold Word of God in the Theology and Ecclesiology of Karl Barth* (Eugene, OR: Pickwick Publications, 2015).

3. Karl Barth, *Church Dogmatics*, I/2, "The Doctrine of God," ed. G. W. Bromiley and T. F. Torrance (Edinburgh: T. & T. Clark, 1957), 879. Hereafter, references to the *Dogmatics* will be as *CD*, followed by volume number/part number, page number (e.g., *CD* II/2, 145).

4. All citations from *CD* II/2 are from Karl Barth, *Church Dogmatics, The Doctrine of God* vol. II, part 2, ed. G. W. Bromiley and T. F Torrance, trans. Bromiley et al. (Edinburgh: T. & T. Clark, 1957).

5. *CD*, I/1, 111–12.

6. Ibid., 205.

Chapter 1: The Oddness of God

1. These three paintings are perfect complement to the vocation of Matthew. The one who is called must constantly receive revelation and suffer martyrdom precisely because of his vocation as apostle.

2. A point made well by James K. A. Smith in his book on the thought of Charles Taylor. James K. A. Smith, *How (Not) to Be Secular: Reading Charles Taylor* (Grand Rapids: Wm. B. Eerdmans, 2014), 26–28, 98.

3. Here I presume to follow the argument that Karl Barth made in *God in Action*, Barth's spirited defense of his actions related to the "German Christians" and the Nazis in 1934 (Eugene, OR: Wipf and Stock, 2005). I first read this lecture during the Black Panther Trial in New Haven, Connecticut, in 1970, and for the first time saw the

accommodationist nature of our vaunted "social action." That is, the Black Panthers seemed closer to the politically disruptive gospel than we moderate liberals who were urging the police to go easy on the Panthers.

4. In the first pages of *The Epistle to the Romans* (trans. Edwyn C. Hoskyns [London: Oxford University Press, 1933]), Barth noted that human subjectivity is powerless to challenge our given situation because our subjectivity is a product of the given situation. "No new reality *can* be generated out of the present reality." Politics of the right or of the left cannot devise new solutions because even what we call "revolutionary" is a product of the world as it is.

5. Friedrich Schleiermacher, *On Religion: Speeches to Its Cultured Despisers,* trans. John Oman (New York: Harper and Row, 1958), 27. Ironically, Schleiermacher hoped to win Christianity a public hearing and public significance with his refashioning of the faith into interiority.

6. William Carl Placher, *The Domestication of Transcendence: How Modern Thinking about God Went Wrong* (Louisville, KY: Westminster John Knox Press, 1996), 7.

7. Ibid., 6. Hauerwas definitively demonstrates how the theology of Reinhold Niebuhr attempted to remove the oddness of the gospel by showing that "Christianity consisted in . . . universal and timeless myths about the human condition that made Christianity available to anyone without witness" and thereby made Christianity "a 'truth' for the sustenance of social orders in the West" (Hauerwas, *With the Grain of the Universe*, 39).

8. "God in the Dock," in Lesley Walmsley, ed., *C. S. Lewis: Essay Collection and Other Short Pieces* (London: HarperCollins Publishers, 2000), 36. I wish I had thought of this quotation from Lewis when I did my scathing review of Bart Ehrman's, *God's Problem.* Ehrman convicts God of a failure to respond adequately to the questions of a tenured professor of religious studies.

9. Marcus Borg, "What's Christianity All About?" in *Day One*, February 6, 2011, http://day1.org/2544-whats_christianity all about.

10. John Webster's Barthian formation is evident when Webster states that God's holiness is found in God's mercy rather than in God's transcendence. "God is holy precisely as the one who in majesty and freedom and sovereign power bends down to us in mercy. God is the Holy One. But he is the Holy One 'in your midst,' as Hosea 11:9 put it." John Webster, *Holiness* (Grand Rapids: Wm. B. Eerdmans, 2003), 45.

11. Charles Taylor's response to the lamentable "closed world structures" of modern secularists is to plead for "Jamesian open space" whereby secularists might at least concede that, though we have explained just about everything, there might be room for more. This argument for a vague transcendentalism as a cure for the limitations of atheism sounds suspiciously like the old "God of the gaps" appeal to disbelievers. I believe that the cure for secularism/atheism is stress upon election, the God who is surprisingly *pro nobis*, not more distancing of God from humanity. Charles Taylor, *A Secular Age* (Cambridge: Harvard University Press, Belknap Press, 2007), 551–55.

12. *Atheism* (does God exist?) eventually became *nihilism* (do *we* exist?), which validates Barth's claim that humanity exists only as those who are addressed.

13. One of Dawkins's charges against religious people is that we do not meet generally accepted standards of human rationality.

14. Taylor, *A Secular Age*, 3.

15. Richard Dawkins, *The God Delusion* (Boston: Houghton Mifflin, 2006). Christopher Hitchens, *God Is Not Great: How Religion Poisons Everything* (New York: Warner Books,

2007). Both Dawkins and Hitchens are eloquently dismissed by David Bentley Hart in his *Atheist Delusions: The Christian Revolution and Its Fashionable Enemies* (New Haven, CT: Yale University Press, 2009).

16. The story is told by Alasdair MacIntyre, *The Religious Significance of Atheism* (New York: Columbia University Press), 24. If you wonder why Barth rejected apologetics, read a recent attempt by Francis Spufford, *Unapologetic: Why, Despite Everything, Christianity Can Still Make Surprising Emotional Sense* (London: Faber and Faber, 2009). The God being advocated by Spufford looks suspiciously like us and our yearnings and is therefore all too easily dismissed.

17. Eberhard Busch, *Barth* (Nashville: Abingdon Press, 2008), 17. It is curious that Busch called this section the "highlight" since it occurs barely a fourth of the way into the *Dogmatics*. But it is fitting that this "highlight" comes early; Barth believed that all the necessary work to bring us back to God had already been accomplished by God. Human decision and action are anticlimactic after God's election of humanity. All thinking about God is *Nachdenken,* "thinking after." We cannot be for God except post God's being God for us. Eberhard Busch, *Drawn to Freedom: Christian Faith Today in Conversation with the Heidelberg Catechism* (Grand Rapids: Wm. B. Eerdmans, 2010), 3.

   I don't know what to do with all of Barth's masculine designators except to call attention to them as the way scholars talked six decades ago but not now. The reflexive "himself" when applied to God seems important for the following discussion but the neologism "Godself" is awkward.

   Election is at the heart of Barth's "revolution" as Bruce McCormack (our best interpreter of Barth on election) puts it (Bruce McCormack, "Grace and Being: The Role of God's Gracious Election in Karl Barth's Theological Ontology," in John Webster, ed., *The Cambridge Companion to Karl Barth* [Cambridge, England: Cambridge University Press, 2000], 93–97). McCormack says, "I am confident that the greatest contribution of Karl Barth to the development of Church doctrine will be located in his doctrine of election." Through his surprising reworking of election, Barth brought about "a revolution in the doctrine of God. . . ." (Ibid., 223).

   Douglas Sharp, in his dissertation, "The Doctrine of Election in Karl Barth's '*Die Kirchliche Dogmatik,*'" argues that the doctrine of election, rather than Christology, is *the* hermeneutical key to the *Dogmatics*. While I'm not sure why Sharp plays Christology off against election in Barth, he makes a thoroughgoing case for election as a chief organizing principle in the *Dogmatics* (Unpublished dissertation, Graduate Theological Union, 1988). As Robert Jenson says, "Jesus Christ is therefore the basis of the doctrine of election. All statements [about election] must be statements about him" (Robert W. Jenson, *Alpha and Omega: A Study of the Theology of Karl Barth* [Eugene, OR: Wipf & Stock, 2002], 144).

18. Busch, *Barth*, 17.

19. Andreas Pangritz, *Karl Barth in the Theology of Dietrich Bonhoeffer* (Grand Rapids: Wm. B. Eerdmans, 2000), 62–63.

20. Ibid., 119.

21. *CD*, IV/1, 32.

22. Ibid., 32–33.

23. Ibid. I find much of Barth's treatment of Israel in *CD* II/2 troubling, though his constant stress on "unfaithful" Israel is contextualized by his discussion of Judas. Election is given in our unfaithfulness, not in our potential faithfulness; we are all unfaithful as the elect.

In spite of his many affirming statements about Israel, Barth seems to have little place for Israel except as precursor for and included within the church. Barth would more carefully craft his comments about Israel later in *CD* and even repent of some of his incipient anti-Jewish statements. Still, Barth's tendency to continue earlier Christian rhetoric against the Jews is indefensible. See Katherine Sonderegger, *That Jesus Christ Was Born a Jew: Karl Barth's "Doctrine of Israel"* (University Park: Penn State Press, 1992).

24. Eberhard Busch defines *theology* relationally as "the relationship between God and humanity," and the *gospel* itself as, "God has brought and continues to bring Godself into relationship with us." Busch, *Drawn to Freedom*, 4.

25. *CD* II/2, 354–409.

26. Ibid., 364.

27. Ibid., 308.

28. Ibid., 322.

29. David Kelsey, *Eccentric Existence: A Theological Anthropology*, vol. 1 (Louisville, KY: Westminster John Knox, 2009), 528–29. I am indebted to Kelsey for this discussion of election in Scripture.

30. "In the New Testament election is the divine ordination to discipleship, to the apostolate, to the community" (*CD* II/2, 16).

31. In John Howard Yoder's first days as a student of Barth he read *CD* II/2 and was disturbed by the "occasionalism" in Barth's first discussion of ethics in *CD*. Yoder was troubled that some in America read Barth on election as a "rejection of all possible general statements about right behavior and as skepticism about whether in the field of ethics we can say anything specific about the shape and will of God." Yoder eventually made Barth's thought a basis of his own ethics. John Howard Yoder, "Karl Barth: How His Mind Kept Changing," *How Karl Barth Changed My Mind*, ed. Donald McKim (Grand Rapids: Wm. B. Eerdmans, 1986), 166–71.

32. Marilynne Robinson, *Gilead* (New York: Farrar, Straus, and Giroux, 2004), 149–50.

33. Barth criticizes Augustine's "movement away from the biblical testimony" in Augustine's idea of a "double divine decision from all eternity" because this "parallelism" of God's determination implies yes and no (*CD/* II/2, 16).

34. Here I follow "Predestination," Mathijs Lamberigts, in *Augustine through the Ages: An Encyclopedia*, ed. Allan D. Fitzgerald, O.S.A. (Grand Rapids: Wm. B. Eerdmans, 1999), 677–79.

35. Augustine and Calvin struggle with this "all" in 2 Timothy. Augustine says that "all" here could mean all the predestined or that every sort of person is found among the predestined or that "all" refers simply to a divine longing that all might be saved (St. Augustine, "On Rebuke and Grace," *A Select Library of the Nicene and Post-Nicene Fathers of the Christian Church*, ed. Philip Schaff [Grand Rapids: Wm. B. Eerdmans, 1956], 5:489–91). Calvin says that "all" refers to all conditions of people. Barth simply takes "all" to mean what it says and glories in the sweeping "Yes," of divine determination to save. I've explored issues of salvation in William H. Willimon, *Who Will Be Saved?* (Nashville: Abingdon Press, 2008).

36. John Calvin begins his exposition of the election in the *Institutes of the Christian Religion* (trans. Henry Beveridge [Grand Rapids: Wm. B. Eerdmans, 1989], 2.22.1) saying that the purpose of the doctrine is to teach us "to put our trust wholly in the mercy of God," to demonstrate to us "the glory of God in its full grandeur," and to incline "us to a true humility." Quoted by Barth with approval, *CD* II/2, 37.

37. "Calvin's doctrine of election, for Barth, can be summarized as follows. God the Father was, so to speak, the legislative branch. God the Son, the executive branch, and God the Holy Spirit the judicial branch. Calvin's deep mistake was not to include the entire antecedent Trinity in the legislative branch, where the pretemporal decision of election was made. Instead, Jesus became the object and the executor of election. He did not belong to the legislative branch. Therefore the decision of election or predestination was not determined by him as an active subject" (George Hunsinger, *Reading Karl Barth with Charity: A Hermeneutical Proposal* [Grand Rapids: Barker Academic, 2015], 33). Barth's great contribution (and correction of Calvin) was to make Jesus Christ not only the object but also the subject of election. In Jesus Christ "we have to do not merely with elected man but with the electing God" (*CD* II/ 2, 108).
38. Unsurprisingly, I find Paul Helm's discrediting of Barth's critique of Calvin on election unconvincing. See Paul Helm, *John Calvin's Ideas* (Oxford: Oxford University Press, 2004).
39. Charles Taylor says that a major impetus for the creation of secularity's "exclusive humanism" with its "closed consciousness" is Christianity's "hyper-Augustinianism" that assumes that "the majority of the human race will be damned" (Taylor, *A Secular Age*, 652).
40. John Milton, *Paradise Lost*, http://knarf.english.upenn.edu/Milton/pl2.html, 2.557–61.
41. Barth's brief comments on Arminius suggest that he knows more about the later Arminians' mistakes than the more carefully dialectical thought of Arminius himself.
42. "Free Grace," in *The Sermons of John Wesley: A Collection for the Christian Journey*, ed. Kenneth J. Collins and Jason E. Vickers (Nashville: Abingdon Press, 2013), 26.
43. Methodist theologian Tom Oden gives a succinct definition of the classical, Wesleyan Arminian view of synergistic salvation: "The promise of glory is conditional on grace being received by faith active in love" (Thomas C. Oden, *The Transforming Power of Grace* [Nashville: Abingdon, 1993], 135). Years ago Geoffrey Wainwright said that the best hope of a rapprochement between Wesley and Calvin was Karl Barth (*Geoffrey Wainwright on Wesley and Calvin* [Melbourne, Australia: The Joint Board of Christian Education, 1987]).
44. When Barth discusses (briefly) the Remonstrants' challenge to Calvin's predestination, he accuses them of "medieval semi-Pelagianism" and of being precursors of "modern Christianity," making "the criterion or measure of all things . . . [humanity's] conception of that which is right and rational, and worthy" (*CD* II/2, 67). Barth seems to know Arminius only through the Remonstrants.
45. Roger C. Olson, *Arminian Theology: Myths and Realities* (Downers Grove, IL: IVP Academic, 2006), 42. See also Roger Olson, *Against Calvinism* (Grand Rapids: Zondervan, 2011).
46. Olson, *Arminian Theology*, 73. Donald Bloesch says, "In Calvin all is of grace, but grace is not for all. In Luther and Wesley all is of grace and grace is for all, but not all are for grace. In Barth grace is the source of all creaturely being and goes out to all, but every[one] is set against grace. Yet every[one] is caught up in the movement of grace even in the case where there is continued opposition to Christ . . . those who defy grace are claimed by grace and remain objects of grace despite their contumacy and folly" (*Jesus Is Victor! Karl Barth's Doctrine of Salvation* [Nashville: Abingdon, 1976], 70). My chief concern about what Bloesch says about grace is that his thought on grace is not Christologically governed.

47. John Piper, "Pastoral Thoughts on the Doctrine of Election" (sermon, November 30, 2003), http://www.desiringgod.org/sermons/pastoral-thoughts-on-the-doctrine-of -election.
48. Olson, *Arminian Theology*, 99.
49. Barth saw the Calvinistic Synod of Dort as defeating Arminian synergism but at the "great cost" of a weakening of the Reformed "doctrine of grace and justification." Dort reduced the joyful Reformed witness to the gracious covenanting God to that of "sinister heralds of an even more sinister deity." Still, Barth is happier with the fathers of Dort than with the Arminians, whose thought, filtered through the Enlightenment, "relapsed into a fairly crude semi-Pelagianism of a pietist-rationalist type," about the worst Barth could say of anyone's theology (*CD* III/3, 116).
50. Charles G. Finney, "Sermon X: Doctrine of Election," http://www.gospeltruth .net/1836SOIS/10sois_election.htm. Ted Smith does a wonderful job of showing how Finney decisively (and detrimentally) altered American theology (Ted A. Smith, *The New Measures: A Theological History of Democratic Practice* [New York: Cambridge University Press, 2007]).
51. I am indebted to Stephen Gunter for the demonstration of Wesley's faithful rendition of Arminius.
52. Sydney E. Ahlstrom, *A Religious History of the American People* (New Haven and London: Yale University Press, 1972), 845.
53. Tim Keller, "Grateful for Everything," http://timkeller.info/other/excerpts/ (accessed April 2015), emphasis added.
54. Charles Taylor has a fine discussion of *choice* as the central characteristic of what he calls our godless "Age of Authenticity" in which the only value "is choice." I am who I choose to be; what I choose is good because I have chosen (*A Secular Age*, 478).
55. Olson, *Arminian Theology*, 30.

Chapter 2: Karl Barth and Election

1. Eberhard Jüngel opens his book on the Trinitarian significance of Barth's thought with a deceptively simple sentence, "Barth thinks as a theologian" (Eberhard Jüngel, *God's Being Is in Becoming*, trans. John Webster [Grand Rapids: Wm. B. Eerdmans, 2001], 59–60). God is not the result of our theological assertions but prior to them. God's being goes before anything we know or say about God. We raise no question about God before God questions us. God precedes us. Knowledge of God is linked to worship of God.
2. John Calvin, "The Knowledge of God and of Ourselves, http://www.monergism .com/thethreshold/sdg/knowledgegod.html.
3. *CD* II/2, 4.
4. *Evangelical Theology: An Introduction*, trans. Grover Foley (New York: Holt, Rinehart and Winston, 1963), 12. David Kelsey begins his magisterial theological anthropology by asking, "Does Christian faith bring with it any convictions about human being that are so rock bottom for it that they are, so to speak, nonnegotiable in intellectual exchange with anthropologies shaped by other traditions?" Kelsey gives a softer affirmative answer than does Barth, but shows that election plays a key role in any Christian definition of personhood (*Eccentric Existence*, 7). For Barth's anthropology, see Daniel J Price, *Karl Barth's Anthropology in Light of Modern Thought* (Grand Rapids: Wm. B. Eerdmans, 2002).
5. *CD* II/2, 419–49.

6. Bruce McCormack wonders if we are now beyond debates between Calvinists and Arminians. Fewer people are knowledgeable enough to participate in the fine nuances of these positions. Also, Barth has given us a way to move forward from this not-too-fruitful debate. See McCormack's lecture at https://www.youtube.com /watch?v=enHkl69OYL0.

7. *CD* II/2, 95.

8. Ibid., 88.

9. *CD* I/1, 247.

10. As I was completing this book, George Hunsinger's, *Reading Karl Barth with Charity: A Hermeneutical Proposal* (Grand Rapids: Baker Academic, 2015) appeared. Hunsinger criticizes Bruce McCormack and other "Barth revisionists" for misrepresenting Barth's views on election, particularly in regard to the *Logos asarkos*. The revisionists seem to deny that election is a primordial act of God, Father, Son, and Holy Spirit from all eternity. The revisionists believe that Barth turned the Trinity into a consequence of pretemporal election. The debate quickly becomes very technical, very complicated, and (in my judgement) not directly relevant to the concerns of my attempt to relate Barth and election to preaching.

11. Quoted in Herbert Hartwell, *The Theology of Karl Barth: An Introduction* (Philadelphia: The Westminster Press, 1969), 109.

12. Karl Barth, *Deliverance to the Captives* (New York: Harper and Collins, 1978), 86–87. Douglas Campbell's comments on Romans 11:32 wonderfully undergird Barth's interpretation of this text. See Campbell, *The Deliverance of God: An Apocalyptic Rereading of Justification in Paul* (Grand Rapids: Wm. B. Eerdmans, 2009), 90–94.

13. *CD* II/2, 176.

14. Ibid., 76.

15. Ibid., 77.

16. A major objection of Barth to Calvin's predestination is its obscurity—making both God and humanity "unknown quantities" (Ibid., 146).

17. Taylor, *A Secular Age*, 551.

18. *CD* II/2, 104.

19. Ibid. Statements like this very soon led Reformed critics such as Van Til to complain that Barth had restricted God to only one attitude toward humanity, and that Barth had ignored straightforward biblical passages on eternal damnation that did not fit into his theological scheme. Above all, Van Til accused Barth of denying that Scripture gives direct revelation of God. I find it odd that evangelical critics are bothered that Barth is so relentlessly Christological. See Cornelius Van Til, *Christianity and Barthianism* (Grand Rapids: Baker Book House, 1962), 108–9, 164–65.

20. *CD* II/2, 104.

21. Ibid., 146.

22. John Milton, *Paradise Lost*, http://knarf.english.upenn.edu/Milton/pl2.html, 12:640–46, 49-50.

23. *CD* II/2, 13–14. This is quite a statement from a theologian who opposed modern theology's attempt to reduce thick biblical narrative to some contrived "essence."

24. Ibid., 14 (italics mine).

25. Ibid., 12.

26. Bonhoeffer, quoted in Kelsey, *Eccentric Existence*, 531.

27. *CD* II/2, 94.

28 Ibid., 164.
29. Gerald McKenny describes the repetitious nature of Barth's *Dogmatics* as a lengthy "series of nonidentical repetitions" (Gerald McKenny, *The Analogy of Grace: Karl Barth's Moral Theology* [Oxford: Oxford University Press, 2010]).
30. *CD* IV/3, 3–4.
31. *CD* IV/1, 36, 37, 67.
32. John Calvin, *Commentary on 1 John 4*.
33. George Hunsinger notes that the longest quote in the *CD* is from Athanasius.
34. The current debate on "Open Theism" is insufficiently Christological. Beginning with Christ, with the Chalcedonian formulation, rather than with abstract "theism," enables Barth to render an active, resourceful, personal, revealing God and a truly responsive human agent. Barth condemned theology that works from generalities and abstractions about God in *CD* II/2, 48.
35. Ibid., 311.
36. Emil Brunner, *The Christian Doctrine of God: Dogmatics*, vol. I, trans. O. Wyon (London: Lutterworth, 1949), 314. More recent evangelical scholars have taken up Brunner's charge of indefensible exegesis by Barth in his treatment of election. See Suzanne McDonald, *Re-Imaging Election: Divine Election as Representing God to Others and Others to God* (Grand Rapids: Wm. B. Eedmans, 2010).
37. Bruce L. McCormack and Clifford B. Anderson, eds., *Karl Barth and American Evangelicalism* (Grand Rapids: Wm. B. Eerdmans, 2011). See the astute, yet critical evangelical assessment of Barth on election by D. A. Carson, *Divine Sovereignty and Human Responsibility: Biblical Perspectives in Tension* (London: Marshall, Morgan & Scott, 1981), 214–16.
38. Though Barth calls Ephesians 1:3, "the strongest presentation of predestination in the New Testament," he mentions Ephesians 1:4 only once in his five hundred pages on election! However, Barth certainly demonstrates that while he is a close reader of Scripture, he is an imaginative, *theological* reader. Barth is the major figure in the advent of theological exegesis as it is now widely practiced in the seminary where I teach. See Mary Kathleen Cunningham, *What Is Theological Exegesis: Interpretation and Use of Scripture in Barth's Doctrine of Election* (Valley Forge, PA: Trinity Press International, 1995). In comparing Barth's exegesis with that of standard historical critics, Cunningham says that Barth "deals with critical scholarship in an ad hoc fashion" and never allows any of the critics' insights to blur Scripture's true, unified focus, "Jesus Christ" (75).
39. Pangritz, *Karl Barth in the Theology of Dietrich Bonhoeffer*, 119.
40. Kelsey, *Eccentric Existence*, 532. "The doctrine of predestination is corrupted when we project back onto God the kind of logical or causal connections . . . which we have here on earth, for then we make it into some kind of pre-determinism or fatalism, which is very wrong, and quite unchristian" (Thomas F. Torrance, Robert T. Walker, eds., *Incarnation: The Person and Work of Christ* [Downers Grove, IL: InterVarsity Press, 2008], 258). For an astute (though critical of Barth), concise discussion of the history and current challenges of predestination teaching, see Matthew Levering, *Predestination: Biblical and Theological Paths* (Oxford: Oxford University Press, 2011), 135-76.
41. Rebecca Schuman, in a clever article, "Hanging Up on a Calling" (*The Chronicle of Higher Education*, January 27, 2014), chastises her fellow academics for speaking of the professorship as a "vocation" and a "calling." Schuman says that this way of speaking about a life in higher education leads to sick servility and people who are "expected

to work for free." I would have thought that being a professor is such hard work one ought never attempt it without a sense of vocation. Perhaps Schuman's criticism of "calling" shows that it was a mistake for theologians like Calvin to speak of a person's job as a "vocation." Vocation in the *Christian* sense is Jesus' call to discipleship, of which the call to be a Servant of the Word is a subspecies.

42. In criticizing Augustine on election I have perhaps been unfair. What Augustine said on election, he said, as I have noted, in the heat of controversy with the Pelagians. What Calvin made of Augustine later may be a distortion. If one wants to know what Augustine really believes about God's agency and prior, seeking, determined love for humanity, one ought to read his *Confessions*, not his *Retractions*.

43. *CD* I/1, 159.

44. Karl Barth, *Dogmatics in Outline*, trans. G. T. Thomson (New York: Harper & Row, 1959), 15.

45. Ibid., 16. That's why it's not right to say, at someone's death, "she has gone to a better place." God is not a place; God is personal, relational. In death we come to the God who, in Jesus Christ, from all eternity elected to come to us.

46. *CD* II/2, 670.

47. Ibid., 500. "God claims this [person] and makes [this person] willing and ready for His service" (*CD* IV, 503).

48. The presence of Christ as agent in preaching has been masterfully explored by James F. Kay in his *Preaching and Theology* (St. Louis: Chalice Press, 2007).

49. Barth speaks of the worldly, evil "regime of balance" whereby we attempt "to comfort and justify and safe-guard" ourselves from God (*Christian Life Church Dogmatics*, IV/4; *Lecture Fragments*, trans. Geoffrey W. Bromiley [Grand Rapids: Wm. B. Eerdmans, 1981], 197).

50. *CD* II/1, 286.

51. *CD* II/2, 458–506. See Paul McGlasson's study of Barthian exegesis related to Judas in his book *Jesus and Judas: Biblical Exegesis in Barth* (Scholars Press, 1991).

52. *CD* II/2, 458.

53. Ibid., 459.

54. Ibid., 460.

55. Ibid., 463.

56. Ibid., 471.

57. Ibid., 472.

58. Ibid., 477.

59. Ibid., 321.

60. Ibid., 411.

61. Ibid., 414.

62. Ibid., 479.

63. Ibid., 502.

64. Ibid., 480–504 contains Barth's discussion of "handing-over" (*paradunai*). This is a wonderful performance of Barth's narratively based theology in which the movement of the story itself is essential to the theological claim. As he ends his excursus on Judas, Barth takes a swipe at Carl Daub's book, which "could make no more of Judas than repeatedly to condemn and decry him as a 'sinner without equal,'" which for Barth shows "the blindness and impotence of German Idealism to the central truth of the New Testament."

65. Ibid., 305. Ubiquitous mercy as the thematic unity of both testaments surely is why most of Barth's detailed exegesis in *CD* II/2 is of passages from the Old Testament.
66. Ibid., 208.
67. Ibid., 209.
68. Ibid., 641.
69. Ibid., 504.
70. Ibid., 505.
71. Ibid., 28. "Grace is the Nevertheless of the divine love to the creature. The election consists in this Nevertheless. . . . Against our No [God] places [God's] own Nevertheless."
72. Preached September 18, 2011, Duke University Chapel.
73. Thomas Keneally, *Schindler's Ark* (London: Hodder & Stoughton, 2009).
74. Quoted in *The Writer's Almanac*, October 7, 2014, http://writersalmanac.publicradio .org/index.php?date=2014/10/07.
75. James Joyce, "Grace," in *Dubliners* (Viking, 1958), 173–74.
76. *CD* II/2, 509.
77. Ibid., 535.
78. Ibid., 510.
79. Ibid., 25.
80. Ibid., 145.
81. Ibid., 518.
82. Ibid., 510.
83. Ibid., 512.
84. Ibid., 30.
85. Ibid., 32.
86. Genesis 9 certainly implies that, although Israel is in a special covenant with God, all creatures have been elected to be in covenant.
87. *CD* II/2, 172.
88. Ibid., 176. "God pledges and commits . . . to be the God of [humanity]" (177).
89. Ibid.
90. Colin E. Gunton, *The Barth Lectures*, ed. P. H. Brazier (London: T & T Clark, 2007), 118.
91. Jonathan Franzen, *Freedom* (New York: Farrar, Straus, and Giroux, 2010).
92. *CD* IV/1, 499.
93. Ibid., 465.
94. *CD* II/2, 162.
95. *CD* IV/1, 89–90.
96. *CD* III/3, 105.
97. CD IV/4, 29.
98. *CD* IV/1, 499.
99. Kelsey, *Eccentric Existence*, 309.
100. *CD* II/2, 315.

Chapter 3: The Vocation of the Elect

1. Charles Taylor, *The Sources of the Self* (Cambridge, MA: Harvard University Press, 2007), 29–30.
2. Marilynne Robinson, *Lila* (New York: Farrar, Straus & Giroux, 2014).

3. *CD* II/2, 182. Deism is predictable when God is accused of making a primal, static "decree" that predestines some for salvation, some for damnation, and then retires offstage into obscurity.

4. *CD* III/4, 663. The perils and pitfalls of laying an abstract, metaphysical system (in this case, Process Theology) over a Christological reading of the doctrine of election are demonstrated by Donna Bowman, *The Divine Decision: A Process Doctrine of Election* (Louisville, KY: Westminster John Knox Press, 2002).

5. *CD* II/2, 410.

6. Ibid.,16.

7. Kelsey, *Eccentric Existence*, vol. 2, 953.

8. See Stanley M. Hauerwas and William H. Willimon, *Holy Spirit* (Nashville: Abingdon Press, 2015).

9. Eugene Peterson, *The Pastor* (New York: HarperCollins, 2011).

10. "Heidelberg Catechism," http://www.heidelberg-catechism.com/en/lords-days/1.html #sthash.EMkBoBFO.dpuf.

11. Rainer Maria Rilke, *Letters to a Young Poet*, trans. Charlie Louth (New York: Penguin Books, 2013).

12. We can learn from nontheological anthropologies such as psychology, sociology, or gender studies, but their insights are limited to descriptions of human phenomena (or "symptoms" as Barth delightfully calls the insights of the social sciences), not to the core our humanity.

13. For Barth's later reflections on "God is God" see his *The Humanity of God* (Richmond: John Knox Press, 1963), 42–43.

14. *CD* II/2, 106.

15. Ibid., 53.

16. Ibid., 196–97. I'm not sure what Barth means by the church "forfeiting" election.

17. Ibid., 419–23.

18. Ibid., 414.

19. Thus John Webster characterizes Barth's doctrine of election as "not fate but form . . . election is to that form of human life which Jesus Christ himself establishes" (John Webster, ed., *The Cambridge Companion to Karl Barth* [Cambridge: Cambridge University Press, 2000], 91–92).

20. *CD* II/2, 183.

Chapter 4: Called for Mission

1. Bernard of Clairvaux initiated the Second Crusade by preaching from a hill not thirty yards from this door in 1146, a reminder of the ambiguity of the church's participation in the *missio Dei*.

2. Lesslie Newbigin, *The Open Secret: Sketches for a Missionary Theology* (Grand Rapids: Wm. B. Eerdmans, 1995).

3. Hunsberger calls Newbigin's version of the doctrine of election a "unique perspective" of decisive missionary significance for the church (George R Hunsberger, *Bearing the Witness of the Spirit: Lesslie Newbigin's Theology of Cultural Plurality* [Grand Rapids: Wm. B. Eerdmans, 1998], ch. 3). I am indebted to Hunsberger for my interpretation of Newbigin on election.

4. Hunsberger, *Bearing the Witness of the Spirit*, 84.

5. For election as vocation, see *CD* 11/2, 343, 410, 414, 449.

6. *CD* II/2, 13.
7. Barth has been criticized for allowing his Christocentrism to slip into "Christomonism." While Barth cites Abraham as a significant first move in the history of election, Newbigin's even stronger Abrahamic emphasis wonderfully grounds election in God's covenant with Israel.
8. James Gustafson says that the notion of election is incompatible with both modern science and theism in its assertion that God would choose one species over any other. Rosemary Radford Ruether says that Christianity's use of election to denigrate Judaism as particularistic and exclusivistic and to elevate itself as a universalistic religion is imperialistic. For Judith Plaskow, election is inherently hierarchical and sexist with its "stubborn implication of privilege" and encourages passivity in women. Mary Potter Engel says, "All talk of election must be approached with suspicion." See her short survey of the alleged dangers in election in Mary Potter Engel, "Election," in Donald W. Musser and Joseph L. Price, eds., *New and Enlarged Handbook of Christian Theology* (Nashville: Abingdon Press, 2003), 153–55.
9. Bryan Stone, *Evangelism after Christendom: The Theology and Practice of Christian Witness* (Grand Rapids: Brazos Press, 2007), 66. Christopher J. H. Wright makes election the grand narrative that runs through all of Scripture, the very foundation for mission in his *The Mission of God: Unlocking the Bible's Grand Narrative* (Downers Grove, IL: InterVarsity Press, 2006), 262–64.
10. Lesslie Newbigin, *Christian Witness in a Plural Society* (London: British Council of Churches, 1977).
11. Quoted in Hunsberger, *Bearing the Witness of the Spirit*, 106.
12. I doubt that Barth would support such a high view of the church and its necessity for God's saving intent. Is Barth's hesitancy to ascribe to the church so active a role in mission the reason for Barth's relative lack of attention to mission in his *CD*?
13. Quoted by Hunsberger, *Bearing the Witness of the Spirit*, 93.
14. In his article "The Good Samaritan as Metaphor," Robert Funk says that the parable of the Good Samaritan is not a moral lesson in behavior but a metaphor for the odd manner in which we receive deliverance. It is not a story about those to whom I ought to offer help but rather a story that asks, "From whom am I willing to receive help?" *Semeia* 2 (1974): 77–81. It's the same question that ought to be asked by listeners to a sermon.
15. Quoted in Hunsinger, *Bearing the Witness of the Spirit*, 13.
16. See Seock-Tae Sohn, *The Divine Election of Israel* (Grand Rapids: Wm. B. Eerdmans, 1991).
17. Dean G. Stroud, *Preaching in Hitler's Shadow: Sermons of Resistance in the Third Reich*, trans. Dean G. Stroud (Grand Rapids: Wm. B. Eerdmans, 2013), 67, 72. Dean Stroud, in his annotations to his translation of this sermon, notes that Barth's play on the German *nehmen* ("take") as in his use of *aufnehmen, annehmen, mitnehmen, hinnehmen*, highlights our essentially passive reception of God's electing grace. We are "to receive one another," "to see each other as Christ sees us."
18. Newbigin, *Open Secret*, 26.
19. Ibid., 73–74. Modernity attempts to include (i.e., subsume) the particular within the universal whereas Scripture portrays universality achieved through divine use of the particular.
20. Ibid., 14. Newbigin noted this now-hackneyed universalist objection long before Dawkins, Hitchens, Eck, and Hick.

21. Hunsberger, *Bearing the Witness of the Spirit*, 98.
22. Joseph M. Webb, "A Revolution in Christian Preaching: From the 'Old Testament' to the 'Hebrew Bible,'" *Quarterly Review* 20 (2000): 256–57. See the critique of Webb's essay by Amy-Jill Levine: "[T]erms like Hebrew Bible and Jewish Scriptures serve ultimately either to erase Judaism (since 'Jews' are not 'Hebrews' and the synagogue reads not the 'Hebrew Bible' but the Tanakh . . .) or to deny Christians part of their own canon. . . . The so-called 'neutral' term is actually one of Protestant hegemony" (A.-J. Levine, "Jewish-Christian Relations from the 'Other Side,'" *Quarterly Review* 20 [2000]: 298).
23. In numerous sermons, Martin Luther King Jr. spoke of the black church's messianic assignment, "To save the soul of the nation." King, "I See the Promised Land," *A Testament of Hope: The Essential Writings and Speeches of Martin Luther King, Jr.*, ed. James M. Washington (New York: HarperSanFrancisco, 1986).
24. Newbigin, *Open Secret*, 79.
25. Ibid.
26. In Margaret Atwood's dystopian novel *The Handmaid's Tale* (1985), American fundamentalists create a theocracy because America is "chosen" and the rest of the world "reprobate." Does the lie of American exceptionalism account for Barth's fascination with the bloody American Civil War?
27. Quoted in Hunsberger, *Bearing the Witness of the Spirit*, 87 (italics mine).
28. Quoted in ibid.
29. Quoted in ibid., 153.
30. Karl Barth, *CD* IV/3, second half: *The Doctrine of Reconciliation*, (Edinburgh: T. & T. Clark), 573.
31. Ibid., 575.
32. Lesslie Newbigin, *The Open Secret: Sketches for a Missionary Theology* (Grand Rapids: Wm. B. Eerdmans, 1995), 197.
33. *CD* II/1, 482
34. *CD* IV/1, 50–51.
35. Newbigin, *The Open Secret*, 23.
36. Barth, *The Christian Life*, 150.
37. Newbigin, *The Open Secret*, 197.
38. Karl Barth, *Ethics* (Grand Rapids: Wm. B. Eerdmans, 1981), 121.
39. Ibid., 210. I love that Barth consistently viewed what we call "history" as "myth" and what we relegate to "myth" (the witness of Scripture) is true "history."
40. Ibid., 196.
41. Emily Dickinson, *The Letters of Emily Dickinson*, ed. Thomas H. Johnson and Theodora Ward (Cambridge, MA: Belknap-Harvard University Press, 1958), quoted in Magdalena Zapedowska, "Wrestling with Silence: Emily Dickinson's Calvinist God," *American Transcendental Quarterly* 20, no. 1 (2006): 379-98.
42. *CD* IV/ 4, 184.
43. Douglas A. Campbell, *The Deliverance of God: An Apocalyptic Rereading of Justification in Paul* (Grand Rapids: Wm. B. Eerdmans, 2009), 67.
44. Barth begins his explication of Christian ethics in *CD* IV/4 with an examination of the Lord's Prayer. "Our task in Christian ethics is an attempt to portray Christian life under the command of God. . . . God's free act is in [God's] turn to [humanity], that is, baptism with the Holy Spirit, which can only be God's work; and [humanity's] free

act at the beginning is turning to God, that is, baptism with water as the work in which [humanity] begins to respond to the work and word of God" (*The Christian Life*, 49).

45. *CD* I/1, xi.

46. I counted fifty-six occurrences of *control* (*die Beherrschung*) in *CD* II/2. Barth's use of the word increases in volume III and explodes in *CD* IV. Barth's uses *control* in a positive sense when applied to God's providence, almost always using the word negatively when speaking of human attempts to control.

47. Comedian Johnny Carson, in an interview toward the end of his life, said that he went into comedy because he was painfully shy. "On stage, when you are performing, you are in control. When you are not on stage, you are out of control in conversation and encounters with others. I went on stage to gain some control over my life" ("Johnny Carson: American Masters," PBS, May 23, 2014).

48. Daniel Goleman, *Focus: The Hidden Driver of Excellence* (New York: HarperCollins, 2013).

49. Iris Murdoch, *Metaphysics as a Guide to Morals* (New York: Penguin, 1991).

50. I've been aided by Reiner Stach and Shelley Frisch, *Kafka: The Decisive Years* (Princeton: Princeton University Press, 2013).

51. Gilles Deleuze, *Postscript on the Societies of Control* 59 (Winter, 1992), http://links.jstor.org /sici?sici=0162-2870%28199224%2959%3C3%3APOTSOC%3E2.0.CO%3B2-T.

52. Alice Goffman, *On the Run: Fugitive Life in an American City*, Fieldwork Encounters and Discoveries (Chicago: The University of Chicago Press, 2014), xi, 2.

53. Marcus Aurelius, "The Meditations," trans. George Long, http://classics.mit.edu /Antoninus/meditations.html, ch. 17.

54. St. Augustine, *Confessions*, Book II

55. Charles Whitney, *Francis Bacon and Modernity* (New Haven, CN: Yale University Press, 1986) quite successfully presents the modern world as the result of the Baconian revolution seeking control.

56. One last attempt to say a good word for the Enlightenment is Anthony Pagden, *The Enlightenment: And Why It Still Matters* (New York: Random House, 2014). Padgen praises the Enlightenment as producing today's "broadly secular, experimental, individualistic, and progressive intellectual world" and the rejection of religion as a reliable source of information about either humanity or nature.

57. *CD* II/2, 306. Barth locates the beginning of the problem of individualism in Augustine's preoccupation with the question of why some hear the word of God and believe and others don't. Barth would have preferred that Augustine remained focused on the wonder of God's speaking rather than on the mystery of human disbelief. In ways Augustine could never have anticipated, Barth says the *Confessions*, "paved the way for Pietism and Rationalism" and even the perversions of "secular individualism" (308).

58. Taylor, *A Secular Age*, 30–35.

59. Ibid., 36.

60. Ibid., 38–39.

61. James K. A. Smith, *How (Not) to Be Secular*, 31. I am indebted to Smith's lucid reading of Taylor.

62. *Oration* 6.1 found in NPNF vol. II.7 (Nicene and Post-Nicene Fathers, ed. Philip Schaff, [Peabody, MA: Hendrickson Publishers, 1994]) and on a number of websites.

63. Ibid., 12.1.

64. John Wesley, "A Covenant Prayer," in *The United Methodist Hymnal* (Nashville: United Methodist Publishing House), #607.

65. *CD* I/1, 40, 41.

66. This is the Barthian ecclesiology that Reinhard Hütter says reduces the church to "ceaseless critical oscillation," in which the church is "unstable," fragile "moment by moment." Barth would say that Hütter's assessment is just right as a valid, dynamic definition of the church and would probably reject as stolid, Hütter's counter definition of the church as a "way of life, i.e., a distinct set of practices interwoven with normative beliefs, concretely and distinctly embodied." Hütter's critique of Barth's ecclesiology is critiqued by Keith L. Johnson, "The Being and Act of the Church: Barth and the Future of Evangelical Ecclesiology," *Karl Barth and American Evangelicalism*, ed. Bruce L. McCormack and Clifford B. Anderson (Grand Rapids: Wm. B. Eerdmans, 2011), 201–226. I wonder how critics of Barth's ecclesiology would respond to Kimlyn Bender's *Karl Barth's Christological Ecclesiology* (Eugene, OR: Cascade, 2013). Bender portrays Barth's view of the church (building mostly on *CD* IV/2) as the principal way that, "Jesus lives in this His earthly historical form of existence, in the community as the form of His body" (150). As I write this, Pope Francis has made news by charging that the curia has "ecclesiastical Alzheimer's."

67. *CD* IV/2, 696. George Hunsinger says that church, in Barth's thought, "presents not a quandary to be solved, but a miracle to be respected and a mystery to be revered." George Hunsinger, *How to Read Karl Barth: The Shape of His Theology* (New York: Oxford University Press, 1991), 185.

68. The great contemporary Catholic theologian, Hans Urs von Balthasar, in 1951 wrote a fine interpretation of Barth (*The Theology of Karl Barth*) that is still too sedate adequately to present Barth. See also D. Stephen Long, *Saving Karl Barth: Hans Urs von Balthasar's Preoccupation* (Minneapolis: Fortress Press, 2014).

69. I agree with Nicholas Healy that much ecclesiology fails to think rightly about the "living, rather messy, confused and confusing body that the church actually is." *Church, World, and the Christian Life: Practical-Prophetic Ecclesiology* (Cambridge: Cambridge University Press, 2000), 3.

70. Barth, *The Christian Life*, 190.

71. Johannes Weiss, *Jesus' Proclamation of the Kingdom of God*, trans. and ed. Richard Hyde Hiers and David Larrimore Holland (London: SCM Press, 1971).

72. Albert Schweitzer, *The Quest for the Historical Jesus: A Critical Study of Its Progress from Reimarus to Wrede* (London: A&C Black, 1911).

73. See the introduction in William H. Willimon, *The Early Preaching of Karl Barth: Fourteen Sermons with Commentary* (Louisville, KY: Westminster John Knox Press, 2009).

74. Søren Kierkegaard, *The Journals of Kierkegaard*, trans. Alexander Dru (New York: Harper & Row, 1958), 164.

75. Stanley Hauerwas, *Without Apology: Sermons for Christ's Church* (New York: Seabury Books, 2013).

76. C. Kavin Rowe begins his book *World Upside Down: Reading Acts in the Graeco-Roman Age* (Oxford: Oxford University Press, 2009) with reference to Barth's work on election (181n1). Rowe shows the deep destabilization of Roman Imperial order that was occasioned by the Acts declaration that God was in Christ reconciling the world to Himself.

77. Karl Barth, *Evangelical Theology: An Introduction*, trans. Grover Foley (Grand Rapids: Wm. B. Eerdmans, 1963), 134.
78. Fyodor Dostoyevsky, *The Brothers Karamazov*, trans. Andrew H. MacAndrew (Toronto: Bantam, 1981), 299.
79. Barth, *Homiletics*, trans. Geoffrey W. Bromiley and Donald E. Daniels (Louisville, KY: Westminster John Knox Press, 1991), 49.
80. *CD* IV/1, 227.
81. Barth, *Homiletics*, 78.
82. Ibid.
83. *CD* I/2, 530. Barth dismissed any attempt to freeze "the relation between Scripture and revelation" (*CD* I/1, 124). I have some sympathy with evangelical critics of Barth who charge that, in his insistence on the eventful quality of revelation, in his determination to keep God's voice free, Barth offers a rather fuzzy doctrine of scriptural inspiration. Has Barth unintentionally demeaned the authority of Scripture as God's speaking? Still, when one hears some evangelical scholars speak of the authority of Scripture, one hears a tendency towards ossification. See Nicholas Wolterstorff, *Divine Discourse: Philosophical Reflections on the Claim That God Speaks* (Cambridge: Cambridge University Press, 1995) for an astute discussion of Barth and the problem of scriptural authority.
84. Barth, *Homiletics*, 128.
85. Stanley M. Hauerwas, *The Peaceable Kingdom* (Notre Dame, IN: University of Notre Dame Press, 1983), 146.
86. Quoted by Rowe, *World Upside Down*, 101.
87. *CD* I/2, 299.
88. Rowe, *World Upside Down*, 258.
89. *CD* 2/2, 346.
90. David Bentley Hart, *Atheist Delusions: The Christian Revolution and Its Fashionable Enemies* (New Haven: Yale University Press, 2009), 167.
91. *CD* II/2, 302.
92. Rom. 1:25; *CD* I/2, 307.
93. Ibid., 303.
94. Karl Barth, *How I Changed My Mind*, ed. John D. Godsey (Edinburgh: St. Andrews Press, 1969), 37. Christians are not free to conduct a critique of "religion" as if we were not its perpetrators. As noted, we are all too willing to present Christianity as another harmless technique that is good for you.
95. *CD* I/1, 289.
96. Barth, *The Epistle to the Romans*, 389.
97. *CD* I/1, 309.
98. Karen Armstrong in "Speaking of Faith" interview on National Public Radio, November 5, 2009. She now calls her religious posture (quite appropriately) "freelance monotheism." See Karen Armstrong, *The Case for God* (New York: Knopf, 2009).
99. In response to a debate in *The Christian Century* concerning a theological distinction within Christianity, the Reverend Patricia A. Conley cited Marcus Borg's *The Heart of Christianity: Rediscovering a Life of Faith* as providing an end to religious debate because beliefs, after all, don't matter: "Clearly predominant for Borg is the understanding of Christianity as a tradition of practice not predicated on right belief. Throughout the book he presents Christianity as a path, a way of life" (*The Christian Century*, May 5, 2009, 29).

100. See Sermon 16, "The Means of Grace," §V.4, *Works*, 1:396.
101. See Wesley's letter to Count Zinzendorf and the Church at Herrnhut (5–8 Aug. 1740), *Works*, 26:27; and Sermon 16. The three great minds of the sixteenth century were Calvin, Luther, and Ignatius of Loyola. Wesley drew from all but was perhaps most significantly formed by Ignatius and his disciplines.
102. Eberhard Busch, *Barth* (Nashville: Abingdon Press, 2008), 20.
103. Barth, *The Epistle to the Romans*, 533.
104. In making the church the center of Christian ethics, Sam Wells risks displacement of Christ. Samuel Wells, *God's Companions: Reimagining Christian Ethics* (Maiden, MA: Blackwell, 2006).
105. *The Journals and Papers of Soren Kierkegaard*, ed. and trans. Howard V. Hong and Edna H. Hong (Princeton: Princeton University Press, 1967–1978), 3:120, 121, 179.
106. *Philosophical Fragments*, ed. and trans. Howard V. Hong and Edna H. Hong (Princeton: Princeton University Press, 1985), 109.
107. "The greatest obstacle, thinks Kierkegaard, to becoming a Christian in the present age is the illusion that the presuppositions of modern thought are a good place to start" (Murray A. Rae, *Kierkegaard's Vision of the Incarnation: By Faith Transformed* [Clarendon Press: Oxford, 1997]). Professor Rae's work has been instrumental in my thought about Kierkegaard. While I was giving lectures in New Zealand, Professor Rae gave me the idea for this book.
108. *Provocations: Spiritual Writings of Kierkegaard* (Farmington, PA: The Plough Publishing House, 1999), 396–97.
109. Kierkegaard demands not only that we understand his thought but also that we enter into the existential situation which he commends. Truth, Christian truth, must be personal. See Paul Holmer, "On Understanding Kierkegaard," in Howard A. Johnson and Niels Thulstrup, eds., *A Kierkegaard Critique* (New York: Harper, 1962), 40–53.
110. Karl Barth, *The Humanity of God* (Richmond: John Knox Press, 1960).
111. *CD* I/1, 92–93.
112. Ibid., 176.
113. *Göttingen Dogmatics: Instruction in the Christian Religion*, ed. Hannelotte Reiffen, trans. Geoffrey W. Bromiley (Wm. B. Eerdmans, 1990), 1:135.
114. "The relation to God on our side must always be a wrestling like Jacob's [Gen. 32:35] in which constantly is sought only in God and not in us." *Göttingen Dogmatics*, 189.
115. *CD*, IV/2, 23.
116. *CD*, IV/3, 118.
117. Murray A. Rae, *Kierkegaard's Vision of the Incarnation: By Faith Transformed* (Oxford: Clarendon Press, 1997), 178.
118. *CD* II/1, 141.
119. Note that when we say the Creed, we affirm the church as subsequent to, and a product of, the Holy Spirit—"I believe in the Holy Spirit, the Holy Catholic Church. . . ." See Hauerwas and Willimon, *The Holy Spirit*, 32–40.
120. April 6, 2014, Fifth Sunday in Lent, Duke University Chapel.

Chapter 5: The Witness of Preaching

1. *CD* IV/3, 629.
2. Quoted by Barth in *CD* I/1, 122–23.

3. Luther spoke of God's word as a "moving shower" that comes and goes. There is no "receiving, grasping, and seizing" this word because it is the work of the Holy Spirit. "God's Word goes forth and is heard where and how he himself wills. We hear the blowing of the wind, but who knows whence it comes or whether it goes." Quoted by Barth in *The Christian Life*, 28.

4. In his history of early Christian thought, Robert Wilken says, "the Word of God makes its way not by argument but as men and women bear witness to what has happened" (Robert Wilken, *The Spirit of Early Christian Thought: Seeking the Face of God* [New Haven: Yale University Press, 2003]), 6.

5. Michael Wyschogrod says that in answering, "Why did God elect?" "We must avoid an answer that does too much" (Wyschogrod, *Body of Faith* [Seabury Press: New York: 1983], 58). Wyschogrod is a Jewish theologian who has been influenced by Barth, seeing election as essential for the preservation of Israel. Whereas for Christians the Incarnation is the supreme instance of God's earthly activity, for Jews, it's election. Wyschogrod says, "The election of the people of Israel as the people of God constitutes the sanctification of a natural family. God could have chosen a spiritual criterion: the election of all those who have faith or who obey God's commandments. The liberal mind would find such an election far more congenial. But God did not choose this path. . . . The election of Israel is therefore a corporeal election . . . a Jew remains in the service of God no matter what he believes or does . . . a truth that was well understood by those enemies of God who knew that they had to murder the Jewish body along with the teachings of Israel" (xv).

6. David Novak, *The Election of Israel: The Idea of the Chosen People* (Cambridge: Cambridge University Press, 1995), 10. Novak has powerfully demonstrated the necessity of construing Israel's election as a *theological* reality.

7. Ibid., 23.

8. Ibid.

9. Ibid., 78.

10. Ibid., 44. Later, the Nazis cited Jewish claims to be "elect" as a source of their hatred of Jews and spoke about the need for a new and revised theology of election that made the German *Volk* the chosen of God.

11. Some have even argued that the Jewish idea of election led to genocidal actions by Israel in the conquest of non-Israelites. Gerd Lüdemann in *The Unholy in Holy Scripture: The Dark Side of the Bible*, trans. John Bowden (Louisville, KY: Westminster John Knox Press, 1977), 77. Joel S. Kaminsky ("Did Election Imply the Mistreatment of Non-Israelites?" *Harvard Theological Review* [April, 2003]: 397–425) counters that Lüdemann seems unaware that Israel's election "presupposes three categories, rather than two: the elect, the anti-elect, and the non-elect." Israel viewed the non-elect as "fully part of the divine economy, and, in a very real sense, Israel was to work out her destiny in relation to them" (399). There is little biblical or Midrash evidence of Jewish contempt for the non-elect (413). Kaminsky argues that the "most unusual idea" of the election of Israel has a complex theological basis in the Hebrew Scriptures. Israel is elected "for some type of service" in "a large divine plan or purpose" because "the Lord loved you" (Deut. 7:7–8). Kaminsky cites Wyschogrod as praising the notion of Israel's election as guaranteeing "the fatherhood of God toward all peoples, elect and nonelect, Jew and gentile" (Kaminsky, "Did Election Imply Mistreatment?" 425).

Roland Bainton, in *Christian Attitudes towards War and Peace: A Historical Survey and Critical Re-Evaluation* (New York: Abingdon, 1960), relates the history of Christians (such as Henry Bullinger and Cotton Mather), appropriating the Old Testament texts on the conquest of the Amalekites and Canaanites to urge violence against "papists" and Native Americans (165–72).

12. Regina Schwartz, *The Curse of Cain: The Violent Legacy of Monotheism* (Chicago: University of Chicago Press, 1997), charges that the conceit of election is a major source of religious violence.

13. Franz Rosenzweig, *The Star of Redemption*, trans. Barbara E. Galli (Madison, WI: The University of Wisconsin Press, 2005).

14. Ibid., 83.

15. *CD* II/2, 195.

16. Sadly, European Christian laws against Jewish proselyting in the past contributed to the attitude among many Jews that Israel is not a missionary community.

17. Novak, *The Election of Israel*, 160.

18. Ibid., 162. One of the most beautiful contemporary portrayals of the continuing power of election for Jews is Chaim Potok's novel *The Chosen*.

19. Kaminsky, "Did Election Imply Mistreatment?" 425.

20. *CD* IV/3–2, 877.

21. Ibid.

22. Ibid., 878. Barth had less affirming things to say about Jews, Israel, and the synagogue, some of them deeply troubling. The picture is complex. The place to start wrestling with Barth and his perspective on the Jews is with his view of election. See Rein Bos, *We Have Heard That God Is with You: Preaching the Old Testament* (Grand Rapids: Wm. B. Eerdmans, 2008), 73–94, for a judicious discussion of Barth and Israel.

23. Barth, *The Christian Life*, 95.

24. Looking back, I now see how deeply influential the idea of the church as the elect was upon Hauerwas and my *Resident Aliens: Life in the Christian Colony*, exp. ed. (Nashville: Abingdon Press, 2014).

25. Kavin Rowe, *World Upside Down: Reading Acts in the Greco-Roman Age* (New York: Oxford University Press, 2009), 121.

26. Ibid., 122.

27. Douglas Campbell's rescue of Paul's reputation in *The Deliverance of God* helps bring Barth's doctrine of election into focus. I had read Krister Stendahl's, "Paul and the Introspective Conscience of the West" when I was in seminary. The allegedly "Lutheran" reading of Paul (unfair to Luther and many Lutherans) with its misconstrual of Paul as an advocate of a certain kind of justification was unfair to Paul. The conventional justification-by-faith interpretation of Paul's gospel in which "faith" rescues us from Jewish "legalism" sets Christianity against Judaism as a faith plagued by moralistic deficiencies. Campbell sees Paul moving from Christ's appearance to him, back to his beloved Judaism, on toward a sweeping eschatological affirmation of the justification of God to humanity in which God has taken the initiative and set things right, not only for Israel, but for all.

28. James Davison Hunter, *To Change the World: The Irony, Tragedy, and Possibility of Christianity in the Late Modern World* (Oxford: Oxford University Press, 2010).

29. Stanley Hauerwas, *Without Apology: Sermons for Christ's Church* (New York: Seabury Books, 2013), 89–90.

30. Quoted in Kelsey, *Eccentric Existence*, 333.
31. Barth, *The Christian Life*, 96.
32. Speaking at his retirement banquet, Barth said that Christ has already won the war. As for his contribution, he was no more than a passenger on the baggage cart, at a safe distance following the army after the victorious battle.
33. *CD* II/2, 196–97.
34. Ibid., 415.
35. Ibid., 417.
36. *CD* I/1, 188.
37. *CD* II/2, 320.
38. Ibid., 324–25.
39. Ibid., 349.
40. Barth, *The Christian Life*, 105.
41. *CD* II/2, 206.
42. *CD* III/3, 226.
43. Ibid., 225.
44. Richard Lischer, "Why I Am Not Persuasive," *Homiletic* 24, no. 2 (Winter 1999): 13–16.
45. Hauerwas, *With the Grain of the Universe*, 146.
46. Stanley Hauerwas, *Disrupting Time: Sermons, Prayers, and Sundries* (Salem, OR: Cascade Books, 2004), 228–32.

Chapter 6: Preaching as Public Truth

1. Kavin Rowe shows how Christian practices "must inevitably appear strange" to the Graeco-Roman world because the Romans had "no preexistent category or tradition of inquiry within which the phenomenon of Christian mission could be rightly perceived." Festus had no means for thinking about Christian witnesses other than to say that they were "crazy" (i.e., odd) (Rowe, *World Upside Down*, 125).
2. Duke Memorial United Methodist Church, January 19, 2014.
3. Dan Wakefield, *Returning: A Spiritual Journey* (New York: Doubleday,1988).
4. *CD* IV/3, 611.
5. Ibid., 566.
6. Ibid., 576.
7. I work this theme of preaching as repetition in chapter 3 of William H. Willimon, *Undone by Easter* (Nashville: Abingdon Press, 2009).
8. *CD* IV/3, 627, 629.
9. Ibid., 114–15.
10. Ibid., 119.
11. Ibid., 662.
12. Ibid., 615.
13. Ibid., 645.

Chapter 7: Homiletical Implications of Election

1. Karl Barth, "The Need and Promise of Christian Preaching," in *The Word of God and the Word of Man* (New York: Harper Brothers, 1957), 123.
2. An early commentator on Barth's doctrine of election ends his book by saying, if preachers took election seriously, "There will be greater optimism in the pulpit," with

"greater emphasis in what Christ has done for us rather than what we have to do" (William John Hausmann, *Karl Barth's Doctrine of Election* [New York: Philosophical Library, 1969], 87–88).

3. I have in mind Michael Pasquarello, *Christian Preaching: A Trinitarian Theology of Proclamation* (Grand Rapids: Baker Academic, 2006); David J. Lose, *Confessing Jesus Christ: Preaching in a Postmodern World* (Grand Rapids: Wm. B. Eerdmans, 2003); Richard Lischer, *A Theology of Preaching: The Dynamics of the Gospel* (Durham, NC: Labyrinth Press, 1992); Thomas G. Long, *The Witness of Preaching* (Louisville, KY: Westminster John Knox Press, 2005); Mary Catherine Hilkert, *Naming Grace: Preaching and the Sacramental Imagination* (New York: Continuum, 1997); Charles L. Campbell, *Peaching Jesus: New Directions for Homiletics in Hans Frei's Postliberal Theology* (Grand Rapids: Wm. B. Eerdmans, 1997); James F. Kay, *Preaching and Theology* (St. Louis: Chalice Press, 2007); Fleming Rutledge, *And God Spoke to Abraham: Preaching from the Old Testament* (Grand Rapids: Wm. B. Eerdmans, 2011).

4. *CD* IV/3, 2, 877.

5. "God has selected a single people out of all the nations of the world in order to make this people a sign of salvation" (Gerhard Lohfink, *Jesus and Community: The Social Dimension of the Christian Faith*, trans. J. P. Galvin [Philadelphia: Fortress Press, 1984], 28).

6. I find it revealing that the word *salvation*, used infrequently in Acts, is used in this verse precisely at the point when the church is amazed by the scope of God's elective intent.

7. Campbell, *The Deliverance of God*, 71.

8. Mark Galli, *Karl Barth: An Introductory Biography for Evangelicals* (Grand Rapids: Wm. B. Eerdmans, forthcoming). "If Evangelicalism requires that somebody *must*—of *necessity*, either due to eternal divine decree or divine righteousness in the face of sinful creaturely agency—suffer eternal damnation, then Barth will never be evangelical enough for evangelicals. And, of course, he will be extremely reassured and gratified by his exclusion from those ranks. If, however, Evangelicalism is indeed about good news . . . neither Reformed Orthodoxy nor Arminian or Pietist traditions are evangelical enough" (Chris Boesel, "Better News Hath No Evangelical than This," in Christian T. Collins Winn and John L. Drury, eds., *Karl Barth and the Future of Evangelical Theology* [Eugene, OR: Cascade Books, 2014], 189). Stephen N. Williams adds little to evangelical theology's criticism of Barth as perpetrator of dreaded "universalism" in his treatment of Barth on election in his *The Election of Grace: A Riddle without a Resolution?* (Grand Rapids: Wm. B. Eerdmans, 2015). Williams continues the evangelical criticism that Barth is "unbiblical." Williams's chief concern seems to be that we cannot speak of election without someone, of necessity, suffering eternal damnation.

9. Thomas G. Long, *Preaching from Memory to Hope* (Louisville, KY: Westminster John Knox Press, 2009); Brian K. Bount, *Invasion of the Dead: Preaching Resurrection* (Louisville, KY: Westminster John Knox Press, 2013); Richard Lischer, *The End of Words: The Language of Reconciliation in a Culture of Violence* (Grand Rapids: Wm. B. Eerdmans, 2005).

10. Stanley M. Hauerwas, *Approaching the End: Eschatological Reflections on Church, Politics, and Life* (Grand Rapids: Wm. B. Eerdmans, 2013).

11. We are privileged to preach in a time when the promise that God will draw all to Zion's mount is being fulfilled in the drawing in of that "multitude that no one can number" (Rev. 7:9), in the astounding, unprecedented spread of Christianity in the South and the East.

12. Michael Bush, ed., "Matthias Barth," in *This Incomplete One: Words Occasioned by the Death of a Young Person* (Grand Rapids: Wm. B. Eerdmans, 2006) 17–20.
13. William Butler Yeats, "The Second Coming," in *The Collected Poems of W. B. Yeats* (New York: Macmillan, 1951), 184–85.
14. *CD* II/2, 417; IV/3, 478.
15. *CD* II/2, 422.
16. Ibid., 457.
17. Ibid., 320. An evangelical commentator says that "Barth's doctrine of election serves powerfully to encourage a potent proclamation of the gospel, focusing on the gracious initiative of God exemplified in the objective atoning death of Jesus Christ for all humanity. The Church can, indeed must, press the message of the universality of God's love and call without hesitance or reservation: all are chosen and have been claimed without exception for God's Kingdom, and are thereby called to yield themselves with unreserved dependence upon God in grateful response for his grace" (Michael O'Neil, "Karl Barth's Doctrine of Election," *Evangelical Quarterly* 76, no. 4 [2004]: 311–26).
18. "Within theological thinking generally unconditional priority must be given to thinking which is attentive to the existence of the living person of Jesus Christ" (*CD* IV/3, 175).
19. "We may believe that God can and must only be absolute in contrast to all that is relative, exalted in contrast to all that is lowly, active in contrast to all suffering, inviolable in contrast to all temptation, transcendent in contrast to all immanence. . . . But such beliefs are shown to be quite untenable, and corrupt and pagan by the fact that God does in fact be and do this in Jesus Christ" (*CD* IV/1, 186).
20. Lesslie Newbigin, *The Household of God: Lectures on the Nature of the Church* (London: SCM Press, 1953).
21. Barth, *Deliverance to the Captives*, 76–77.
22. *CD* I/1, 299.
23. *CD* IV/3, 623.
24. Ibid., 616.
25. *CD* II/2, 514.
26. Ibid., 520.
27. The oddity of divine election means that preachers "cannot translate the truth and reality of the divine command into a necessary element of [humanity's] spiritual life" (Ibid., 522).
28. Ibid., 521. Barth emphasizes this in his (unfair?) criticism of "Roman Catholic co-ordination of moral philosophy and moral theology" (528–35).
29. Ibid., 641.
30. Barth, *Homiletics*, 80.
31. Barth, *The Epistle to the Romans*, 428–29.
32. Cited by Barth in *CD* II/2, 525.
33. Ibid., 522.
34. Stanley Fish, *Is There a Text in This Class? The Authority of Interpretive Communities* (Harvard: Harvard University Press, 1980).
35. The rabbis taught that when Moses went up Sinai, Yahweh gave him a choice: He could either bear the weight of the mountain or the weight of Torah; Moses chose the heavier burden.

36. Harry G. Frankfurt, *On Bullshit* (Princeton: Princeton University Press, 2005), 64–67.
37. *CD* I/1, 64.
38. Barth says that the truth of the gospel is not dependent on "whether we know and receive it or not. . . . The preaching of the Gospel can only proclaim and show that this is how things stand objectively . . . that our existence as characterized and modified and established by the judgment of God can be lived only in faith" (*CD* II/2, 766).
39. Ibid.
40. Ibid., 780.
41. Ibid., 766.
42. Ibid., 767.
43. Ibid., 781.
44. Søren Kierkegaard, *Philosophical Fragments*, trans. H. V. Hong and E. H. Hong (Princeton: Princeton University Press, 1985), 109.
45. *CD* III/2, 607.
46. Paul Tillich, *Systematic Theology* I (Chicago: University of Chicago Press, 1951), 8. See David Kelsey, *Eccentric Existence*, 112–19.
47. James F. Kay, *Preaching and Theology* (St. Louis: Chalice Press, 2007), 35.
48. Barth, *Göttingen Dogmatics*, 7.
49. Karl Barth, "Church and Culture," in *Theology and Church*, trans. L. P. Smith (London: SCM, 1962), 339.
50. Karl Barth, "*Theologische Existenz heute!*" in *Theologische Existenz heute* vol. 1 (Munich: Chr. Kaiser Verlag, 1933), 4–5.
51. Quoted in Stroud, *Preaching in Hitler's Shadow*, 33.
52. Angela Dienhart Hancock, *Karl Barth's Emergency Homiletic, 1932-1933: A Summons to Prophetic Witness at the Dawn of the Third Reich* (Grand Rapids: Wm. B. Eerdmans, 2013).
53. *CD* I/1, xiv.
54. Andy Crouch, *Culture Making: Recovering Our Creative Calling* (Downers Grove, IL: InterVarsity Press, 2008).
55. *CD* II/1, 190.
56. *CD* II/2, 41.
57. *CD* III/4, 607.
58. *CD* I/1, 181.
59. Ibid., 206.
60. *CD* IV/3,1, 97.
61. *CD* II/1, 227.
62. See George Hunsinger, "Beyond Literalism and Expressivism: Karl Barth's Hermeneutical Realism," in *Disruptive Grace: Studies in the Theology of Karl Barth* (Grand Rapids: Wm. B. Eerdmans, 2000), 210–25.
63. *CD* II/1, 233.
64. Søren Kierkegaard, *Philosophical Fragments*, trans. David Swenson (Princeton: Princeton University Press, 1962), 69.
65. Barth, *Homiletics*, 69.
66. Ibid., 78.
67. Flannery O'Connor, *A Good Man Is Hard to Find: And Other Stories* (New York: Signet Books, The New American Library, 1961), 88-91.

Index of Names

Abraham, 12, 57, 59, 64, 65, 67, 68–69, 108–9
Achtemeier, Betty, 137
Achtemeier, Paul, 137
Adam, 16, 29, 67
Ahlstrom, Sydney A., 22
Allen, Woody, 8
Ames, Reverend, 50
Aquinas, Thomas, 14
Aristotle, 10, 155
Arminius, Jacob, 16–17, 23, 168nn41, 44
Armstrong, Karen, 93, 179n98
Astor, John Jacob, 21
Athanasius, 32, 171n33
Atwood, Margaret, 176n26
Augustine, 14, 32, 34, 35, 79, 167nn33, 35; 172n42, 177n57
Aurelius, Marcus, 79

Bainton, Roland, 181–82n11
Barth, Karl v, ix, x, xi, 9–11, 15, 25–49, 54–55, 60–61, 69, 81, 83–85, 87–89, 91, 94, 96, 105–7, 110, 115, 118, 119, 120–22, 124, 134–37, 141, 143, 144–45, 148–51, 153–54, 159–60, 164nn1 (intro.), 3 (chap. 1); 165nn4, 12; 166nn16, 17, 23; 167nn31, 33, 35, 36; 168nn37, 38, 41, 43, 44, 46; 169nn49, 1 (chap. 2), 4; 170nn6, 10, 16, 19; 171nn29, 34, 36, 38; 172nn49,

64; 173n65, 174nn12, 16, 19; 175nn7, 12, 17; 176nn26, 39, 44; 177nn46, 57; 178nn66, 67, 68, 76; 179n83, 181nn3, 5; 182nn22, 27; 183nn32, 2 (chap. 7); 184n8, 185nn17, 28, 186n38
Barth, Matthias, 144–46
Bender, Kimlyn, 178n66
Bentham, Jeremy, 77
Bernard of Clairvaux, 174n1
Blount, Brian, 142
Boesel, Chris, 184n8
Bonhoeffer, Dietrich, 9, 12, 30, 33, 157, 160
Borg, Marcus, 5, 8, 179n99
Bowman, Donna, 174n4
Bloesch, Donald, 168n46
Brooks, Philips, 134
Brunner, Emil, 26, 33, 171n36
Bullinger, Henry, 182n11
Busch, Eberhard, 9, 166n17, 167n24

Caesar, 3, 147
Calvin, John, 14–17, 23–26, 27, 29–32, 34, 110, 167nn35, 36; 168nn37, 38, 43, 44, 46; 170n16, 172nn41, 42; 180n101
Campbell, Douglas A., 69, 114, 140, 170n12, 182n27
Campbell, Will, 121
Caravaggio, Michelangelo, 1–2

Carson, Johnny, 177n47
Chesterton, G. K., v
Christ, 3, 11, 13, 22, 25–26, 28–31,
    36, 54–56, 65, 97, 105, 114, 117,
    140, 141, 143, 146, 152, 158, 161,
    171, 178n76, 183nn32, 2 (chap. 7);
    185nn17 , 19
Conley, Patricia A., 179n99
Cornelius, 99
Crossan, John Dominic, 8
Cunningham, Mary Kathleen, 171n38

Dante, 27
Daub, Carl, 172n64
David, 11, 58
Dawkins, Richard, 8, 16, 165nn13, 15;
    175n20
Deleuze, Gilles, 76–78
Del Monte, Cardinal Francesco, 1
Descartes, René, 50
De Tocqueville, 77
Dickinson, Emily, 67
Domitian, 89
Dostoyevsky, Fyodor 87, 151
Duns Scotus, 14, 27

Echo, 74
Eck, Diana, 175n20
Ehrman, Bart, 8, 165n8
Elisha, 130
Elizabeth, 124
Engel, Mary Potter, 175n8
Esau, 12
Eusebius, 89
Eve, 29
Ewer, William Norman, v

Festus, 183n1 (chap. 6)
Feuerbach, Ludwig, 54
Fey, Tina, 8
Finney, Charles G., 20–22, 169n50
Fish, Stanley, 152
Foucault, Michel, 76
Francis, Pope 2, 148, 178n66
Frankfurt, Harry G., 152–53
Franzen, Jonathan, 47
Frederick the Great, 61

Freud, Sigmund, 10, 50, 124
Funk, Robert, 175n14

Galli, Mark, 141–44
Goffman, Alice, 78
Goleman, Daniel, 74
Goliath, 11
Grand Inquisitor, 87
Gregory of Nazianzen, 82
Grunewald, Matthias, 105
Gunter, Stephen, 169n51
Gunton, Colin, 47
Gustafson, James, 175n8

Hancock, Angela Dienhart, 156
Hardy, Thomas, 8
Hart, David Bentley, 91–92, 166n15
Hauerwas, Stanley M., 86–89, 91, 100,
    102, 116–17, 121, 122–23, 142, 151,
    164n1 (intro.), 165n7
Healy, Nicholas, 178n69
Heidegger, 50
Helm, Paul, 168n38
Hick, John, 175n20
Hitchens, Christopher, 8, 165–66n15,
    175n20
Hitler, Adolph, 9, 61, 121, 156
Homer, 27
Hunsberger, George R., 59, 174n3 (chap. 4)
Hunsinger, George, 168n37, 170n10,
    171n33, 178n67
Hunter, James Davison, 115
Hütter, Reinhard, 178n66

Isaac, 68

Jacob, 12, 36, 180n114
James, 80
Jenson, Robert, 166n17
Jeremiah, 10, 12, 36, 162
Jesus, 1, 2, 12, 20, 23, 30, 32, 37–38,
    41–43, 48, 58, 69, 74, 81, 86, 99, 108,
    112, 116, 119–20, 123–24, 129–30,
    144, 146, 148–49, 155, 168n37,
    172nn41, 45, 178n66
John, 38
Johnson, Keith L., 178n66

John the Baptizer, 57, 105, 107, 108, 133
Joyce, James, 44–45
Judas Iscariot, 38–41, 139, 166n23, 172nn51, 64
Jüngel, Eberhard, 27, 169n1
Juno, 74

Kafka, Franz, 74–75
Kaminsky, Joel S., 112, 181n11
Kay, James F., 155, 172n48
Keller, Tim, 23–24
Kelsey, David H., 12, 49, 51, 169n4,
Keneally, Thomas, 44
Kierkegaard, Søren, 64, 67, 68, 85–86, 94–95, 97, 143, 154, 159, 180nn107, 109
King, Martin Luther, Jr., 48, 56, 176n23

Lamberigts, Mathijs, 167n34
Lazarus, 101–2
Lenin, 151
Levering, Matthew, 171n40
Levine, Amy-Jill, 176n22
Lewis, C. S., 5
Lischer, Richard, 121, 142
Locke, John, 50
Lohfink, Gerhard, 184n5
Long, Thomas G., 142
Loyola, Ignatius of, 180n101
Lüdemann, Gerd, 181n11
Luke, 129–30
Luther, Martin, 15, 28, 33, 54, 106, 151, 180n101, 181n3, 182n27

MacIntyre, Alasdair, 81, 166n16
Mark 2, 13, 92
Marquis D'Argens, 61
Martensen, Hans, 95
Martha, 101
Marx, Karl, 124
Mary, 101, 131
Mary Grace, 162
Mather, Cotton, 182n11
Matthew 1, 13, 164
Matthias, 40
McCormack, Bruce, 32, 166n17, 170nn6, 10

McGlasson, Paul, 171n51
McKenny, Gerald, 171n29
McSwain, Jeff, 141–42
Meir, Golda, 121
Michelangelo, 2
Milton, John, 16, 29
Moses, 185n35
Murdoch, Iris, 75
Mynster, Bishop, 95

Narcissus, 74
Newbigin, Lesslie, 58, 59, 60, 62–66, 147, 174n3, 175nn7, 20
Niebuhr, Reinhold, 4, 165n7
Nietzsche, Friedrich, 10
Noah, 64
Nouwen, Henri, 131–32
Novak, David, 109–12, 181n6

Obama, Barack, 48
Oden, Thomas C., 168n43
Odysseus, 27
O'Connor, Flannery, 162–63
Olson, Roger, 17, 19, 24
Osteen, Joel, 107, 150

Pagden, Anthony, 177n56
Paul, 12, 13, 52, 53, 58, 69, 90, 93, 111, 113, 114, 119, 120, 140, 143, 158, 161, 182n27
Peter, 38, 97–98, 113
Peterson, Eugene, 53
Piper, John, 17–18
Placher, William Carl, 5
Plaskow, Judith, 175n8
Plato, 106, 124
Potok, Chaim, 182n18
Proust, Marcel, 135
Purdon, Father, 44–45

Rae, Murray A., 180n107
Ratzinger, Joseph, 93
Rayburn, Jim, 141–42
Reagan, Ronald, 65
Rhoda, 116
Rilke, Ranier Maria, 54
Ritschl, Albert, 85

Robinson, Marilynne, 13, 50–51
Rosenzweig, Franz, 110–11
Rosten, Leo, v
Rowe, C. Kavin, 113–14, 178n76, 183
Ruether, Rosemary Radford, 175n8

Sarah, 64
Saul, 11, 12, 40
Schindler, Oskar, 44
Schleiermacher, Friedrich, 4, 69, 150,
    151, 165n5
Schuman, Rebecca, 171–72n41
Schwartz, Regina, 182n12
Schweitzer, Albert, 70, 85
Sharp, Douglas, 166n17
Smith, James K. A., 3, 81, 164n1
Smith, Ted A., 169n50
Spain, Jimmy 70–71
Spinoza, Baruch, 109–10
Spong, John Shelby, 8
Spufford, Francis, 166n16
Stone, Bryan, 59
Stroud, Dean G., 175n17
Suhard, Cardinal Emmanuel Celestin, 118

Taylor, Charles, 3, 28, 50, 81, 165n11,
    168n39, 169n54
Tillich, Paul, 84, 153, 154–55
Tolstoy, 151
Torrance, Thomas F., 171n40
Turpin, Ruby, 162–63

Van Til, Cornelius, 170n19
Virgil, 27
von Balthasar, Hans Urs, 178n68

Wainwright, Geoffrey, 168n43
Wakefield, Dan, 131–32
Walker, Robert T., 171n40
Warren, Rick, 107
Webb, Joseph M., 63–64
Webster, John, 165n10, 174n19
Weiss, Johannes, 85
Wells, Samuel, 180n104
Wesley, Charles, 139
Wesley, John, 4, 15–17, 22, 82–83,
    93, 128, 168n, 43, 46; 169n51,
    180n101
Whitney, Charles, 177n55
Wilken, Robert, 181n4
Williams, Stephen N., 184n8
Willimon, William H. 70–71, 101–2, 119,
    122–23
Wittgenstein, Ludwig, 7
Wright, Christopher J. H., 175n9
Wyschogrod, Michael, 181nn5, 11

Yeats, William Butler, 145
Yoder, John Howard, 167n31

Zachariah, 124

Index of Subjects

analogy, 83–4

anthropology, 18, 25, 50, 155, 169n4

apocalyptic, 52, 146–51

Arminianism/Arminians, 9, 16, 17, 19–20, 22, 54, 141, 168n41, 169n29, 170n6, 184n8

atheism, 3, 7, 16, 165n11

balance, 172n49

baptism, 48, 82, 99, 177n44

call (see vocation)

Calvinism/Calvanist, 9, 15–17, 19–20, 22, 23, 54, 65, 73, 141–42, 169n49, 170n6

Catholicism, 83–6, 93

choice, 2, 12, 22, 34, 36, 50, 55, 58, 66, 97, 112, 169n54

Christology, 11, 22, 36, 69, 106, 108, 151–52, 156, 158, 166n17

church, 12, , 59–60, 62, 151, 157, 159, 175n12, 178nn66, 67, 69; 180nn104, 119; 182n24

conflict, 89–91, 115–16, 146–51

control, ix, 53–54, 73–89, 93–94, 97–99, 101–4, 117, 123, 157, 160, 177 n46

conversion, 40, 90, 153, 156

correlation, 154–55

covenant, 10, 30–32, 34, 40–1, 46–51, 61, 66–67, 69, 82–83, 96, 110–11, 150, 169n49, 173n86, 175n7

Deism, 47, 159, 174n3 (chap. 3)

election (*gnadenwahl*), ix–x, 9, 51, 63–6, 95, 106–9, 114–17, 119–20, 128–30, 137–63, 166n17, 167nn29, 30, 31, 36; 168nn37, 38; 169n4, 170n10, 171nn36, 38; 172n42, 173n71, 174nn4 (chap. 3), 16, 19, 3 (chap. 4); 175nn7, 8, 9; 178n76, 181nn5, 6, 10, 11; 182nn12, 18, 22, 27, 183n2 (chap. 7), 184n8, 185nn17, 27

dangers, 59, 65, 175n8

history, 14–17

modernity, 34–37, 64, 74, 81–82

Scripture, 10–14

Enlightenment, 81, 90, 109–10, 169n49, 177n56

eschatology, 114, 116–17, 142–43

ethics, 46, 176–77n44

eucharist, 39, 51, 56, 158–59

evangelicals, 141–42, 184n8

evil, 74

exegesis, 171nn36, 38; 173n65

explanation, 121–23

faith, 36–37, 86, 96
freedom, 31, 47, 80

God, knowledge of, 3–4, 6–7, 26–28, 30,
   34, 37–39, 54–56, 156–57
grace, 25–27, 37–40, 44–45, 139, 162–63,
   175n17

hearing, 139–41
heaven, 55
holiness, 165n10

idealism, 172n64
Incarnation, 26, 29, 33, 96, 123–27, 158,
   181n5

Jews, v, 9, 60–64, 108–15, 121, 138, 147,
   166–67n23, 176n22, 181nn5, 10;
   182nn16, 18, 22

lectionary, 151, 153
Liberalism, v, 3, 5, 6, 7, 20, 21, 42, 63, 70,
   85, 90, 139, 142, 149

marriage, 13
Methodism/Methodist v, x, 4, 20, 23, 41,
   54, 70–71, 82–84, 88, 104, 118, 119,
   126, 128, 135, 138,
mission, 12, 57–104, 111–13, 147–48,
   154
moralism, 139, 151

narcissism, 74–75
Nazis, 60–61, 77, 91, 156, 164n3
   (chap. 1)
nihilism, 165n12

objectivity, 154

particularity, 63–65, 66
Pietism, 4
practice, 92–96, 179n99, 183n1 (chap. 6)
preachers, 8, 87–88, 137, 147–48, 183–
   84n2 (chap. 7)
preaching, ix–x, 9, 47, 87–88, 106–9, 117,
   120, 128–63

predestination, 11–14, 142, 151, 168n37,
   171nn38, 40
   Arminian, 16–17, 19–20, 22–23, 54
   Augustinian, 14–15
   Calvinism, 14–16, 19, 20–21, 28, 34, 35,
      48, 51, 54, 168n44, 170n16
   Lutheran, 15
   monergism, 15
   Paul, 52
   Pelagianism, 17, 22, 24, 35, 150
   synergism, 16
preparation of sermons, 157–58
prisons, 26, 78, 148–49

racism, 56
reconciliation, 3–33, 35, 55, 65, 96, 141,
   146
religion, 4, 62, 90, 92–93, 95, 179n94
resurrection, 113–14, 117
revelation, ix, x, 7, 26, 28, 32–37, 54–55,
   60, 70, 81, 84, 88, 92, 93, 95–96, 99,
   109–10, 113, 120, 123–24, 128, 134,
   137, 141, 149–53, 157–59, 162–64,
   170n19, 179n83
rhetoric, 155–56

salvation, 14–17, 19– 23, 27, 29–30, 35,
   51, 59, 60, 62, 64–65, 82, 84, 99, 102,
   111, 112, 119, 139, 141, 144, 146,
   148, 150, 158, 159, 168n43, 174n3,
   184nn5 , 6
sanctification, 66
Scripture, 28, 44–45, 53, 58, 68, 70,
   87–89, 105, 110–11, 122–24, 129–32,
   138–39, 147, 150, 153, 156, 158,
   167n29, 170n19, 171n38, 176n22,
   179n83, 181n11
sermon, ix, xi, 106–08, 117, 132–35,
   136–63
sin, 17, 32, 36, 39–40, 56, 153, 161
sincerity, 152–54
spirituality, 4, 150
state, the, 2–4, 48, 136
Stoicism, 79
Supralapsarianism, 13, 26, 46
surveillance, 76–78

theodicy, 87
time, 101–04
Trinity, 27–28, 32, 92
truth, 57, 77, 82, 84, 85, 86,87, 88, 97,
    98, 99, 101, 111, 117, 121–23, 127,
    133–41, 143, 145–47, 152, 158, 161,
    165 n7

universality, 64, 175n19, 185n17

vocation, 2–3, 38, 50–56, 65, 67–68,
    70–73, 82–83, 116, 132, 135, 150,
    162, 171–72n41

Wesleyanism 15, 17–19, 22, 93
witness, ix, 65–66, 105–27, 134–35,
    157–60